Ferrari

Ferrari

Rainer W. Schlegelmilch
Hartmut Lehbrink
Jochen von Osterroth

h.f.ullmann

Inhalt
Contents

Vorwort

Ferrari und Rennen: Das sind die beiden Seiten derselben Münze, schon in der Natur des Mannes Enzo Ferrari begründet, der lebte, um zu siegen, als Rennfahrer, als Rennleiter, als Produzent von Rennautos. Vom Grand-Prix-Monoposto, jener radikalsten Abstraktion des Automobils, bis hin zum viersitzigen Granturismo der Marke sind es stets nur wenige Schritte.

Man kann das hören: Jede Ferrari-Maschine, selbst wenn ihr die strengsten Emissionsgesetze Bürgerrecht zugestehen, erzählt von Le Mans, Monza und der Targa Florio, stellt ihre eigene Story in die Tiefe von fünfzig Jahren Motorsport. Und man kann es lesen, in der beredten Sprache der Ferrari-Formen, geschaffen von Künstlern wie Michelotti und Pininfarina, damit die Prototypen und Rennsportwagen und Reisewagen im Zeichen des schwarzen Pferdchens so zügig vom Start zum Ziel oder von Lübeck nach Lugano gelangen können als möglich.

Von ihrer wechselseitigen Beeinflussung und der Evolution ihrer Linien, geboren, um schnell zu sein, berichtet dieses Buch in Wort und Bild – und davon, dass immer der Rennsport der Vater aller Dinge war. Es erzählt von Motoren und Modellen und ein bisschen auch von den Männern im Hintergrund.

Dabei findet sich der Höhepunkt nicht unbedingt am Schluss: Am Anfang stand ein Barchetta, ein Barchetta steht nahezu am Ende, und der Weg dazwischen ist gesäumt von Zeugnissen purer Schönheit und der erregenden Ausstrahlung, die das Ding Auto haben kann. Der Weg ist das Ziel – bei Ferrari allemal.

Besonders angesichts der kreativen Fülle der Anfangsphase mussten sich die Autoren jedem Anspruch auf enzyklopädische Vollständigkeit versagen und verfuhren notgedrungen repräsentativ. Dass dabei auch subjektive Gesichtspunkte ins Spiel kamen, ließ sich nicht vermeiden.

Preface

Ferrari and motor racing are two sides of the same coin, deeply etched into the very nature of the man Enzo Ferrari. He lived to win whatever the stakes, whether as a driver, a team manager or a constructor. It is but a short step from a Ferrari Grand Prix car, the most radical expression of the car maker's art, to a Grand Tourer of the same marque.

It is obvious to the ear, because a Ferrari, any Ferrari, even one built to comply with the most stringent and mundane emission control regulations, still has a whisper of the legend of Le Mans, Monza and the Targa Florio. It is a legend based on a fifty-year history in motor sport.

It is equally obvious to the eye. Designed by artists like Michelotti or Pininfarina, the prototypes, the sports cars and the road-going coupés that bear the black prancing horse coat of arms have a unique style that speeds them on their way from the start to the chequered flag or from Paris to Rome in the blink of an eye.

These famous lines have evolved out of the search for performance and this book traces that story in words and images. While covering the cars, the engines and the men who made them, it also underlines the fact that competition is the mother of invention.

This is an on-going story that does not necessarily reach a climax at its conclusion. At the beginning, just as at the end, we find a Barchetta. The path that links them is strewn with the most powerful images of pure beauty and charisma that can be conjured up in the name of the motor car.

Given the abundance of creativity that marked the beginning of our story in particular, the authors have not attempted to portray the complete picture, but have contented themselves with producing an outline sketch. This has sometimes led to a subjective view of the story.

Vorwort von Luca di Montezemolo

Jedesmal, wenn ein neues Buch über Ferrari erscheint, frage ich mich, wie es trotz der Einseitigkeit dieses Themas noch interessant wirken kann. Das vorliegende Werk hat mich überrascht durch präzise Information und ausdrucksstarke Bilder.

Wann immer man mich fragt, was ich von Ferrari-Fahrzeugen halte, antworte ich, dass ich sie bewundert habe, so lange ich denken kann. Das war also schon so, bevor ich Leiter des Rennstalls wurde, und ist erst recht so zwanzig Jahre später als Präsident der Firma Ferrari.

Immer hat mich die unwiderstehliche Faszination angerührt, die jedes Geschöpf mit dem springenden Pferd ausströmt, und oft habe ich mich nach den Ursachen gefragt. Nun, da ich dieses Phänomen aus der Nähe kenne und von innen her miterlebe, glaube ich, es verstanden zu haben.

Ferrari sind tausendfach beschrieben worden, und die Fantasie der Autoren enthält kein Adjektiv mehr, das nicht schon im Repertoire der Anerkennung und des Lobes enthalten gewesen wäre.

Seine Autos seien Verkörperungen schöner Mechanik für Männer, die den Wunsch haben, sich selber zu belohnen, einen Traum zu erfüllen und dem Leben noch für lange Zeit jugendliches Feuer abzugewinnen - dies war die Lieblingsdefinition unseres Firmengründers Enzo Ferrari. Im Lauf der Jahre hat sich dieses romantische Bild überschnitten mit vielen anderen, mit Konzepten und Vorstellungen aus Zivilisation, Kultur und Kunst.

So viel Hochachtung stellt für uns eine große Herausforderung dar. Wir wollen uns ihrer würdig erweisen, damit das Erlebnis Ferrari, das jeden ergreift, der damit in Berührung kommt, weiter so intensiv empfunden wird. Gerade dieser sentimentale Aspekt verstärkt eine meiner persönlichen Überzeugungen: Die heutige Ferrari-Welt ist die logische Entwicklung einer fünfzigjährigen Tradition, und die Formel für diesen Erfolg besteht darin, Objekte der Emotion zu schaffen und zu verkaufen.

Preface by Luca di Montezemolo

Every time a new book appears about Ferrari, I ask myself why a subject that has been covered so often can still be so interesting. As for this book, it has impressed me above all with the quality of the text, the accuracy of the information and the clarity of the illustrations.

When I am asked what I think of the cars designed and built by Ferrari, I reply that I have always liked and admired them. That is to say, a long time before I became the Scuderia's Sporting Director, and then, twenty years later, the President of the company.

I too have fallen under the spell that emanates from every creation bearing the sign of the cavallino rampante, and I have often asked myself why. Now

that I am directly involved with this phenomenon and can see it from the inside, I think I have found the answer.

Ferraris have been described in a thousand and one ways, and the imagination of the writers who have tackled the subject has already used up all the superlatives.

"The epitome of mechanical beauty acquired by men who want to turn their dreams into reality and inject their life with a long period of youthful passion" was a favorite expression of our founder, Enzo Ferrari. With time, other concepts were added to this romantic image, such as the advance of civilization, culture and the arts.

Luca Cordero di Montezemolo

This high regard presents us with a great challenge in our work, because we have to prove ourselves worthy of it so that what might be called the "Ferrari effect" will never lose its spell. It is precisely this sentimental aspect which reinforces a deeply held personal conviction: Ferrari today embodies the logical evolution of a tradition based on its fifty-year history. The secret of success is to continue to develop and to put forward objects that bear the stamp of emotion.

Ferrari

Der Mann   The Man

Drei Männer haben das Jahrhundert des Automobils stärker geprägt als irgendwer sonst: Henry Ford war für die Prosa zuständig, indem er die Massen mobil machte, Ettore Bugatti und Enzo Ferrari für die Poesie, weil sie den Stoff schufen, aus dem die Träume sind, in Gedanken liebkost von vielen, wirklich zugänglich nur wenigen Glücklichen. Rivalen sind die beiden lediglich im zeitlosen Zauberreich der Legende – im realen Leben fuhr der große Italiener Ende der vierziger Jahre da fort, wo der große Franzose italienischer Herkunft aufgehört hatte.

Weltmann insofern, als die Welt zu ihm kam und sein Ruhm in alle Welt abstrahlte, war Enzo Ferrari gleichwohl von einer bemerkenswerten Bodenständigkeit. In Modena wurde er am 18. Februar 1898 in mittelständisch-behaglichen Wohlstand hineingeboren. Im magischen Dreieck zwischen Modena, Maranello und Fiorano, einem säkularen Vatikan gewissermaßen, blieb er zeit seines langen Lebens befangen. In Modena starb er am 14. August 1988.

»Ich nähere mich der Ziellinie«, hatte er bei der Vierzigjahresfeier seines Unternehmens 1987 gesagt, und seine Zuhörer waren gerührt. Das Bild machte Sinn, und so baute es der italienische Aristokrat Graf Giovanni Lurani Cernuschi, Rennfahrer, Journalist und Freund des Alten seit 60 Jahren, in einem Nachruf aus: »Immer stand Ferrari auf der Pole Position, als Rennfahrer, Teamchef, Produzent von Prestigeautos und Rennwagen – und als Agitator von Menschen und Ideen.«

Enzo Ferraris Rennkarriere erstreckte sich über zwei Halbzeiten, säuberlich voneinander geschieden durch eine Inkubationsphase von zwei Jahren, in der sein Ehrgeiz schwelte und schließlich erneut aufflackerte. Die erste begann am 5. Oktober 1919 eher bescheiden, fünfte Position in seiner Klasse, die zwölfte insgesamt beim Bergrennen Parma–Poggio di Berceto, auf einem CMN (für Costruzioni Meccaniche Nazionali), der aus Isotta-Fraschini-Teilen zusammengeschraubt war. Sie kulminierte 1920 mit einem zweiten Platz bei der Targa Florio. Da war Ferrari bereits Werksfahrer bei Alfa Romeo, und er hätte gewinnen können, hätte ihn seine Hintermannschaft über den Verlauf der Dinge auf der Berg- und Talbahn durch die sizilianische Madonie besser auf dem Laufenden gehalten. Sie endete im Mysterium: Für den Grand Prix von Europa in Lyon 1924 gemeldet, fuhr er einige Trainingsrunden und setzte sich dann auf den Zug heim nach Modena. Niemand erfuhr warum.

Der zweite Versuch ließ sich 1927 furios an mit Siegen in Alessandria und Modena, hielt im folgenden nicht, was diese versprochen hatten, und klang 1931 auf dem Circuito delle Tre Province mit einer Schmach von unübersehbarer Symbolik aus: Ferrari unterlag, wenn auch knapp, dem »fliegenden Mantuaner« Tazio Nuvolari, der Boss seinem Bediensteten. Denn am 1. Dezember 1929 hatte man, verbrieft und besiegelt in der Kanzlei des stadtbekannten Anwalts Enzo Levi, in Modena die Società Anonima Scuderia Ferrari aus der Taufe gehoben, für Alfa Romeo die Fortsetzung des Sportprogramms mit anderen Mitteln unter Ferraris Stabführung.

Stets dem Superlativ als dem Maß aller Dinge verpflichtet, hatte dieser die besten Piloten rekrutiert, und zu diesen zählte Nuvolari, seinerseits auf dem Wege in den Mythos. Obwohl sich an seinen Namen drei der größten Siege der Scuderia knüpfen, bei der Targa Florio 1932, bei der Mille Miglia 1933 und beim Großen Preis von Deutschland 1935 auf dem Nürburgring, also mitten im Reservat der Silberpfeile, knisterte und kriselte es zwischen den beiden - Urmodell für die vielen Fehden, die Ferrari später mit seinen Fahrern austrug.

More than any others, three men have made a lasting impression on a century of the motor car: Henry Ford provided the prose, in that he produced transport for the masses; Ettore Bugatti and Enzo Ferrari on the other hand provided the poetry, deliberately dedicating themselves to realising our dreams. These two men were only rivals in the timeless world of legend, the Italian colossus beginning his work at the end of the 1940s when the French giant of Italian descent was coming to the end of his career.

Enzo Ferrari was a man of the world in as much as the world came knocking on his door, while his reputation spread far and wide. However he was very much a local boy. He was born on 18 February 1898 in Modena, into a reasonably well-off family, and for most of his life he stayed within the magical triangle of Modena, Maranello and Fiorano; a sort of secular Vatican, and indeed it was in Modena that he died on 14 August 1988.

"I am coming up to the finishing line," he said in 1987 as he celebrated his company's fortieth birthday. Even though they could see the sense in his remark, it was an emotional moment for his audience. The aristocratic Count Giovanni Lurani Cernuschi, a racer and journalist who had been Ferrari's friend for sixty years, put this remark into perspective, writing after his death: "Ferrari was always in pole position, whether as a driver, a team owner, a constructor of racing and prestigious cars, or a motivator of men and ideas."

Enzo Ferrari's career as a driver was played out in two distinct halves, separated by a two year gap when he sharpened his talent and polished his act. He made a modest debut on 5 October 1919, finishing fifth in class and twelfth overall at the Parma–Poggio di Berceto hillclimb. He was at the wheel of a CMN (Costruzioni Meccaniche Nazionali) made from a collection of Isotta-Fraschini parts. The high point of this part of his career came in 1920 when he finished second in the Targa Florio. By that time Ferrari was already an official Alfa Romeo driver and he could have actually won the race if he had been better informed by his team as to what was going on in the hills and valleys of Madonia. The curtain came down on this part of his life in mysterious circumstances during the 1924 Grand Prix of Europe at Lyon. In practice, he completed a few laps then left the circuit and returned to Modena by train. No explanation was ever forthcoming.

The second half kicked off with a bang in 1927, with wins in Alessandria and Modena. Unfortunately this early promise was not fulfilled and the final act was played out in 1931 on the Three Provinces track. In what was to prove a symbolic humiliation, Ferrari was beaten by a whisker by Tazio Nuvolari. In other words the boss had had to give way to the employee. On 1 December 1929, in the presence of the well-known man of law, Enzo Levi, the Società Anonima Scuderia Ferrari, (the Ferrari Team) had been founded. This organization was tasked to run a motor sport program on behalf of Alfa Romeo, under the leadership of Enzo Ferrari. Committed to succeed, Ferrari decided to hire the best possible drivers. One of them was Tazio Nuvolari, then embarking on what would be a glorious career. Despite great wins in the 1932 Targa Florio, the 1933 Mille Miglia, and the 1935 German Grand Prix at the Nürburgring, where Nuvolari beat a whole host of Silver Arrows, conflict was always on the cards between Enzo Ferrari and Tazio Nuvolari. This conflict was to set the tone for the *Ingegnere*'s future relationships with his drivers.

1935 signalled the first brief appearances of his own cars: two twin-engined single-seaters with front and rear-mounted eight cylinder Alfa

In das Jahr 1935 fiel auch der kurze Auftritt seiner ersten eigenen Kreationen, zweier Bimotor-Monoposti mit Achtzylinder-Maschinen vorn und hinten von Alfa Romeo, die deshalb von dem in Portello ansässigen Konzern urheberrechtlich für sich vereinnahmt wurden. Sie waren über 300 Stundenkilometer schnell und zuverlässig, entwickelten indessen einen schier unstillbaren Heißhunger auf Reifen.

Am 1. Januar 1938 ließ Alfa Romeo wissen, man werde das Rennteam unter dem Namen Alfa Corse in die eigene Regie überführen. Zugleich trug man Enzo Ferrari an, seine Tätigkeit als Rennleiter in dieser neuen Konstellation fortzusetzen. Seine Unterschrift unter dem Vertrag löste gleichsam einen Zeitzünder aus, der Ferrari und tüchtige Mitarbeiter wie Luigi Bazzi und Alberto Massimino im November 1939 von Alfa Romeo lossprengte. Der Anlass für diese Scheidung auf Italienisch war ein latenter Zwist mit Alfa-Manager Ugo Gobbato, der sich schließlich an Ferraris Unmut über den spanischen Techniker Ricart entzündete. Seinen Groll erregten bereits Äußerlichkeiten: Des Spaniers Haar sei glatt und ölig gewesen, rümpfte er noch viel später die Nase, und seine Rechte habe bei der Begrüßung schlaff nachgegeben, ein Stück Fleisch ohne Knochen, leblos wie die Hand einer Leiche.

Auch in dieser Hinsicht war Ferrari Ästhet, der das allzu Menschliche scharf beobachtete und mit seltsamer Eindringlichkeit und kafkaeskem Gespür für unappetitliche Details zu Papier brachte: »Sein Körper war über und über bedeckt mit schwarzem Flaum, unter dem rosig seine Haut hervorschaute. In den Härchen glänzten fast immer Schweißperlen«, schrieb er halb angewidert über Giuseppe Campari, einen der Starpiloten seiner Scuderia, dem er gleichwohl in herzlicher Freundschaft verbunden war.

Die Ursachen lagen indessen viel tiefer: Ferrari war zu Subordination nicht länger bereit. Außerdem, befand er, lähme es die Initiative, wenn man zu lange für das gleiche Haus arbeite. Dennoch erfüllte ihn begreifliche Rachsucht. Die Alfa-Oberen hatten ihm zur Auflage gemacht, vier Jahre lang unter seinem Namen kein Fahrzeug zu bauen oder einzusetzen. Also gründete er in Modena eine Firma mit der unverfänglichen Bezeichnung Auto Avio Costruzioni und baute für die Mille Miglia 1940 zwei schöne Spider vom Typ 815, eingekleidet von der Carrozzeria Touring und dem Alfa Romeo 2300 6C verdächtig ähnlich. Und noch im Juli 1951, als Ferrari-Pilot Froilán González, genannt der Pampas-Stier, die bis dahin fast unschlagbaren Alfetta 159 beim Großen Preis von England niedergerungen hatte, frohlockte Ferrari: »Ich habe meine Mutter ermordet.«

Der erste Zwölfzylinder, der seinen Namen trug, entstand 1946. Geburtshelfer waren die Motoreningenieure Gioacchino Colombo und Luigi Bazzi. Es war ein 1,5 Liter, und jede Verbrennungseinheit hatte rund 125 Kubikzentimeter, die dem Modell seinen Namen gaben: 125. Zylinder im Dutzend – das passte kaum in die Trümmerwüste der unmittelbaren Nachkriegszeit, aber Ferrari plante weit in die Zukunft hinein, schätzte die legere Großzügigkeit der Zwölfzylinder von Delage und Packard und hatte sich verliebt in das »Lied der zwölf«, wie er es nannte, die italienische Interpretation dessen, wie sich eine solche Maschine anzuhören habe.

Damit war das Fundament gezimmert zum Faszinosum Ferrari. Dem taten nicht einmal die Folgen der Begegnung zwischen dem Commendatore von Mussolinis Gnaden und Fiat-Chef Giovanni Agnelli am 18. Juni 1969 Abbruch, als Ferrari die Hälfte seiner Anteile an die Turiner Auto-Hydra veräußerte und zugleich zum bloßen Statthalter auf vormals eigenem Territorium degradiert wurde. Seine alljährliche Pressekonferenz

Romeo engines, even though the Portello based marque adopted them as their own. These cars were extremely reliable and capable of over 185 miles (300 km) per hour, but were handicapped by excessive tire wear.

On 1 January 1938 Alfa Romeo announced its intention to run its own race team under the Alfa Corse banner. At the same time Enzo Ferrari was offered the position of Sporting Director in this new organization. His signature on the contract was a time bomb which in 1939 led to him leaving the company with some of his closest colleagues like Luigi Bazzi and Alberto Massimino. The reason for this divorce, Italian style, was the constant tension existing between Ferrari and Alfa Romeo director, Ugo Gobbato. But the final detonator for his departure was Ferrari's lack of respect for Ricart, the Spanish engineer. Ferrari did not hide his disdain for the Spaniard, going so far as to accuse him of having lank oily hair and of shirking his responsibilities. He went further, saying that shaking hands with the Spaniard was like holding a soft piece of boneless meat, as lifeless as a corpse.

When it came to appearances Ferrari was always an esthete. He would make a caustic study of his entourage, taking persistent delight in revealing unsavory details about people. He had this to say, with a note of disgust in his voice, when describing Giuseppe Campari, a star driver for the Scuderia, with whom he enjoyed a cordial and friendly relationship. "His body was covered with black down which hid his pinkish skin, almost always shining with beads of perspiration."

But in the case of his split with Alfa Romeo, the reasons for the disagreement went much deeper: Ferrari was no longer disposed to be a subordinate. Furthermore he felt that if one stayed too long working for the same company, one lost the sense of initiative. Finally he had legitimate reasons for seeking revenge.

The directors of Alfa Romeo had forbidden him to build or to race any car at all under his own name for a period of four years. Despite this, back in Modena, Enzo Ferrari formed a company under the anodyne name of "Auto Avio Costruzioni" and built two very handsome spider-type 815s with bodywork by Touring, to compete in the 1940 Mille Miglia. For all that, these cars bore an uncanny resemblance to the Alfa Romeo 2300 6C. On 14 July 1951, when Froilán González—"The Pampas Bull"—won the British Grand Prix at the wheel of a Ferrari 375 F1 defeating the previously invincible Alfetta 159s, Enzo Ferrari had no hesitation in announcing: "I have killed my own mother!"

The first twelve-cylinder engine to carry his name appeared in 1946 and was the brainchild of engine specialist Gioachino Colombo and engineer Luigi Bazzi. The power unit had a capacity of one and half liters; each cylinder displacing 125 cc. This produced its model name: the 125. Cylinders by the dozen were not common currency in the post-war years, but Ferrari was something of a visionary and was prepared to bet on the future. He had admired the qualities of the twelve-cylinder engines produced by Delage and Packard and had fallen in love with this sophisticated piece of machinery and with what he described, in true Italian style, as the "song of the twelve." Thus the way was paved for a lifelong fascination.

Nothing seemed to rattle Enzo Ferrari. On 18 June 1969 Giovanni Agnelli, the powerful boss of the Fiat group, acquired half the shares of the Ferrari company, but the man himself, now relegated to the role of controller of an empire that had once been his own, was still as vigorous, vital and brilliant as ever. His annual press conference remained, as ever, a meeting

blieb, was sie immer gewesen war, ein Meeting mit einem Monument. Termine unter vier Augen bewahrten Audienzcharakter. Und selbst Royalty, Geldadel und missliebige Prominenz hielt Ferrari auf Distanz mit der simplen pädagogischen Praktik des Wartenlassens, ein Renaissancefürst des 20. Säkulums, der seinen Machiavelli gut gelesen hatte.

Für Leute, die von ihm abhängig und in Ungnade gefallen waren, insbesondere jedoch für Piloten, die nicht länger zum höheren Ruhme seines illustren Hauses beitrugen oder beizutragen schienen, hielt er längst ein fein gestuftes Sortiment von Grausamkeiten bereit - vom Skalpell bis hin zum Schafott. Die Meriten von gestern zählten nie - Ikonen des Sports wie John Surtees und Jacky Ickx können ein Lied davon singen. Sich den Zorn eines Mannes von seiner Statur zuzuziehen war furchtbar, zumal Enzo Ferrari - wie der Commendatore in Mozarts *Don Giovanni* - alle Fäden in der Hand hielt. Niemand hat gern Krach mit einem Denkmal.

Dass Ferrari schon zu Lebzeiten wie ein solches erschien, dazu trug er durchaus selbst bei, retuschierte gern ein bisschen an der Realität, fügte hier etwas hinzu, nahm da etwas fort. So verschwimmt die Geschichte des *cavallino rampante*, des schwarzen Hengstes vor dem Kanariengelb der Stadt Modena im Ferrari-Wappen, im Zwielicht. Er selbst erzählte sie so: Nach seinem Sieg auf der Savio-Rundstrecke bei Ravenna am 25. Mai 1923 - vor Nuvolari - seien die Eltern des italienischen Kriegshelden Francesco Baracca auf ihn zugekommen. Baracca war Kampfflieger, ein Idol seines Landes mit 34 Abschüssen, bis ihn selbst jemand gegen Ende des Ersten Weltkriegs über den Höhen von Montello herunterholte. Sein Emblem war ein sich bäumendes Pferd. Die Gräfin Paolina Baracca habe ihm die heraldische Kostbarkeit spontan zum Hausgebrauch anvertraut, mit den Worten: »Ferrari, nimm dies und tue es auf deine Autos. Es wird dir Glück bringen.«

Diese große Geste, rügen manche, sei indessen gar nicht statthaft gewesen - bei dem Pferdchen habe es sich um das Zeichen von Baraccas Staffel gehandelt, und noch nach dem Zweiten Weltkrieg habe es eine Aerobrigata im Schilde geführt. Zumindest eine andere Ferrari-Story hält seriöser Nachfrage nicht stand: Bei seiner ersten Targa Florio 1919 sei sein CMN im Wagentross des italienischen Präsidenten Vittorio Orlando hängengeblieben, der in Campofelice eine Rede gehalten habe. Orlando war an jenem Tage in der Tat in Sizilien, aber in Termini Imerese, einem beliebten Logis der Targa-Teilnehmer.

Sich dem Profil Enzo Ferraris mit den Techniken von Holz- und Scherenschnitt zu nähern, wäre gänzlich verfehlt: Seine Persönlichkeit war zwar nicht schillernd oder zwielichtig, aber vielschichtig und komplex bis hin zur Synthese des scheinbar Unvereinbaren. Obwohl das Klischee vom Mann der Tat geradezu auf Ferrari gemünzt zu sein schien, war ihm ein fatalistischer Grundzug eigen, und er war traurig wie viele kreative Menschen. »Ich fühle mich verloren, preisgegeben an die Willkür des Schicksals«, klagte er mit einem latinischen Hang zum Pathos.

Zum Tod pflegte er ein fast intimes Verhältnis. Man kannte einander gleichsam vom Sehen, eine »Nodding acquaintance with death«, wie es Stirling Moss genannt hat. Den Verlust seines Sohnes Alfredo, der 1956 an Leukämie starb, hat er nie verwunden, benannte zahlreiche Motoren, Rennwagen und Straßensportwagen zum bleibenden Gedächtnis mit dessen Kosenamen Dino. Die Schar der Rennfahrer, die im Zeichen des *cavallino rampante* ums Leben kamen, ließe sich zu einem kompletten posthumen Starterfeld auflisten: Giuseppe Campari, Alberto Ascari,

with a monument; a private meeting, the equivalent of a papal audience. He was a Renaissance prince of the twentieth century with a grasp of the teachings of Machiavelli. He could keep royalty, celebrities and the monied classes at bay by following to the letter the simple expedient of keeping them waiting.

For those who depended on him but had the misfortune to fall from grace, particularly drivers who no longer contributed or appeared not to contribute to the grand reputation of his company, he reserved a whole host of atrocities, from the simple scalpel cut to the scaffold. Past achievements counted for nothing. Motor racing masters like John Surtees and Jacky Ickx have both felt his anger. Incurring the wrath of a man of Enzo Ferrari's stature was to experience a reign of terror, as he knew how to pull strings in his favor, knowing that no one likes to cross a monument.

His own experience had taught Ferrari how to manipulate reality, and he worked on and polished this image with well thought-out brush strokes. A case in point is the uncertain origin of the little black horse emblem prancing on the yellow background of the town of Modena. He himself came up with the following explanation: on 25 May 1923, after winning at the Savio track near Ravenna, he was sought out by the parents of war hero Francesco Baracca. Baracca was a legendary airman who had shot down 34 enemy aircraft before being shot down himself in the hills of Montello shortly before the end of the war. His emblem was a prancing horse and according to Ferrari, the countess Paolina Baracca presented him with this heraldic device on the spur of the moment, saying, "Ferrari, take this. Put it on your cars and it will bring you luck."

Some people claim that this chivalrous gesture exceeded the countess' competence; that the little horse was simply the emblem of the squadron and was still being used as a coat of arms by an *aerobrigata* after the Second World War.

There is yet another dubious legend in the myth that is Ferrari. The story goes that, while competing in his first Targa Florio in 1919, his CMN got stuck in the procession of cars following the Italian President, Vittorio Orlando, on his way to make a speech in Campofelice. The record shows that Orlando was definitely in Sicily that day, but in Termini Imerese, a particularly popular resort with Targa Florio competitors.

Finally, there is a third anecdote that would seem to be quite simply the result of an overactive imagination. During one particular race we are to believe that Ferrari got caught in a snow storm and was attacked by wolves. A situation that is hard to imagine, even for the most ardent fan of winter rallying!

It is impossible to describe Ferrari's character in conventional terms. Not that it was uncertain or lacked glamor. The biggest problem is that he was an extremely diverse character and impossible to categorize. While the made-to-measure cliché of a realist fits Ferrari perfectly, he nevertheless had a fatalist streak, and like many creative people he suffered from a degree of melancholia. "I feel lost and subject to the whim of destiny," he would sometimes complain with typical Latin self-pity.

He seemed to have an almost intimate relationship with death and knew it by sight as it were, "a nodding acquaintance with death," as Stirling Moss put it.

Enzo Ferrari never got over the death of his son, who died of leukemia in 1956, and in his honor several engines and cars bore the shortened version of his name—Dino. The list of drivers who died carrying the Ferrari emblem

Eugenio Castellotti, Luigi Musso, Peter Collins, Ken Wharton, Alfonso de Portago, Wolfgang Graf Trips, Tommy Spychiger, Lorenzo Bandini oder Gilles Villeneuve sind nur prominente Beispiele.

Er litt daran wie Joe Keller in Arthur Millers Drama *All My Sons* am Sterben der Flieger, die er auf dem Gewissen hat, obwohl Ferrari-Unfälle meistens auf das Versagen des Störfaktors Mensch zurückzuführen waren. Und er laborierte am streng ritualisierten Aufschrei der Presse in diesen Fällen, zog sich dann noch tiefer in seine Modeneser Eremitage und in sich selbst zurück. Bis auf ein paar Stippvisiten in Monza blieb er den Rennen fern, nicht aus Distanz, sondern im Gegenteil, weil für ihn seine Wagen lebten und weil er ihren Fahrern in Liebe oder Hass zugetan war. Wenn er liebte, verzieh er viel, nannte etwa den tollkühnen Kanadier Gilles Villeneuve beinahe zärtlich seinen Prinzen der Zerstörung.

Seine selbst gewählte Isolation – John Surtees, Weltmeister 1964 auf Ferrari, vergleicht das Maranello der sechziger Jahre gern mit einer Burg mit Graben und Zugbrücke – führte zu einem Doppeleffekt: Die Außenwelt, häufig redigiert und gefiltert durch seine Mitarbeiter, drang nur herein, soweit es dem alten Herrn bekömmlich war. Andererseits ließ man lediglich verlauten, was die Leute draußen wissen sollten. Damit war ein permanenter Konflikt mit der rastlos recherchierenden Zunft der Journalisten vorprogrammiert. Zumindest schieden sich an der Person des gusseisernen Autokraten die Geister. Franco Lini, selber Journalist und ab 1966 Ferrari-Rennleiter für zwei Jahre, bescheinigte ihm, er habe Menschen lange observiert, um herauszufinden, ob sie für seine Pläne taugten oder nicht, habe Schwächen und Eitelkeiten durchschaut wie auf einem Röntgenschirm.

Gegenüber ehrlichen Mitarbeitern sei er loyal gewesen – jedenfalls solange sie im Dienst der Firma waren.

An eben dieser Aufrichtigkeit ließ und lässt es Niki Lauda, Champion für Ferrari in den Jahren 1975 und 1977, in erfrischender Weise nicht mangeln: »Enzo Ferrari? Ein altertümliches Standbild mit eisernen Prinzipien. Man musste ihn nehmen, wie er war – sonst hätte man es keinen Monat in seinem Betrieb ausgehalten.«

Giancarlo Baghetti hingegen, später Direktor der Zeitschrift *Auto Oggi* in Mailand, lernte die Sphinx Ferrari mit all ihren Facetten kennen: »Unser erstes Treffen fand im Januar 1961 statt. Er war frostig, fast wie jener Tag. Aber ich machte offenbar einen guten Eindruck, und er nahm mich in sein Team auf.«

Baghetti revanchierte sich mit einer statistischen Einmaligkeit, gewann mit dem Großen Preis von Frankreich jenes Jahres den ersten Grand Prix seiner Karriere. Später sei das Verhältnis vereist, da Baghetti gekündigt habe. Indessen: »Am Freitag vor dem Gran Premio d'Italia 1966, im ersten Jahr der Dreiliterformel, sah ich ihn in Monza wieder. Ich fühlte mich schuldig und unbehaglich, wie ein ertappter Deserteur. Aber Ferrari war jovial und herzlich.« Baghetti hatte sich im ersten Training auf einem Lotus-BRM mehr schlecht als recht geschlagen. »In Maranello«, habe Ferrari gesagt, »steht noch ein Dino 246. Wollen Sie den fahren?« Baghetti habe sprachlos genickt.

Am nächsten Morgen stand der Wagen für ihn bereit.

reads like a huge posthumous race grid, Giuseppe Campari, Alberto Ascari, Eugenio Castellotti, Luigi Musso, Peter Collins, Ken Wharton, Alfonso de Portago, Wolfgang von Trips, Tommy Spychiger, Lorenzo Bandini and Gilles Villeneuve to name but a few.

Just like Joe Keller in Arthur Miller's *All My Sons*, who is ridden by pangs of remorse because of the pilots that have died through his fault, so too Enzo Ferrari suffered terribly. But in fact, most accidents to Ferrari drivers were caused by human error. Each time he would react to the standard barrage from the media by hiding ever more deeply in his Modena hermitage, where he could go to find himself. Apart from a few lightning visits to Monza, he hardly ever came to the track. Not because he disliked travel, but because, in his mind, his cars were living things, and also because he either loved or hated his drivers. When he loved them he was forgiving, which is why he called the daredevil Gilles Villeneuve his Prince of Destruction.

His self-imposed solitude had a double effect. On the one hand the old man's view of the world came to him filtered and described by his colleagues in a way that suited him, while on the other hand the outside world would only hear what he felt they wanted to hear. John Surtees, who was World Champion with Ferrari in 1964, compared Maranello in the sixties to a castle surrounded by a moat with only a drawbridge for access.

This led to a constant conflict with the press who were ceaselessly searching for information. But at least opinions on the iron-willed autocrat were divided. Franco Lini, a journalist who was also Ferrari's Sporting Director for two years from 1966, claims that Ferrari would devote a lot of time to studying people to see if they could be useful to him, and to study their strengths and weaknesses, as if he X-rayed them.

He would remain loyal to faithful colleagues, or at least for as long as they were in his service.

With his usual frankness and no beating about the bush, Niki Lauda, World Champion at the wheel of a Ferrari in 1975 and 1977, declares: "Enzo Ferrari? An ancient statue with a will of iron. You had to take him at face value, either that or you would last no longer than a month in his company."

As for Giancarlo Baghetti, later a director of *Auto Oggi* in Milan, he learnt all there was to learn about the sphinx that was Ferrari. "Our first meeting took place in January 1961. His welcome was as icy as the weather that day. But I suppose I made a good impression as he took me into the team."

Baghetti rewarded him for this in a way that remains unique in the statistic books. He won the French Grand Prix at Reims that year, his maiden Grand Prix. After a while their relationship cooled as Baghetti left the Scuderia of his own accord. "I saw him again for the first time at Monza, during practice for the 1966 Italian Grand Prix. It was the first year of the three-liter Formula One cars. I felt ill at ease, a bit like a deserter. But Ferrari was cheerful and pleasant with me." During first practice, Baghetti, at the wheel of a Lotus-BRM, had not done particularly well, and Ferrari came to talk to him. "There is still one Dino 246 at Maranello. Would you like to drive it?" Silent with emotion, Baghetti could only agree.

The next day the car was at his disposal.

Ferrari

Das Werk   The Marque

Am Anfang stand der Motor, ein Zwölfzylinder. Das war 1946 und ein stolzes, helles Signal mitten hinein in den italienischen Neubeginn nach dem Krieg. Es war auch ein Symbol, etwa dafür, wie Enzo Ferrari angesichts des nörgelnden Chors seiner Kritiker unbeugsam seinen Weg ging.

Die Realität gab ihm recht: Rennerfolge und überall Nachahmung, bekanntlich ja die subtilste Form der Schmeichelei. Und es war ein frühes Zeichen dafür, dass sich Ferrari als Exponent der Maschine verstand – erst dann kam das Chassis, und für die Karosserie waren andere zuständig. »Einer von uns«, pflegte Battista Farina zu sagen, Ferraris bevorzugter Couturier ab 1952, »schaute aus nach einer berühmten, schönen Frau, die er ausstatten wollte, der andere nach einem Schneider der Weltspitzenklasse, der Kleider für sie machen konnte«.

Ein Phantombild des Ferrari opus 1, das im Winter 1946/47 die Runde machte in der italienischen Presse, war gleichsam programmatisch: Bis ins Detail sind Triebwerk, Rahmen und Aufhängung zu erkennen, die Silhouette – die eines Coupés – bleibt vage und verschwommen. Tatsächlich handelte es sich bei dem Erstling im Zeichen des cavallino rampante, der im Frühjahr 1947 durch das Werkstor in Maranello rollte, um einen Spider, der die gefälligeren Linien künftiger Barchetta-Versionen im Ansatz vorwegnahm. Der 125 Sport war ein Fehdehandschuh in Ferrari-Rot. Die Zielsetzung war klar, scharf umrissen das Feindbild: Alfa Romeo musste geschlagen werden, dort, wo es wirklich weh tat – in der Formel 1.

Die Kampagne selbst bereitete Enzo Ferrari mit durchtriebener Sorgfalt und strategischer Umsicht vor: an allen erdenklichen Fronten, auf vielen Nebenkriegsschauplätzen wie bei den Sport- und GT-Wagen, der Formel 2 und der Formula Libre. Zugleich rüstete er auf, kongenial unterstützt von den Ingenieuren Gioacchino Colombo, einem Mann der ersten Stunde, der bis 1951 blieb, und Aurelio Lampredi, der seinem schwierigen Brotherrn von 1948 bis 1955 die Stange hielt: von den 125 und 159 cm³ je Verbrennungseinheit im Geburtsjahr 1947 über deren 166, 195, 212, 225, 275, 340 bis hin zu den 375 cm³ im Jahre drei nach Gründung der Firma.

Wie immer in jener Phase fanden sie sich in den Typenbezeichnungen seiner Wagen wieder und ergaben, mit der magischen Zahl zwölf multipliziert, das Gesamtvolumen der Maschine. 1950 waren folglich jene 4,5 Liter ausgeschöpft, die das Grand Prix-Reglement bis einschließlich 1951 gestattete, als Alternative zu den 1,5 Litern mit Kompressor, mit denen die feindlichen Alfetta 158 und 159 ins Gefecht geworfen wurden. Ironie des Schicksals: Indem er sie bekämpfte, rannte Ferrari gegen seine eigene Vergangenheit an – ihr Konzept in den Enddreißigern stammte von ihm selbst, Colombo und Luigi Bazzi.

1950, im ersten Jahr der modernen Grand-Prix-Geschichte, endete der Kampf der alten gegen die neue Zeit noch mit einem vernichtenden 5:0. Mitten in der Saison 1951 jedoch vollzog Ferrari mit den Siegen von Gonzalez in Silverstone und von Alberto Ascari am Nürburgring und in Monza den Dreisprung in die Unsterblichkeit.

Da hatte das Wort – ein Dutzendname in Italien, ein Kultbegriff, sowie er auf einem Auto steht – längst einen guten Klang im Rennsport. Am 25. Mai 1947 hatte der 44-jährige Franco Cortese das zweite Rennen des 125 Sport gewonnen, auf der Caracalla-Rennstrecke in Rom. Der erste internationale Ferrari-Sieg, mit dem zweiplätzigen 159 S am 11. Oktober des gleichen Jahres in Turin, ging auf das Konto des Franzosen Raymond Sommer, den

In the beginning there was an engine, a twelve-cylinder. It was 1946, and in its own way this engine epitomised the rebirth of Italy after the war. But it was also a symbol of Enzo Ferrari's single-minded will to follow his chosen path, with no consideration for any obstacles put in his way. It would not take long for events to prove him right, events in the shape of his success in competition and the fact that he spawned imitators more or less all over the place—surely the sincerest form of flattery. Right from the beginning, Ferrari, as a constructor, made the engine his priority with the chassis coming second. For the bodywork he looked elsewhere. As Battista Farina, who was Ferrari's favorite coachbuilder from 1952, liked to say, "one of us was looking for a beautiful and famous lady to dress, and the other was trying to find a tailor who would produce made-to-measure garments for her."

The sectional drawing of Ferrari opus 1, published in the Italian press in the winter of 1946/47, proved this concept: while every precise detail of the engine, the frame and suspension was clearly visible, the silhouette of a coupé was vague and sketchy. In fact the first car to come out of the Maranello factory carrying the prancing horse badge was a spider which predicted the lines of future "barchettas."

The 125 Sport was a Ferrari-red challenge. His aim was obvious. He had to beat the enemy, Alfa Romeo, where it would hurt the most, in other words in Formula 1. Enzo Ferrari planned the campaign down to the last detail, refining his strategy and involving himself in every aspect of the task in a variety of classes including Sports Cars, Grand Touring cars, Formula 2 and Formula Libre.

At the same time he strengthened his position with the solid support of engineers like Gioacchino Colombo, who had been with him in the early days and would stay with Ferrari until 1951, and Aurelio Lampredi who never deserted his post from 1948 to 1955. They were the creators of the 125 and 159 models and later of the 166, 195, 212, 225, 275, 340 and 375. These numbers denoting the different versions simply indicated the capacity of a single cylinder. One only has to perform the simple task of multiplying them by the magic number 12 to find the cubic capacity of the engine. By 1950 the maximum capacity allowed for a normally aspirated engine of 4.5 liters was reached and this rule would apply until the end of the following year. The Alfetta 158 and 159 ran with 1.5-liter supercharged engines under the equivalence rule. The irony of this was that Ferrari was now battling with his own past, as this concept, dating back to the thirties, had been created by himself, Gioacchino Colombo and Luigi Bazzi.

In 1950, the first season of the modern era of Grand Prix racing, the battle ended in a humiliating five-nil defeat. But in the course of the following season, during which Ferrari triumphed at Silverstone with Froilán González and with Alberto Ascari at both Nürburgring and Monza, the great leap towards immortality had been made.

By now the Ferrari name—very common in Italy but enjoying cult status when applied to a motor car—had a good ring to it in competition circles. On 25 May 1947, 44-year-old Franco Cortese had won the 125 Sport's second ever race on the Caracalla circuit in Rome.

The first international win for a Ferrari followed on 11 October of the same year at Turin, with Raymond "Lionheart" Sommer at the wheel of a two-seater 159 S. When Froilán González won the British Grand Prix on 14 July 1951, the victory could be seen as a fitting epilogue to innumerable victories in sports car events: the 1949 Targa Florio with Biondetti/

sie Löwenherz nannten. Dem Durchbruch an der Grand-Prix-Front am 14. Juli 1951 gingen Siege bei den Vorzeige- und Prestigeveranstaltungen für Sportwagen voraus: bei der Targa Florio 1949 durch Biondetti/Benedetti, bei der Mille Miglia 1949 durch Biondetti/Salani, 1950 durch Giannino Marzotto, den mittleren der drei rennfahrenden Erben des Tuch-Imperiums, mit Beifahrer Marco Crosara, und 1951 durch Villoresi/Cassani, in Le Mans 1949 durch das Gespann Luigi Chinetti/Lord Selsdon. Enzo Ferrari, der 1950 bereits 200 Mitarbeiter beschäftigte, war kein reicher Mann, durchaus angewiesen auf den Ertrag, den der Sport an Startprämien und Preisgeldern einspielte.

Werkspiloten, selbst Stars wie Tazio Nuvolari, Alberto Ascari oder Felice Bonetto, mussten 50 Prozent ihrer Honorare abliefern. Das deckte kaum die Unkosten. Folglich wagte er bald den Ausfallschritt auf ein zweites Standbein, die Produktion von Straßensportwagen, die bis auf den heutigen Tag die Renn-Aktivitäten der Firma mitträgt: Auf einer Pressekonferenz im Februar 1995 anlässlich der Vorstellung des 412 T2 für die neue Saison mutmaßte Ferrari-Präsident Luca di Montezemolo, nur 55 Prozent des Renn-Budgets werde von Sponsoren finanziert, den Rest müsse man sich schon selbst verdienen.

In den ersten vier Jahren verwischte sich der Unterschied zwischen den Rennfahrzeugen und den Gran Turismos der Marke allerdings bis hin zur Identität, obwohl ihnen jeweils gerade beziehungsweise ungerade Chassisnummern zugeteilt wurden: Gianni Marzotto zum Beispiel startete zweimal auf der Mille Miglia mit den Autos, die er auch auf der täglichen Fahrt zum Büro benutzte.

Anfänglich betreute Ferrari seine Kunden persönlich, begann aber bald, seine Fäden zu spinnen hin zu wichtigen Vorposten wie New York (Luigi Chinetti) und London (Colonel Ronnie Hoares, Maranello Concessionaires).

Broschüren gab es selten, Werbung war im Grunde überflüssig: Der Renn-Ruhm schon der frühen Jahre wirkte wie ein Magnet. Und überdies sprach das noble Produkt aus Norditalien, eingekleidet von Formkünstlern wie Vignale, Ghia, Touring oder den altehrwürdigen Stabilimenti Farina, für sich mit dem beredten Idiom von Kraft, Klang und Schönheit, jeder Ferrari maßgeschneidert und ein Unikat.

Zur Gelenkstelle in der Geschichte beider Unternehmen geriet eine Begegnung zwischen Enzo Ferrari und Battista »Pinin« Farina sowie dessen Sohn Sergio 1951 in einem Restaurant in Tortona, dem ein zähes Tauziehen vorangegangen war: Ferrari mochte Maranello nicht verlassen, Farina beharrte auf seiner Garnison Turin als Treffpunkt, bis man sich auf neutrales Territorium einigte. Man kannte sich seit dem Bergrennen Aosta - Grand St. Bernard 1921 und hatte den Erfolg des jeweils anderen sozusagen aus dem Augenwinkel beobachtet. Obwohl begleitet von den Unkenrufen der Branche, die beiden zusammen, das sei wie zwei Primadonnen in einer Oper oder zwei Pfarrer in einem Sprengel, entspann sich bei diesem Arbeitsessen ein Dialog auf Lebenszeit: Man ergänze einander, schrieb Farina später, wie die Komplementärfarben blau und gelb.

Der Pakt der Konsuln, wie sie in Italien genannt wurden, trug umgehend Früchte, ein Cabriolet mit strengen Formen für den Genfer Rennstallbesitzer Georges Filipinetti, weitere Einzelstücke und Gruppen von Kundenwagen wie den 375 America und den 250 GT Europa. Erst der 250 GTE 2+2 von 1960 hingegen erfuhr mit insgesamt 955 Exemplaren eine solche Verbreitung, dass man von einer Serie sprechen konnte.

Benedetti; 1949 Mille Miglia, with Biondetti/Salani and the Mille Miglia yet again in 1950 with Giannino Marzotto (one of three racing heirs to a textiles empire) partnered by Marco Crosara; and still the Mille Miglia the next year with Villoresi/Cassani; as well as Le Mans in 1949 with the Luigi Chinetti/Lord Selsdon pairing.

By 1950 Enzo Ferrari already employed 200 people, but he was still not a rich man, as he depended to a large extent on fees and prize money from his wins. Even such famous factory drivers as Tazio Nuvolari, Alberto Ascari and Felice Bonetto had to hand over fifty percent of their winnings, which in fact only barely covered expenses.

So Ferrari decided to add a second string to his bow to fill his coffers, namely the production of high-speed road cars which, to this day, continue to support the company's racing activities. At a press conference in February 1995 to launch the 412T2 single-seater for that season's racing, Ferrari President Luca di Montezemolo explained that 55 percent of the competition budget came from sponsors and the factory had to find the rest.

For the first four years it was hard to spot the difference between the racing cars and the grand touring cars, except that the latters' chassis were always given odd numbers. To prove the point, Gianni Marzotto twice ran in the Mille Miglia in cars which he used on a daily basis to drive to work.

At first Enzo Ferrari looked after his customers personally, but he soon put a network into place with major local dealers like Luigi Chinetti in New York and Colonel Ronnie Hoare of Maranello Concessionaires in London. Sales brochures were rare and unnecessary as the cars were much loved thanks to their reputation in competition. Effectively this thoroughbred product from the Emilia Romana region with its bodywork produced by such metalwork masters as Vignale, Ghia, Touring, and the master builder Stabilimenti Farina was its own best advertisement for power, fame and beauty. Each Ferrari was made to measure and virtually unique.

In 1951 in a Tortona restaurant a crucial meeting took place between Enzo Ferrari, Battista "Pinin" Farina, and his son Sergio. The planning of this meeting led to some argument. Ferrari did not want to leave Maranello and Farina wanted to stay in his kingdom of Turin. Finally they met on neutral ground. The two men knew one another since the Aosta-Grand St. Bernard hillclimb in 1921 and they had followed one another's fortunes ever since, although neither would admit as much. The prophets of doom had predicted that a meeting of these two strong personalities would be akin to putting two operatic prima donnas on the same billing. As things turned out it would lead to a lifelong dialogue. "We go together as well as the colors of blue and yellow," Farina would later write.

Known in Italy as the "Consular Treaty," the fruits of this meeting were not long in coming, in the shape of a simple cabriolet destined for the Genevan team owner, Georges Filipinetti, followed by other one-offs and cars produced in small numbers such as the 375 America and the 250 GT Europa which were sold to a wealthy clientele. It was not until 1960 and the launch of the 250 GTE 2+2, of which 955 were built, that one could really talk in terms of a production car.

That year there was one other important sign that Ferrari had decided to move with the times. Until then, the company revolved around the man, but now it was transformed into a limited company—Società Esercizio Fabbriche Automobili e Corse, or S.E.F.A.C.

Enzo Ferrari reckoned he had three distinctly different types of customer; the fifty-year-old who had done well in life; the motor sport

Noch in anderer Hinsicht huldigte Ferrari in diesem Jahr dem Geist der neuen Zeit: indem er sein Unternehmen, das bislang strikt auf seine Person bezogen war, in eine AG umwandelte, die Società Esercizio Fabbriche Automobili e Corse, kurz S.E.F.A.C. Seinen Kundenkreis teilte er nicht ohne Sarkasmus in drei Segmente auf: den arrivierten Fünfzigjährigen, den Mann aus dem Umkreis des Rennsports, der seine eigenen Fähigkeiten als Autofahrer als außergewöhnlich einschätzte, und den Poseur, dessen attraktive Freundinnen bei Betriebsbesichtigungen in Maranello die Arbeit der Werktätigen zum Erliegen brachten. Gleichwohl lagen schwierige Zeiten vor ihm: Die S.E.F.A.C. verzettelte sich mit ihrem Engagement in der Formel 1, bei den Prototypen und in der GT-Klasse. Häufige Änderungen des Regelwerks durch die CSI in Paris kamen die Hersteller teuer zu stehen. Und auf dem schmalen Sektor der schnellen Produktionswagen erwuchs massive Konkurrenz durch Firmen wie Porsche, Maserati, Jaguar und Aston Martin.

Da empfahl sich die tröstliche Anlehnung an die Schulter eines der Giganten im Autogeschäft. Henry Ford der Zweite, der selber einen schwarzen Ferrari Barchetta besaß, bot sich an. Aber ein für den 20. Mai 1963 geplanter Deal platzte, weil sich der Koloss aus Dearborn vorbehielt, in Enzo Ferraris ureigenstes Rosengärtlein hineinzuregieren – die Rennabteilung. Just diese bekam denn auch Fords Zorn unmittelbar und elementar zu spüren. Bereits 1964 gewann das Daytona Coupé des Ford-Satelliten Carroll Shelby die Grand-Tourisme-Kategorie in Le Mans, und der Gesamtsieg der neuseeländischen Riege Chris Amon und Bruce McLaren 1966 mit dem mächtige Siebenliter entpuppte sich als Auftakt zu einer vierjährigen Ford-Hegemonie über den französischen Klassiker. Zugleich erwies sich die Ferrari-Baureihe 275/330 als großer Wurf.

Aber die Turbulenzen blieben und mündeten in Ferraris Canossagang ins Fiat-Hauptquartier Turin am 18. Juni 1969, wo er einem aufgeräumten und wissbegierigen Gianni Agnelli 50 Prozent der Anteile der S.E.F.A.C. überantwortete. 40 weitere würden bei seinem Ableben folgen, die restlichen zehn in der Familie bleiben, bei seinem Sohn Piero Lardi Ferrari.

Er verließ die Chefetage im achten Stockwerk des Komplexes Corso Marconi 10 dennoch guten Mutes, da er die Kontinuität seines Lebenswerks gesichert und in guten Händen sah, als zukünftiger Ehrenvorsitzender keineswegs aufs Altenteil gesetzt war und in der Rennabteilung nach Belieben schalten und walten konnte wie bisher. Die Ehe hatte kurioserweise die CSI gestiftet: Auf der Suche nach einem Triebwerk für zwei sportliche Modelle feineren Zuschnitts, ein Coupé und ein Cabriolet, waren zwei Fiat-Emissäre im Januar 1965 in Maranello vorstellig und auch fündig geworden. Denn dort röhrte ein kompakter Zweiliter-V6 des Motoreningenieurs Franco Rocchi auf dem Prüfstand. Man war sich rasch einig, da Fiat verhieß, eine Serie von 500 Maschinen bis Ende des Jahres aufzulegen, just die Population, die die Rennsport-Legislative für die Verwendung in der Formel 2 ab 1967 vorgeschrieben hatte.

Dem Daytona, dem ersten Straßen-Ferrari unter Fiat-Kuratel und zugleich letzten Exponenten der Frontmotor-Ära, war umgehender und anhaltender Erfolg beschieden, der sich in einer Rekord-Auflage von 1395 Exemplaren zwischen 1968 und 1973 niederschlug.

Danach knickte, trotz einer geschickt gefächerten Modellpalette vom 308 GT4 bis zum BB 512, die Erfolgskurve ein, als Folge der kunstvoll inszenierten Energiekrise, fiebriger Unruhe in der italienischen Arbeiterschaft und allgemeiner Verunsicherung durch den Terror der Roten Brigaden.

enthusiast who felt he was an exceptional driver; and the playboy whose seductive girlfriend would bring everything to a standstill when she visited the workshop. But difficult times loomed on the horizon. S.E.F.A.C. had diversified into Formula 1, Sports Prototypes and GT racing. Frequent changes to the technical regulations introduced by the CSI, the Paris-based sporting authority of the day, caused considerable expense for the constructors. There was also a growth of strong competition in the high-performance road-car market from companies like Porsche, Maserati, Jaguar, and others such as Aston Martin.

It was at this point that one of the giants of the motor industry offered Ferrari its support. Henry Ford II, who was known to drive a black Ferrari when off-duty, approached the Commendatore. But the agreement which should have been signed on 20 May 1963 never saw the light of day as the Dearborn deity refused to allow Ferrari a free hand when it came to his pet project—the competition department.

Henry Ford did not take kindly to being snubbed in this way and swore he would get his revenge on Ferrari's favorite battleground. In 1964 a Daytona coupé prepared by one of Ford's partners, Carroll Shelby, won the GT category at Le Mans. Two years later, Chris Amon partnered by Bruce McLaren took overall victory in this legendary event at the wheel of a powerful Ford, powered by an impressive seven-liter V8. A Ford four-year hegemony at the Le Mans 24 Hours had thus begun. This did not stop the Ferrari 275 P and the 330 P (later the P2, P3 and P4) from winning several other endurance races.

This was not enough to calm the turbulent financial waters, however, and Ferrari was forced to humbly follow the road to Canossa, in this case to Turin, and to be precise to the Fiat headquarters. On 18 June 1969, the king of Maranello sold fifty percent of the shares in S.E.F.A.C. to Gianni Agnelli, who was at all times polite and showed no sign of gloating over his acquisition. The agreement stated that on Ferrari's death, forty percent of the shares would revert to the Fiat group and ten percent would remain the property of his son, Piero Lardi Ferrari.

Thus it was that Enzo Ferrari, suitably reassured about the long-term future of his company, left the eighth floor office of the Fiat building at 10 Corso Marconi. Not only was the future of his business guaranteed, but also his position on the board was safe, irrespective of his age, and furthermore he retained personal control of the competition department. Unwittingly the CSI had contributed to this partnership. In January 1965, two representatives from Fiat had visited Maranello with the aim of acquiring an engine to power two high-performance models, a coupé and a cabriolet. It so happened that they arrived just as a compact two-liter V6 engine designed by Franco Rocchi was being bench tested. An agreement was quickly reached and Fiat agreed to produce 500 cars by the end of the year. This was exactly the minimum number stipulated in the regulations, so that a version of this engine could be used in Formula 2 from the beginning of 1967.

The 365 GTB/4 was to be the first Ferrari to see the light of day under the patronage of Fiat, the last front-engined two-seater high-performance coupé. The Daytona, as it was called, was a phenomenal success and no less than 1395 were built between 1968 and 1973.

Then, despite a well planned product range, from the 308 GT4 to the BB 512, the successful sales story faltered slightly. Petrol crises, trouble with the trade unions, terrorist attacks organised by the Red Brigades,

Zumindest eine Genugtuung blieb: Die Baisse der Mittsiebziger wurde kontrapunktisch begleitet von einer anhaltenden Dominanz der Ferrari 312 T in der Formel 1 über die zumeist Ford-getriebene Konkurrenz. Dann aber setzte fast kontinuierlicher Aufschwung ein. Kreationen wie der 288 GTO von 1984 und der F40 im Jubiläumsjahr 1987 gehörten zu den erregendsten Aussagen, die zum Thema Automobil jemals gemacht wurden, zum höheren Ruhme von Mann und Werk.

Der nach Enzo Ferraris Tod im August 1988 befürchtete Einbruch blieb aus, im Gegenteil: Angeheizt durch Spekulanten, eskalierten die Preise für alles, auf dem der Name Ferrari stand, ins Irrwitzige. Für einen F40 wurden 2,2 Millionen Mark verlangt, für einen 250 GTO zahlte 2008 jemand 20 Millionen Euro.

Ebenso rasch und unerwartet beruhigte sich der Markt zu Beginn der neunziger Jahre wieder. Aber selbst die häufige Präsenz der schönen Schnellen auf den Straßen der Welt tat ihrem Nimbus keinen Abbruch. Zu einem sorgfältig bewahrten Bestand kamen 1971 zum ersten Mal über 1000, 1979 über 2000, 1985 über 3000, 1988 mehr als 4000. 1997 beteiligte die Allmutter Fiat Ferrari mit 50 Prozent am schärfsten Rivalen von einst – Maserati, zwei Jahre später dem Beritt des *cavallino* rückstandsfrei angegliedert. Mit den bereits bestehenden Ferrari-Provinzen, der einstigen Carrozzeria Scaglietti in Modena, Ferrari-Territorium seit 1977, dem Hauptquartier der Gestione Sportiva (GeS) in Fiorano seit 1982, direkt neben der 1972 gebauten Teststrecke, auf der sich selbst die Überflutung nach einem Wolkenbruch simulieren lässt, und dem 1988 eingekauften Kurs von Mugello unweit Florenz, fand sich die Marke mit dem Dreizack zu einem schmucken Imperium zusammen. Zentrum der Macht auf einem Areal von 520 000 m² aber ist Maranello. Hier schwingt Ferrari-Fürst Luca di Montezemolo seit 1997 sein Zepter nach der Formula Uomo. Es gilt, Arbeit, Produkt und Umwelt miteinander zu harmonisieren.

Im Mittelpunkt, doziert der smarte Markgraf, stehe allzeit der Mensch. Diese Philosophie bildet sich ab in markanten Zeugnissen des 21. Jahrhunderts, lichten Gebäuden und Anlagen von eigenwilliger Schönheit, eingebettet in das typische Ambiente der Emilia-Romagna mit viel bekömmlichem Grün. Jüngste Attraktionen des Ferrari Village: das neue Gebäude für die Fahrzeugmontage, entworfen von Star-Architekt Jean Nouvel, und das von Star-Architekt Marco Visconti bizarr geformte Ristorante Aziendale.

Die Perfektion von Ferrari drückt sich in funkelnden Bilanzen aus: So erzielte das italienische Vorzeigeunternehmen, zu dessen Verwaltungsrat seit 2012 auch der Apple-Top-Manager Eddy Cue zählt, in jenem Jahr Rekordergebnisse mit 2,4 Milliarden Euro Umsatz, 7318 ausgelieferten Fahrzeugen und einem Handelsgewinn von 350 Millionen Euro. Im Herbst 2012 werden trotz hoher Investitionen 959 Millionen liquider Nettomittel bilanziert. Stärkste Absatzmärkte nach Spitzenreiter USA sind China und Deutschland. Weltweite Zuwächse – nur in Italien selbst sinkt die Kaufkraft für mobile Luxusgüter geradezu drastisch.

Und da ist die unvergleichliche Rolle der Marke im Sport: 15 Fahrer-Championate, 16 Konstrukteurstitel, 218 erste Plätze in der Formel 1, 14 Markenweltmeisterschaften und neun Le-Mans-Siege, acht Erfolge bei der Mille Miglia, sieben bei der Targa Florio. Der Stolz, kein Zweifel, ist berechtigt.

these were all factors which combined to create a general lack of confidence. There was still one ray of hope in the recessionary times of the mid-seventies, however, and that was the dominance of the Ferrari 312 T in Formula 1 against opponents generally using Ford engines.

The momentum that followed this period was characterized by almost constant progress. Cars such as the Ferrari 288 GTO and the F40, introduced to commemorate the fortieth anniversary of the company's existence, passed straight into motoring history, confirming the worth of both the man and his work. While some thought the death of Enzo Ferrari in August 1988 would diminish the value of his creations, they were wrong. In fact quite the opposite was true. Thanks to diehard speculators, the price of anything bearing the Ferrari emblem went through the roof, reaching incredible levels. 1.6 million dollars were paid for an F40—and in 2008, someone else bought a 250 GTO for 28 million dollars.

The market subsided just as quickly and unexpectedly at the beginning of the nineties. But even the frequent presence of the speedy beauty on the world's roads did not destroy the myth. In 1971, for the first time, 1000 of these lovingly created cars were produced; in 1979 over 2000; in 1985 over 3000; and in 1988 the total exceeded 4000. In 1997 Fiat Auto, the "mother of all," sold a 50-percent share in Maserati to Ferrari, Maserati's long-time arch-rival (and Fiat sister company in the Fiat group); and two years later, Maserati was completely reined up behind the Ferrari *cavallino*. The trident marque ended up as an extremely attractive empire consisting of existing Ferrari provinces; the former Carrozzeria Scaglietti in Modena, Ferrari territory since 1977; the head office of the Gestione Sportiva (GeS) in Fiorano since 1982, right next to the test track built in 1972 where even the floods that follow a rainstorm can be simulated; and the Mugello course near Florence, acquired in 1988. The center of power, though, on an area measuring 128.5 acres (52 hectares), is at Maranello. This is where Luca di Montezemolo has been wielding his scepter since 1997, according to the Formula Uomo program. The aim is to achieve a balance of work, product, and environment.

And, as the wise margrave says, everything always revolves around the people who work there. This philosophy is seen in eye-catching 21st century facilities: bright, airy buildings and landscaping of striking beauty, embedded in the typical ambience of the Emilia-Romagna, with plenty of inviting greenery. The latest attractions at the Ferrari Village are the new assembly building, designed by star architect Jean Nouvel, and the bizarrely shaped Ristorante Aziendale created by another star architect, Marco Visconti.

The perfection of Ferrari can be seen in the company's sparkling financial statements: in 2012—the same year that top Apple manager Eddy Cue joined its Board of Directors—the pioneering Italian manufacturer achieved record sales figures of 3.1 billion dollars, shipping 7318 vehicles and making a trading profit of 455 million dollars. In fall of 2012, despite high levels of investment, the company recorded net liquidity of 1.2 billion dollars. After the USA, Ferrari's largest markets are China and Germany. The company has enjoyed global growth—it is only in Italy itself that the purchase power for mobile luxury goods is, quite simply, in drastic decline.

And then there is the marque's incomparable role in sports: 15 drivers' championships, 16 constructors' titles, 218 firsts in Formula 1, 14 World Sportscar Championships and nine Le Mans wins, eight successes at the Mille Miglia, and seven at the Targa Florio. No doubt about it: there's good reason to be proud.

Ferrari

Die Wagen   The Cars

Spider (Barchetta) Touring

Die Zusammenarbeit mit der 1926 ins Leben gerufenen Carrozzeria Touring ging auf das Jahr 1940 zurück, als deren Chef Bianchi Anderloni Ferraris verhohlenes Frühwerk einkleidete, den Auto Avio Costruzioni Tipo 815.

Dann intervenierte der Erste Weltkrieg. Und so folgte der zweite Streich erst auf der Turiner Autoausstellung im September 1948, der Spider Touring 166 MM. Das Kürzel sollte dem Mille-Miglia-Sieg jenes Jahres durch das Ferrari-Gespann Biondetti/Navone ein Denkmal setzen. Aber alle Welt nannte ihn *Barchetta* (kleines Boot), Doppelhit wegen vieler Sporterfolge und einer gelungenen Form, noch bis hin zum AC-Modell Ace (1953) und selbst dem Fiat Barchetta (1995) gern und ausgiebig zitiert. Sie entstand gemäß dem patentierten Superleggera-Prinzip der Anderlonis: Ein Fachwerk von Rohren und Röhrchen über dem Rahmen wurde mit vorgekrümmten Karosserieteilen aus Aluminium beplankt.

Die rundliche Motorhaube des Barchetta beherbergte Maschinen zwischen 166 und 340 cm³ je Zylinder, die ihm

The collaboration with Carrozzeria Touring—founded in 1926—dated back to 1940, when its boss Bianchi Anderloni became involved in the design of Ferrari's little-known first creation, the Auto Avio Costruzioni Tipo 815.

But then the Second World War intervened. So the second model was not unveiled until the Turin Motor Show in September 1948: the Spider Touring 166 MM. The initials were intended to commemorate the winning of that year's Mille Miglia by the Ferrari team Biondetti and Navone. However, everyone called it by the nickname of *Barchetta* (little boat), lauded and revered for its racing successes and fine lines right up to the AC model Ace (1953), and even quoted by the Fiat Barchetta (1995). It was based on the patented Anderloni *Superleggera* principle: a multi-tubular assembly was fitted above the actual frame, and then covered in sheets of pre-formed aluminum.

The curvaceous hood of the Barchetta concealed engines of between 166 and 340 cc, which determined the model number. The 166 MM could already reach

Erschien im September 1948: Der Spider Touring 166 MM mit seiner markanten Front und einer leichten Aluminium-Karosserie, gezeichnet von Touring-Chef Bianchi Anderloni.

Appeared in September 1948: the Spider Touring 166 MM with its striking front and light aluminum bodywork, drawn by Touring boss Bianchi Anderloni.

Der kleine 166 Spider, auch Barchetta (kleines Boot) genannt, überzeugte mit seinen fließenden Linien und ausgewogenen Proportionen. Er wog nur 900 Kilogramm.

seine wechselnden Namen gaben. Schon der 166 MM hatte 140 PS, der 4,1-Liter von 1950 deren 220. Zur Augenweide gesellte sich der Ohrenschmaus: die robusten Klangbilder von Aurelio Lampredis V12 mit seinem markanten langen Block, bekannt aus den Monoposti der Marke. Gleichwohl fanden viele Touring Spider den Weg auf gewöhnliche Landstraßen.

The small 166 Spider, also known as Barchetta (small boat), was very convincing with its flowing lines and balanced proportions. It weighed only 1985 lbs (900 kg).

140 bhp, while the 4.1-liter version of 1950 boasted 220 bhp. A delight for the eyes was accompanied by a treat for the ears: the powerful sound of Aurelio Lampredi's V12 engine with its remarkable long block, already known from the brand's single-seaters. However, many Touring Spiders were also seen on normal country roads.

Ein optischer und akustischer Genuss: Das Zwölfzylinder-Aggregat mit knapp 2,6 Liter Hubraum leistete mit den drei Weber-Vergasern 170 PS.

An optical and aural pleasure: the twelve-cylinder aggregate with scarcely 2.6-liter capacity achieved 170 bhp with its three Weber carburetors.

Coupé Ghia

Anfang der Fünfziger war es für Enzo Ferrari überaus wichtig, den reichen amerikanischen Markt für seine Gran Turismos zu erschließen. Da kam ihm die Carrozzeria Ghia gerade recht, deren Leitung Gründervater Giacinto Ghia kurz vor seinem Tode im Februar 1944 an Mario Felice Boano übergeben hatte. Der und sein Sohn Gian Paolo pflegten gute Kontakte zu Chrysler, die Liaison mit Ferrari blieb allerdings kurz und relativ unergiebig. Auf einen weißen Berlinetta auf dem

At the beginning of the Fifties, it was extremely important to Enzo Ferrari that the American market be exploited for his Gran Turismos. The collaboration with Carrozzeria Ghia was ideal for this; the founder of the company, Giacinto Ghia, had handed over the business to Mario Felice Boano shortly before his death in February 1944. Boano and his son Gian Paolo had a good relationship with the Chrysler company. However, the liaison with Ferrari was to be short and relatively

Chassis des 166 Inter von 1950 folgten 1951 zehn 195 Inter, von Boanos Schwiegersohn Ezio Ellena gefertigt. Zehn (einige Chronisten sprechen von zwölf) 212 Inter und fünf 340 America sowie drei Ghia-Cabriolets, die einzigen auf Ferrari-Chassis, waren 1952 der Anfang einer Entfremdung, aus welcher Konkurrent Vignale seinen Nutzen zog.

unproductive. The white Berlinetta built onto the chassis of the 166 Inter of 1950 was followed in 1951 by ten 195 Inters, built by Boano's son-in-law Ezio Ellena. Ten (although some chroniclers say there were twelve) 212 Inters and five 340 Americas plus three Ghia convertibles—the only ones on a Ferrari chassis—were to mark the end of this collaboration in 1952; the competitor Vignale was to benefit from this parting of the ways.

Eine seltene Erscheinung: Der Ferrari 195 Inter wurde von der Carrozzeria Ghia in Turin eingekleidet. Man spricht von nur zehn produzierten Modellen.

A rare appearance: the Ferrari 195 Inter was kitted out by Carrozzeria Ghia in Turin. It is said that only ten models were produced.

Typische Elemente: Viele
italienische Autos der
frühen fünfziger Jahre
wurden mit Rechtslenkung
produziert, ebenso
charakteristisch waren
der üppige Chromschmuck
am Armaturenbrett oder
die dezent angedeuteten
Heckflossen.

Typical elements: many
Italian cars of the early
fifties were produced with
right-hand drive, just as
characteristic was the
sumptuous chrome work on
the console, or the subtle,
almost suggested, tail fins.

Spider Vignale

Die Verbindung zwischen der Carrozzeria Vignale, ansässig im Turiner Distrikt Vanchiglietta, und Enzo Ferrari bahnte sich im Frühjahr 1950 an, mit dem einflussreichen Mailänder Autohändler Franco Cornacchia als Mittelsmann. Sie florierte fünf Jahre und zeitigte nicht zuletzt zahllose Rennsiege. Am Anfang stand ein 166 MM Coupé im Sommer 1950.

Als kreativer Genius wirkte Alfredo Vignales Freund Giovanni Michelotti. Dessen Ideen wurden zunächst im Verhältnis 1:1

The relationship between Carrozzeria Vignale, situated in the Vanchiglietta district of Turin, and Enzo Ferrari was established in the spring of 1950 through the efforts of the wealthy Milan car dealer Franco Cornacchia, who acted as intermediary. The relationship prospered for five years, and resulted in countless racing victories. It began in the summer of 1950 with a 166 MM Coupé.

The creative genius was Alfredo Vignale's friend, Giovanni Michelotti. His 1:1-scale ideas were transferred

auf Aluminiumblätter übertragen. Dann brachte man die Bleche über Holzblöcken mit Holzhämmern in die rohe und über Sandsäcken in die feine Form, befestigte sie mit Schrauben und Nieten über einem Geäst aus Metall, überzog sie schließlich mit Spachtelmasse. Nach einer pingeligen Politur trug Alfredos Bruder Guglielmo die Farbe auf.

Jedes Vignale-Produkt war somit ein striktes Unikat. Ohnehin führten Vignale und Michelotti eine entschlossene Kampagne gegen die Langeweile, bespielten

onto aluminum sheets and these sheets were hammered into rough shapes over wooden supports, then placed over sacks of sand and hammered into the precise shapes. The pieces of bodywork thus produced were fixed to a metal skeleton using screws and rivets, after which a primer coating was applied. After a thorough polish Alfredo's brother Guglielmo applied the paint.

This meant that every single Vignale product was a one-off. Vignale and Michelotti ran a strict campaign against

Leichte Eleganz: Der 166 MM, karossiert von Vignale-Designer Giovanni Michelotti, begeisterte mit seiner funktionalen Eleganz. Der Regisseur Roberto Rossellini und König Leopold von Belgien fuhren Ferrari mit Vignale-Karosserien.

Light elegance: the 166 MM, bodywork by the Vignale designer Giovanni Michelotti, inspired with its functional elegance. The film director Roberto Rossellini and King Leopold of Belgium both drove Ferraris with Vignale bodywork.

virtuos die ganze Bandbreite zwischen klassisch-schlicht und barock-überfrachtet und scheuten selbst vor Ausrutschern in den Art déco nicht zurück. Ihr Füllhorn an Formen, verschwenderisch entleert über insgesamt 155 Ferrari-Chassis, war prall voll mit runden und länglichen Luftöffnungen, angeordnet mit einer deutlich erkennbaren Vorliebe für die magische Zahl drei, Hutzen von lediglich schmückender Funktion, unkonventionell gestalteten Türgriffen sowie viel Chrom. Viele prominente Zeitgenossen wussten das zu würdigen.

Auch der Ferrari 195 Inter wirkte mit seiner Vignale-Karosserie grazil und elegant. Typisch für die Vignale-Kreationen jener Zeit waren die filigranen Türgriffe.

anything remotely monotonous, and their virtuosity extended from the truly Classical to the excessively Baroque, and they were not even afraid to delve into the style of Art Deco when the need arose. Their sometimes over-fertile imaginations produced bodywork for 155 Ferrari chassis, full of round and oblong air intakes, with a notable preference for the magic number three, hollows with no function, and fussy door handles, and the whole thing sprinkled liberally with chrome. Many celebrities of the day appreciated this style.

The Ferrari 195 Inter with its Vignale bodywork also had a delicate and elegant appearance. The filigree door handles were typical for Vignale creations of the time.

250 MM Coupé Pinin Farina

Das Auto, mit dem Kettenraucher und Choleriker Giovanni Bracco das 1000-Meilen-Rennen von Brescia an einem abscheulichen Maitag des Jahres 1952 gewann, war ein experimenteller Ferrari 250 S mit der Kurzblock-Maschine von Gioacchino Colombo, der man Zylinderköpfe aufgesetzt hatte, wie sie Aurelio Lampredi an den hubraumstärkeren Maschinen des Hauses verwendete.

Die Karosserie stammte von Vignale. Da sie gute Anlagen aufwies, wurde sie von Francesco Salomone, Designer bei Pininfarina, lediglich retuschiert, bevor man dem Prototyp auf dem Genfer Salon im März 1953 ein Produktions-Coupé namens 250 MM folgen ließ – diesmal zu Ehren von Braccos verwegener Fahrt im Jahr zuvor. 17 weitere folgten, dazu gab es 14 Spider, nicht alle von Farina.

Der 250 MM war kompakt, handlich nicht zuletzt wegen seines kurzen Radstands von 2400 mm und eher flink als schnell: 255 km/h Spitze meldete das Werk, um einiges langsamer also als die 298 des zeitgenössischen Modells 375 MM. Im Gegensatz zu dem Versuchswagen mit seinen fünf unsynchronisierten hatte er vier synchronisierte Gänge. Und anders als jener richtete er im Rennsport nicht übermäßig viel aus. Seiner Beliebtheit tat das keinen Abbruch.

The car in which the chain-smoking and extremely temperamental Giovanni Bracco won the 1000-mile Brescia race in appalling weather conditions in May 1952 was an experimental Ferrari 250 S. It had a short block engine by Gioacchino Colombo, to which he had fitted cylinder heads similar to those used by Aurelio Lampredi on the larger cubic capacity factory cars.

The bodywork was by Vignale. It was only slightly modified by Francesco Salomone, designer at Pinin Farina, before a prototype was displayed at the Geneva Motor Show in March 1953. This was followed by a production coupé, the 250 MM, built to honor Bracco's win the previous year. Seventeen more examples followed, as well as 14 Spiders, although not all were by Farina.

The 250 MM was compact and maneuverable, not least thanks to its short wheelbase of 7'10" (2400 mm), and notable more for its agility than its speed: the factory claimed a top speed of 158 mph (255 kph), quite a lot slower than the 185 mph (298 kph) of its contemporary, the 375 MM. Unlike the first prototype, the gearbox had four synchromesh gears rather than five crash gears. And unlike the other car, it was by no means a competitive beast in races, but it was much appreciated all the same.

Vater des Erfolgs: Im 250 MM (Mille Miglia) kam zum ersten Mal ein Dreiliter-V12 zum Einsatz, wie er die Sportwagenrennen der Fünfziger und frühen Sechziger beherrschen sollte.

Father of success: the 250 MM (Mille Miglia) was the first car to have the 3-liter V12 engine that dominated international motor sport in the fifties and sixties.

Charakteristisch für den von Battista Pinin Farina gestalteten
250 MM war das große Panorama-Heckfenster. Drei Weber-
Doppelvergaser versorgten die zwölf Zylinder mit dem richtigen
Kraftstoff-Luft-Gemisch.

250 GT Europa Pinin Farina

Die beiden Exponate auf dem Stand des französischen Ferrari-Importeurs Autoval während des Pariser Salons im Oktober 1953 wirkten wie Zwillinge, große Autos, hohe Gürtellinien, schmale Glasflächen. Der Schein trog: Der 375 America, für den Export in die USA bestimmt, war ein 4,5-Liter, während sich der 250 Europa, dem alten Kontinent zugedacht, mit 2963 cm³ beschied, unter der Haube wie jener ein Lampredi-Triebwerk, Leistung zwischen 200 und 220 robusten PS.

14 der 18 Chassis zog zwischen September 1953 und Juli 1954 Pinin Farina an, dazu 27 von 44 einer zweiten Generation bis Januar 1956, zunächst wieder Europa, später nur noch Gran Turismo benannt. 1954 wiederum in Paris vorgestellt, war der seinem Vorgänger ganz ähnlich, wahlweise mit Panorama-Heckscheibe oder zwei Dreieckfenstern, im Übrigen stilistisch gestrafft, auch im Umgang mit ihm ein Gewinn: Der lange Radstand von 2800 mm war um 200 mm gekappt worden, da das Chassis den kürzeren Colombo-Motor beherbergte, mit 2953 cm³ und 240 PS.

Der Hauptlängsträger wölbte sich nun über der Hinterachse, vorn ersetzten Schraubenfedern die bisherige Querblattauslegung. Unangetastet blieben die Maße des spartanischen Innenraums.

The two models displayed on the stand of the French Ferrari importer Autoval at the Paris Salon in October 1953 were as alike as two peas in a pod; imposing vehicles with high waistlines and narrow windows. But appearances can be deceptive: the 375 America, intended for export to the USA, had a 4.5-liter engine, while the 250 Europa, which was destined for the Old World, had 2963 cc; both had a Lampredi engine with a power output of between 200 and 220 sturdy bhp.

Fourteen of the 18 chassis built between September 1953 and July 1954 were given bodywork by Pinin Farina. In addition, 27 of 44 second-generation cars were built before January 1956; these were initially designated Europa, but later were simply called Gran Turismo. Unveiled in 1954, again in Paris, this model was almost identical to its predecessor and available with a panoramic curved rear window or two triangular side windows; in all other respects the styling was more compact, and the handling was thus improved: the long wheelbase of 9 ft 2 in (2800 mm) had been shortened by eight inches (200 mm) as the chassis had been built to take the shorter Colombo 2953 cc engine with 240 bhp.

The central beam of the chassis was angled to straddle the rear axle; at the front, helical springs replaced the previous transverse leaf spring. The dimensions of the spartan interior remained unchanged.

Der filigrane Dachaufbau des 250 GT Europa, von Pinin Farina gezeichnet, verlieh ihm die für dieses Modell typische Eleganz.

The filigree roof construction of the 250 GT Europa, designed by Pinin Farina, lent it the elegance that was typical of this model.

Kleine Blinkleuchten vor der großen Panorama-Heckscheibe, die runden Nebelscheinscheinwerfer von Marchal oder die mit schwarzem Schrumpflack verzierten Ventildeckel entsprachen dem Zeitgeist Mitte der fünfziger Jahre.

The small indicators in front of the panoramic rear window, the round fog lights by Marchal, and the cylinder head covers embellished with black wrinkle paint, were all in keeping with the Zeitgeist of the mid 50s.

375 MM Spider
375 Plus Pinin Farina

Siegertyp: Alle fünf Werkswagen 1954 Tipo 375 Plus waren von Farina eingekleidete Spider.

Die Premiere des 4,5-Liter-Rennsportwagens 375 MM von Ferrari ist belegt für die 24 Stunden von Le Mans 1953, achtbar bis zu einem Kupplungsschaden im Morgengrauen. Zwei weitere ebenfalls in Le Mans gestartete 340 MM, wie der größere Bruder Coupés ähnlich dem 250 MM, wurden nach dem Sarthe-Klassiker auf

The debut of the Ferrari 375 MM 4.5-liter racing sports car is recorded as having been at the 1953 24-hour Le Mans, where it survived until suffering clutch damage at dawn. Two 340 MMs also competed at Le Mans—like their big brother, they were coupés that resembled the 250 MM—and these were upgraded to 375 format after the

375-Format nachgerüstet und bildeten dann mit einem 375 MM Spider von Vignale das Werksaufgebot.

Mit Erfolg: Erstsieg für Nino Farina und Mike Hawthorn bei den 24 Stunden von Spa, Erfolg für Farina/Alberto Ascari beim 1000-km-Rennen am Nürburgring, Marken-Titel. Kraftquelle war Aurelio Lampredis V12, Derivat des

Sarthe Classic. Together with a 375 MM Vignale Spider, they made up the company's squad.

Success: the first victory came for Nino Farina and Mike Hawthorn at the Spa 24-hour race; there was also suc-cess for Farina with Alberto Ascari in the 1000 km race at the Nürburgring—leading towards the Manufacturers'

Winning type: all five 1954 Tipo 375 Plus factory cars were Spiders with bodywork by Farina.

Formel-1-Motors von 1951, 80 mm Bohrung, 74,5 mm Hub, 4494 cm³, 340 PS. Am Ende der Saison waren Kundenwagen mit den Zylindermaßen 84 × 68 mm und 4522 cm³ erhältlich, während die Grand-Prix-Kurbelwelle den Hub der Einsatzfahrzeuge 375 Plus für 1954 auf erneut 74,5 mm, ihren Hubraum auf 4954 cm³ sowie ihre Leistung auf 344 PS aufstockte. Dies und ihre de-Dion-Achse machten sie zu formidablen Werkzeugen beim Kampf um den Titel 1954, mit Siegen in Le Mans (mit Froilán González und Maurice Trintignant) und bei der Carrera Panamericana (durch Umberto Maglioli) als wichtige Bausteine.

Der Aluminium-Tank beherrschte den Kofferraum, und das mächtige Zwölfzylinder-Aggregat mit fünf Litern Hubraum leistete 344 PS.

Championship. The power source was Aurelio Lampredi's V12 design, based on the 1951 Formula 1 engine: 80 mm bore x 74.5 mm stroke, 4494 cc, 340 bhp. At the end of the season, customer cars with cylinders of 84 x 68 mm and 4522 cc were available, while for the Grand Prix engine, the stroke of the 375 Plus was increased for 1954 to 74.5 mm, its cubic capacity to 4954, and its output to 344 bhp. This, and its de Dion axle, were formidable tools in the battle for the 1954 title, with wins in Le Mans (Froilán González and Maurice Trintignant), and at the Carrera Panamericana (Umberto Maglioli) being important contributions.

The aluminum tank dominated the trunk while the powerful twelve-cylinder aggregate achieved 344 bhp with its five-liter capacity.

750 Monza

Das Ferrari-Credo zum V12 schien unverbrüchlich, da wies der Commendatore Aurelio Lampredi an, im Winter 1951/52 einen Vierzylinder zu entwickeln. Mit dessen günstigem Drehmomentverlauf reichten vier Fahrstufen und eine Getriebeübersetzung für die meisten Strecken. Ein genügsameres Konsumverhalten von 22–24 Litern je 100 Kilometer und zehn PS mehr gegenüber den 160 des zwölfzylindrigen Tipo 166 für die aktuelle Formel 2 sprangen ebenfalls heraus, Fundament für

The Ferrari creed regarding the V12 appeared to be unwavering, until Commendatore Aurelio Lampredi announced that a four-cylinder would be developed in the winter of 1951/52. Its better torque meant that four ratios in the gearbox were quite sufficient for most race-tracks. A more reasonable mileage of 10 to 11 mpg (22 to 24 liters per 100 kilometers) and 10 more horsepower than from the 160 of the 12-cylinder Tipo 166 were also achieved, the support that would enable Alberto Ascari

Alberto Ascaris strenge Hegemonie 1952 und 1953, als die WM gemäß dem Formel-2-Reglement mit Zweiliter-Wagen ausgefochten wurde.

Eher mickrig machten sich die Derivate dieser Maschine in den Sportwagen, in die sie ab 1953 gemäß einer erprobten Ferrari-Usance transplantiert wurden. Einer davon: der 750 Monza, in drei Exemplaren von Pininfarina und in weiteren 27 von Scaglietti karossiert – nach einer Skizze von Ferraris Sohn Dino. Mit 2999 cm³ war ihr Motor – mit

to have unchallenged superiority in the 1952 and 1953 World Championships which, according to the rules, were fought out between two-liter Formula 2 cars.

However, the derivatives of this engine that were transplanted into the sports car from 1952 onwards, after thorough testing by Ferrari, proved to be rather dull. One of them was the 750 Monza, of which three were built by Pininfarina and a further 27 by Scaglietti, based on a sketch by Ferrari's son Dino. At 2999 cc, the engine—its

A riveted wooden steering wheel with aluminum spokes, and five instruments—the cockpit of the 750 Monza was limited to the basics.

Die Hutze hinter dem Fahrer optimierte die Aerodynamik, der Vierzylinder-Motor mit drei Litern Hubraum brachte es auf 250 PS, die großen Erfolge blieben allerdings aus.

260 PS eher stark als beständig – bis an die Dreiliter-Grenze ausgereizt. Das Getriebe, zunächst fünf und später vier nicht synchronisierte Gänge, war mit dem Differential an der de-Dion-Hinterachse verblockt. Der 750 Monza stieß auf schier unüberwindliche Konkurrenz: die Zwölfzylinder aus dem eigenen Hause, vor allem aber den Mercedes 300 SLR.

Der belgische Rennfahrer und Journalist Paul Frère schmähte ihn gar ein Stück Holz – mit einem prächtigen Motor.

The hump behind the driver optimized the aerodynamics, the four-cylinder motor with its three-liter capacity managed 250 bhp, however, the big success failed to materialize.

260 bhp made it strong rather than enduring—had been pushed to the three-liter limit maximum capacity rule. The gearbox, which initially had five, and then later four unsynchronized ratios, was mated with the differential on the de Dion rear axle. The 750 Monza came up against apparently unbeatable competition: the marque's own twelve-cylinder cars, but above all the Mercedes 300 SLR.

The Belgian racing driver and journalist Paul Frère went so far as to call it a failure, describing it as a "plank of wood with a fabulous engine."

410 S

Thema mit Variationen:
Sowohl als Spider als
auch als Coupé baute
man in Maranello den
mächtigen 410 S.

Variations on a theme: the
powerful 410 S was built in
Maranello as both a spider
and as a coupé.

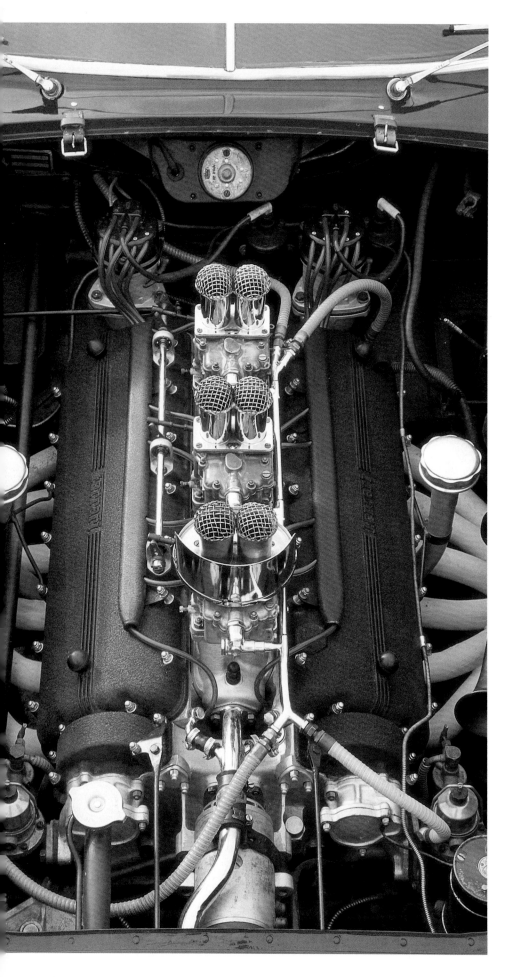

Sie waren technische und optische Delikatessen, die beiden Scaglietti-Spider vom Typ 410 Sport. Ihre Maschinen, enge Verwandte des Triebwerks im 410 Superamerica, wurden wie im 375 F1 von 1951 von 24 Zündkerzen befeuert, mit einer zweiten Reihe auf der Auslassseite der Zylinderköpfe, und auch ihre de-Dion-Achsen wiesen den Weg in die Zukunft.

Eher delikat indessen war ihre Konstitution. Das wurde offenkundig während ihres einzigen Werkseinsatzes am 19. Januar 1956 beim 1000-km-Rennen von Buenos Aires, wo es an beiden Autos Probleme mit der Hinterachse gab. Phil Hill und Olivier Gendebien wurden zweite – im Ferrari 860 Monza, dem man in Maranello fortan die gebührende Zuwendung angedeihen ließ. Die 410 S wurden kurzerhand verkauft. Einer blieb in den Vereinigten Staaten, den Zwilling erstand der Schwede Sture Nottorp. Noch zwei weitere 410 S wurden gebaut, beide mit konventioneller Zündung: ein dritter Spider sowie ein Coupé, das Michel Paul Cavalier in Auftrag gegeben hatte, enger Freund des Commendatore und Verächter automobiler Massenkonfektion.

The two Scaglietti spiders type 410 Sports were the ultimate—both in looks and in technology. Their engines, closely related to that of the 410 Superamerica, had—like the 375 F1 of 1951—24 spark plugs, with a second row squeezed in on the exhaust side of the cylinder heads, and their de Dion axles were also a step into the future.

Their constitution, however, was quite delicate. This was proved in their only official race appearance, on 19 January 1956 at the Buenos Aires 1000 Kilometers, where both had problems with their rear axle. Phil Hill and Olivier Gendebien came second—in the Ferrari 860 Monza, which from then on would play an increasingly important role for the Maranello marque. The 410 Ss were quickly sold; one of them stayed in the US, and its twin was acquired by Sture Nottorp of Sweden. Two further 410 Ss were built, both with a conventional spark plug arrangement. These were a third spider and a coupé, the latter specially commissioned by a close friend of the Commendatore, Michel Paul Cavalier, who despised automobile mass production.

Die klassischen Rund-
instrumente bezog
Ferrari von Jaeger. Drei
Weber-Doppelvergaser
sorgten für die Gemisch-
aufbereitung des 380 PS
starken Zwölfzylinders.

Ferrari obtained the classical
round instruments from
Jaeger. Three Weber double
carburetors took care of
preparing the mixture
for the 380 bhp-strong
twelve cylinders.

Allein schon der große Aluminiumtank, platziert über der Hinterachse, war ein Meisterwerk. Mehrere hundert Nieten wurden von Hand gesetzt, die Bleche gedengelt.

Even the large aluminum tank, placed over the rear axle, was a masterpiece. Several hundred rivets were set by hand, and the aluminum sheets were also honed by hand.

410 Superamerica Series I
410 Superamerica Series II
410 Superamerica Series III

Der 410 SA kam in drei Schüben und 37 Exemplaren, jedes ein Unikat, gemeinsamer Nenner: der Langblock-V12 von 4962 cm³ und erst 340 und schließlich 360 PS, Goodbye-Präsent von Aurelio Lampredi, der die Firma 1955 verlassen hatte. In diesem Jahr kauerte zunächst ein Chassis im Kunstlicht des Pariser Salons. Das komplette Coupé folgte in Brüssel im Januar 1956, zwölf Monate später die zweite Edition auf einem um 200 mm verkürzten Chassis, die man im Umfeld des Aufbaus unauffällig an den Türen eingespart hatte.

Energisch retuschiert zeiget sich der Superamerica der dritten Generation in Paris 1958 den Blicken seiner Bewunderer, mit größeren Bremstrommeln und um 100 mm breiterer Spur, einer Maschine, deren Zündkerzen außen über den Auspuffkrümmern die Verwandtschaft zum Triebwerk des Testa Rossa bezeugten, und einer geglätteten und zeitlos modernen Linie. Seine Scheinwerfer verbargen sich hinter ovalen Abdeckungen oder saßen unmittelbar vorn in den Kotflügeln.

Als der letzte Ende 1959 nach New York eingeschifft wurde, waren formale Konzeption und meist auch Fertigung fast aller Ferrari unversehens in die Regie von Pinin Farina übergegangen. Die Baureihe gipfelte in zwei seiner Superfast-Versionen. Bemerkenswert war vor allem die zweite, 120 mm kürzer und 50 mm höher als der Vorgänger und vergleichsweise europäisch schlicht. Mit dieser ermittelte der Tester von *Sports Cars Illustrated* die besten Werte in der Geschichte des Blatts, Rennfahrzeuge eingeschlossen: bare 5,6 Sekunden für den Sprint auf 60 Meilen, 12,1 auf 100.

The 410 SA was produced in three batches and 37 cars, each one unique but with one common factor: the long-block V12 with 4962 cc, with 340 bhp initially and then 360—a leaving present from Aurelio Lampredi, who had left the company in 1955. The chassis had already been shown in the artificial light of the Paris Salon that same year. The complete coupé was not seen for the first time until the Brussels show in January 1956, followed twelve months later by the second edition with an 8-inch (200-mm) shorter chassis, a saving that had been made on the doors but was hardly noticeable.

Unveiled in Paris in 1958, where it was much admired, the Superamerica had larger brake drums; the track had been widened by four inches (100 mm), and the engine, whose spark plugs were located above the branches of the exhaust manifold, could not hide the fact that it was related to the Testa Rossa engine, and had the smoother lines of a modern classic. Its headlights were either concealed behind oval covers or they appeared directly in the front of the wings.

At the end of 1959, by which time the last Superamerica was on its way to New York, the concept and design of almost all Ferraris were in the hands of Pinin Farina. The series peaked with two Superfast versions. The second one was most remarkable: 4¾ inches (120 mm) shorter and two inches (50 mm) higher than its predecessor, it had a distinctly more European look about it. This was the car that when road-tested by *Sports Car Illustrated* achieved the best figures in the history of the publication—racing cars included: just 5.6 seconds for the sprint to 60 mph (96 kph), 12.1 seconds to 100 mph (160 kph).

Die markante Lufthutze auf der Motorhaube und der Gittergrill kennzeichneten viele Ferrari jener Zeit.

The striking air scoop and the lattice grill characterized many Ferraris of the time.

Das Interieur verwöhnte nicht eben durch üppigen Luxus, die vorderen Entlüftungsgitter wie auch die angedeuteten Heckflossen waren Konzessionen an den amerikanischen Markt.

It was not only the interior that pampered the owner with sumptuous luxury – the front ventilation grille and light tail fins were added as concessions to the American market.

250 GT Boano/Ellena

Vorläufer einer neuen Ferrari-Generation von GTs, auf dem Genfer Salon 1956 von Farina dargeboten, wirkte er ein bisschen massig: wenig Glas, viel Rumpf, ausgeprägte Horizontale zwischen hoch angesiedelten Scheinwerfern und dem Steilabfall des Hecks, großer Kofferraum.

Die ovale Kühleröffnung, von den Rennsportwagen des Hauses wie dem 118 oder dem 121 LM inspiriert, wies zwei Nebelscheinwerfer als Intarsien in den Winkeln auf. Sein Triebwerk war ein Abkömmling des Colombo-Dreiliters aus dem Siegerwagen 250 S bei der Mille Miglia 1952. Mit der Fertigung des Coupés in einer Art Serie wurde zunächst Mario Felice Boano beauftragt, der es sanft retuschierte, vor allem aber den kessen kleinen Hüftknick hinter den Türen abtrug und es in 75 Exemplaren unter die Leute brachte.

Im Frühjahr 1957 trat Boano in Fiat-Dienste als Chef des hauseigenen Centro Stile. Sein früheres Unternehmen an der Turiner Via Collegno hieß fortan Carrozzeria Ellena nach seinem Schwiergersohn, einem der Teilhaber. Deren Interpretation des 250 GT, 1957 in Turin präsentiert, hob sich kaum vom Vorgänger ab: Weg waren die seitlichen Ausstellfenster, vergrößert die Glas- und die Bremsfläche, vertieft das Gepäckabteil, da das Reserverad unter den Boden ausgelagert war, verkürzt der hintere Deckel. 49 Kunden wussten das zu schätzen.

Unveiled at the Geneva Motor Show in 1956 by Farina, the precursor of a new generation of Ferrari GTs appeared somewhat bulky: not much glass, an imposing front, strong horizontal lines between high headlights, the steep line of the rear, the large trunk.

The oval radiator grille took its inspiration from the 118 and 121 LM models, and incorporated two fog lights, one at each end. The engine was based on Colombo's three-liter unit, which had powered the winning 250 S at the Mille Miglia in 1952. Mario Felice Boano was commissioned to create a coupé series; he made a few esthetic changes, in particular removing the cheeky little kick-up behind the doors, and then produced 75 units of the final design.

In the spring of 1957, Boano joined Fiat as chief stylist. His former company on the Via Collegno in Turin was renamed Carrozzeria Ellena—after his son-in-law, one of his partners. His version of the 250 GT appeared at the Turin Motor Show in 1957, but differed only slightly from its predecessor: the quarterlights on the side windows had been removed, the brakes and windows were bigger, the trunk capacity had been increased by positioning the spare wheel under the floor, and the trunk lid had been shortened. These improvements were then shared and enjoyed by 49 happy customers.

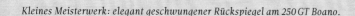

Kleines Meisterwerk: elegant geschwungener Rückspiegel am 250 GT Boano.

A little masterpiece: the elegantly rounded rearview mirror of the 250 GT Boano.

Vom 250 GT Boano entstanden im Jahr 1957 insgesamt 49 Exemplare in den Hallen des Karossiers an der Turiner Via Collegno.

A total of 49 250 GT Boanos were produced in the halls of the coachbuilders on the Via Collegno of Turin in 1957.

250 GT Tour de France

Das Erscheinen des 250 GT 1956 in Genf löste lebhafte Nachfrage aus. Bis 1964 erschien er in etlichen Metamorphosen - wie dieser von 1958.

Vorbereitet durch zwei Prototypen, zeigte sich der 250 GT auf dem Genfer Salon 1956 in seiner vorerst endgültigen Gestalt. Von Pinin Farina stammte der Entwurf, in dem sich zahlreiche Selbstzitate miteinander verquickten. Gefertigt wurde er fast durchweg in Ferraris Werkstätte Scaglietti in Modena, die das Konzept aus Turin noch einmal durchforstete und aufräumte.

After the groundwork had been done with the building of two prototypes, the 250 GT in its provisionally definitive form was shown at the Geneva Motor Show in 1956. Pinin Farina had sketched the outline that contained many of his trademarks. Nearly all the cars were built at Ferrari's Scaglietti works in Modena, where they had fine-tuned the concept delivered to them by the Turin master coachbuilder.

Der Fließheck-Berlinetta war Ferrari pur, selbst mit 130 l Sprit an Bord 1160 kg leicht und kahl wie eine Mönchszelle. Seine Evolution durchlief fünf Stadien, während die Leistung des Dreiliters, System Gioacchino Colombo, stetig von 240 auf 260 PS stieg. Im Bereich des Hecks wandelten sich vor allem Höhe und Profil des Rists über den Hinterrädern. Die Scheinwerfer waren erst ganz vorn angebracht, wenn auch daumenbreit hinter Chromringen, zogen sich

The fastback Berlinetta was pure Ferrari; even with 34 gallons (130 liters) of fuel on board it weighed only 2560 pounds (1160 kg) and was as spartan as a monk's cell. Its evolution went through five stages, while the three-liter engine from the pen of Gioacchino Colombo grew steadily from 240 to 260 bhp. The height and profile of the line above the rear wheel went through several changes, as did the position of the headlights. At first, they were

There was tremendous demand for the 250 GT following its introduction in Geneva in 1956. It appeared in numerous variations right up until 1964—including this one of 1958.

Charakteristisch für den 250 GT Tour de France waren neben
dem Radstand von 2,60 Meter die seitlichen Luftauslässe hinter
den Türen.

dann immer mehr zurück, bis die Rundung der Kotflügel durch Perspex-Kappen wieder hergestellt werden musste, und bezogen am Ende erneut ihre ursprüngliche Position.

Die Heckscheibe aber, zu Beginn der Produktion panoramisch nach vorn gekrümmt, wurde bereits im November 1956 aus dem Umfeld der Seitenfenster verbannt und dort durch sich nach hinten verjüngende Abdeckungen ersetzt, zunächst mit 14, später mit drei Schlitzen, die schließlich einem einzigen Luftauslass wichen, aus Aluminium wie der Rest des Aufbaus.

Auf das Konto des 250 GT gingen zwischen 1956 und 1959 vier Gesamtsiege bei der Tour de France. Sein Kriegername erklärt sich damit selbst.

right at the front of the car behind a small circle of chrome no wider than a thumb, but then placed further back until the rounded shape of the fenders had to be replaced by Perspex caps, before they were finally returned to their original positions.

In the initial stages of production the panoramic rear window extended round to the sides, but this design was abolished in November 1956. The sides then became panels made of aluminum, like the rest of the bodywork. These panels tapered to the rear, initially with fourteen slits in them, later with three, and then with just one.

Between 1956 and 1959 the 250 GT enjoyed four overall wins at the Tour de France. Which explains its name.

Characteristic of the 250 GT Tour de France were, apart from the 2.60-metre (8'6") wheelbase, the side air outlets behind the doors.

*Das Dreiliter-Aggregat
leistete im Tour de France
260 PS bei 7000 Touren,
und der mit einem
Aluminiumverschluss
abgedeckte Tank fasste
130 Liter Kraftstoff.*

*The three-liter aggregate
achieved in the TdF 260 bhp
at 7000 rpm, while the tank,
sealed by an aluminum cap,
held 34 1/2 gallons (130 liters)
of fuel.*

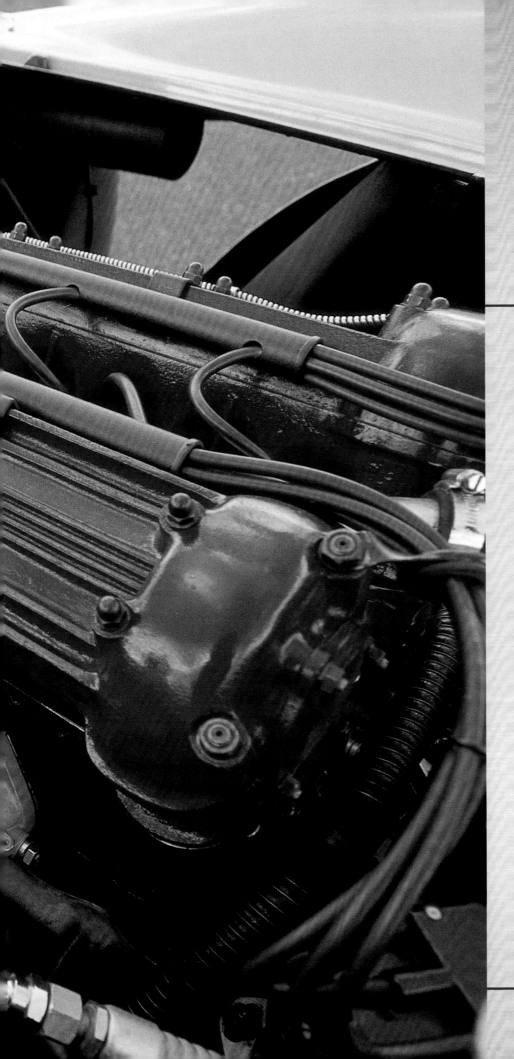

500 Testa Rossa
500 TRC
250 TR
TR 59
TR 60
TR 61
TR 62

Testa Rossa, Rotkopf hieß er, weil seine Zylinderkopfdeckel mit rotem Lack dubliert waren. 13 bedeutende Rennsiege gingen auf sein Konto und die drei Weltmeisterschaften 1958, 1960 und 1961. Das Projekt begann 1956 mit dem Zweiliter 500 TR, einem Vierzylinder von 190 PS. Ende 1956 folgte der TRC, mit Konzessionen an den Appendix C des Sportgesetzes wie eine Tür für den Beifahrer oder ein Reserverad. Das Design stammte wie bereits beim TR von Pinin Farina, die Ausführung von Scaglietti, und die gesamte Auflage fand ihren Weg in die Hände von zufriedenen Kunden.

Testa Rossa—"red head"—was so called because the cam covers on the cylinder heads were painted red. It had no fewer than 13 major wins to its credit, plus three world championships in 1958, 1960, and 1961. The first car in the project appeared in 1956: the 500 TR, with its two-liter, four-cylinder, 190 bhp engine. The TRC followed at the end of 1956 with concessions to Appendix C of the sporting regulations, such as a passenger door and a spare wheel. As was the case with the TR, the bodywork was designed by Pinin Farina and it was built by Scaglietti, and the entire production run was bought by very satisfied customers.

Der Name war Programm: Rot lackierte Zylinderkopfdeckel zierten diese Modellreihe, beginnend mit dem vierzylindrigen 500 TR.

The name says it all: red-painted cylinder head covers embellished the engines of this model range, beginning with the four-cylinder 500 TR.

Der 500 TRC erschien Ende 1956, die Karosserie wurde bei Scaglietti in Modena gefertigt, und der Vierzylindermotor mit zwei oben liegenden Nockenwellen brachte es auf 190 PS.

Der 250 Testa Rossa entstand 1957, komponiert aus dem Chassis des 290 MM, dem V12 des 250 GT und der Karosserie des TR. Die käufliche Version hob sich ab durch tiefe Auskehlungen hinter den Vorderrädern zur Kühlung der riesigen Bremstrommeln, das synchronisierte Viergang-Getriebe und deftige 100 PS je Liter Hubraum. Der TR 59, Entwurf wiederum Farina, Konstruktion Medardo Fantuzzi, war kompakter und mit 306 PS stärker, hatte fünf Fahrstufen und Scheibenbremsen. 1960, kenntlich durch das Kürzel TRI, hatten einige Modelle unabhängig aufgehängte Räder. In Analogie zum aktuellen Tipo 156 für die Formel 1 war der TRI 61 erkennbar am Doppelnüstern-Layout der Frontpartie und trug einen Spoiler auf dem Heck. Der letzte Testa Rossa war 1962 ein 330 TRI/LM, ein Vierliter also mit 360 PS.

The 250 Testa Rossa appeared in 1957, based on the chassis of the 290 MM, the V12 of the 250 GT, and the bodywork of the TR. The production version differed in that it had spectacular cut-away fenders, designed to allow the cooling of the huge drum brakes, a four-speed synchromesh box, and an impressive 100 bhp per liter cubic capacity. The TR 59, also designed by Farina, with construction by Medardo Fantuzzi, was more compact and more powerful with 306 bhp. It had a five-speed gearbox, and disk brakes. In 1960, some models, identified by the model number TRI, had independent suspension. The TRI 61 was in some ways similar to the Tipo 156 Formula 1 car; it was easily recognizable by the radiator grille with two apertures, and it had a rear spoiler. The last Testa Rossa appeared in 1962, a 330 TRI/LM with a four-liter engine providing 360 bhp.

The 500 TRC appeared at the end of 1956, the bodywork was manufactured by Scaglietti in Modena, and the four-cylinder engine with its two overhead camshafts achieved 190 bhp.

Der 500 TR war bei den Sportwagen-Rennen in der zweiten Hälfte der fünfziger Jahre kaum zu schlagen.

The 500 TR was almost unbeatable in sports car racing of the second half of the 1950s.

(Folgende Doppelseite) Ein Rennen der historischen Traumwagen in England: Der 250 TR von 1958 steht schon in Startposition. Wenig später wird Phil Hill den Dreiliter-Zwölfzylinder besteigen — und den Sieg nach Hause fahren.

(Overleaf) The historic dream automobile at a race in England: the 1958 250 TR is already in starting position. A little later Phil Hill gets behind the steering wheel of the 3-litre 12-cylinder to win the race.

*Typisch für den 250 Testa
Rossa von 1958 waren
die tiefen Auskehlungen
hinter den Vorderrädern zur
Kühlung der Bremstrommeln.*

*The deep recesses behind the
front wheels for cooling the
brake drums were typical of
the 250 Testa Rossa of 1958.*

Mit dem 330 TRI siegten
Olivier Gendebien und Phil
Hill beim prestigeträchtigen
24-Stunden-Rennen in
Le Mans. Unter der Haube
agierte ein 360 PS starker
V12-Motor.

Phil Hill and Olivier
Gendebien won the
prestigious Le Mans 24 hours
in the 330 TRI. A 360 bhp
V12 engine was on operation
under the hood.

290 S
315 S
335 S

Mehr als bei irgendeinem anderen schwingen in dem Ferrari-Kürzel 335 S Glanz und Elend des Rennsports mit. Denn der Sieg des 51-jährigen Piero Taruffi 1957 bei seiner 13. Mille Miglia, der letzten überhaupt, war erkauft mit dem Tod seines Teamkollegen Fon de Portago und seines Beifahrers Ed Nelson im gleichen Modell. Auch zehn arglose Zuschauer starben.

1957 zogen Viernockenwellen-V12 ein in die Rennsport-wagen des Hauses, entwickelt vom Ingenieurs-Team Jano, Massimino, Bellantani und Fraschetti, nachdem man als solide Grundlage das Beste aus den Motoren von Lampredi und Colombo miteinander verschnitten hatte im Typ 290 MM. Am Anfang stand der 290 S mit 330 PS, dann erfolgte eine zügige Hubraum-Expansion über den 315 S

More than any other Ferrari model number, the 335 S sums up the highs and lows of motor sport. In 1957, at the wheel of one of these machines, 51-year-old Piero Taruffi won the 13th and very last Mille Miglia—while his team colleague Fon de Portago and co-driver Ed Nelson met their deaths in the same model. Ten innocent bystanders also died.

In 1957 the marque's racing cars were fitted with four overhead camshafts, developed by a team of engineers consisting of Jano, Massimino, Bellantani, and Fraschetti, who had combined the best of the Lampredi and Colombo engines used in the 290 MM. At first there was the 290 S with 330 bhp, then a sharp increase in cubic capacity in the 315 S with 360 bhp, and finally the 335 S, which began

In diesem Cockpit lenkte Piero Taruffi am 12. Mai 1957 den 335 S zum Mille-Miglia-Sieg, sein Teamkollege de Portago verunglückte beim gleichen Rennen mit einem 335 S tödlich.

In this cockpit Piero Taruffi steered the 335 S to the Mille Miglia victory on 12 May 1957. His team colleague de Portago suffered a fatal accident in his 335 S in the same race.

mit 360 PS, gipfelnd im 335 S mit seinen anfänglich 390 PS. Taruffis Mille-Miglia-Sieg war indessen die Schwalbe, die noch keinen Sommer machte, zu schnell waren die Maserati 450 S, zu überlegen die privat eingesetzten Jaguar in Le Mans. Erst ein Vierfach-Erfolg in Caracas - zwei 335 S vor zwei Testa Rossa - sicherte Ferrari die Weltmeisterschaft jenes Jahres.

life with 390 bhp. Taruffi's Mille Miglia win was the swallow that didn't make a summer; the Maserati 450 S were far too fast, and the privately entered Jaguars at Le Mans were far superior. But a quadruple success in Caracas—two 335 S ahead of two Testa Rossas—secured that year's world title for Ferrari.

Aggressiv wirkte der große Gittergrill des 335, insgesamt galt Pinin Farinas Kreation indes als elegant und formal ausgewogen.

The large lattice grill of the 335 gives it an aggressive appearance; in general, however, the Pinin Farina creation is considered elegant and balanced in form.

Die sechs Weber-Vergaser vom Typ 42 DCN übernehmen die
Gemischaufbereitung des 390 PS leistenden Zwölfzylinder-
Aggregates mit vier Litern Hubraum.

The six Weber type 42 DCN carburetors are responsible for
preparing the mix for the 390 bhp twelve-cylinder aggregate with
four-liter capacity.

250 GT Cabriolet Series I
250 GT Cabriolet Series II

Nach einigen Jahren der Zurückhaltung auf dem Cabrio-Markt bereiteten Ferrari und Farina die Wiedereröffnung ihrer Modelle gewissenhaft vor, durch einen roten Prototyp etwa auf dem Genfer Salon 1957. Noch drei weitere Vorläufer kündigten das endgültige 250 GT Cabriolet an. In Ganzstahl gehüllt, fußte es auf den Coupés von Boano und Ellena, ein bisschen fad gegenüber dem rivalisierenden Spider. Abhilfe geschah auf der Pariser Schau 1959 mit dem Cabriolet der zweiten Baureihe, das sich formal und mechanisch offensichtlich nach Farinas neuem 250 GT Coupé richtete. In den letzten Exemplaren der alten Serie mit ihrem ausgeprägten Hang zum rechten Winkel war das bereits angeklungen.

Angesagt waren nun Luxus, Komfort und kommodes Reisen. Die Kerzen waren von außen in die Zylinderköpfe geschraubt, was Lebenserwartung und Zugänglichkeit erhöhte. Doppelzündung, Vierganggetriebe mit elektrischem Overdrive und Scheibenbremsen werteten den gediegenen Beau weiter auf, dazu Modifikationen wie eine höhere und steilere Frontscheibe und mehr Glas hinter dreieckigen Ausstellfensterchen, mehr Platz für die Passagiere und mehr Kofferraum sowie eine gefälligere Linienführung des Stoffdachs, ab 1960 wahlweise durch ein Hardtop ersetzbar.

After a number of years of seeming reticent towards the idea of the cabriolet, Ferrari and Farina meticulously prepared a campaign to relaunch their models, such as with the red prototype introduced at the Geneva Motor Show of 1957. There were three more models before the arrival of the final 250 GT Cabriolet. With a body made entirely of steel, its design was based on the Boano and Ellena coupés, although it was a little less exciting than its rival the Spider. This was remedied at the Paris Salon of 1959 with the second-series Cabriolet, the shape and mechanics of which were obviously based on Farina's new 250 GT Coupé. This had already been heralded in the final versions of the old series with their distinct fondness for right angles.

The whole concept tended towards luxury, comfort, and pleasant traveling. The spark plugs were screwed into the cylinder heads from outside, which increased their longevity and simplified maintenance. Double ignition, a four-speed gearbox with electric overdrive, and disk brakes added to the effect, as did modifications such as a taller windshield with less rake; quarter lights and bigger side windows; more room for passengers, a bigger trunk; and an attractive styling of the fabric roof, which from 1960 could be replaced with a hardtop.

Das 250 GT Cabriolet, natürlich wieder von Pinin Farina gezeichnet und gebaut, zählt zu den schönsten Automobilen seiner Zeit.

The 250 GT Cabriolet, designed and built once again by Pinin Farina of course, is considered one of the most beautiful automobiles of its time.

Klassisch die Proportionen mit der langen Front und dem knapp geschnittenen Cockpit. Chrom-gefasste, ansonsten schnörkellose Rundinstrumente informieren den Fahrer über das Wohlbefinden des auch optisch eindrucksvollen Zwölfzylinders.

The long front and scantily cut cockpit are of classical proportions. Six unadorned round instruments inform the driver of the well-being of the optically impressive twelve-cylinder engine.

250 GT California Spyder Series I
250 GT California Spyder SWB

Seine Entstehung hat der 250 GT California Spyder der Initiative amerikanischer Ferrari-Händler zu verdanken. In seiner formalen Geschlossenheit zählt der California auch heute noch zu den Design-Ikonen aus dem Haus Pininfarina.

Er entstand auf Anregung der nordamerikanischen Ferrari-Händler, im Dezember 1957 als Prototyp, ab Mai 1958 ging er in Produktion. Er war dem geschlossenen GT wie aus dem Gesicht geschnitten, abgesehen von einer höheren Windschutzscheibe und dem erotischen Hüftknick. Farina hatte ihn aufs Reißbrett geträumt, Scaglietti ließ ihn Realität werden, Objekt zugleich von Modellpflege und Variation: Scheinwerfer auf den Spitzen der Kotflügel oder hinter Plexiglas-Schalen, Änderungen an den Rückleuchten und dem Kofferraumdeckel,

This car was created in response to a request by the North American Ferrari concessionaires; the prototype was produced in December 1957, and it went into production in May 1958. It was virtually a copy of the hardtop GT, apart from the taller windshield and a silhouette that resembled the female form. Farina had sketched out the plans on his drawing board, and Scaglietti turned them into reality, an object of beauty and variation: headlights on the tips of the fenders or behind Perspex; modifications to the rear lights and trunk lid, and—occasionally—no side

gelegentlich Verzicht auf die Lufteinlässe hinter den Vorderrädern. Ende 1959 kam der Übergang zu Dunlop-Scheibenbremsen. Die Kerzen steckten nun von außen in den Zylinderbänken des V12 wie im Testa Rossa.

Der Vorbote einer zweiten Serie auf dem Genfer Salon 1960 entpuppte sich als Abkömmling des Berlinetta SWB, zu dem allerdings jede äußere Ähnlichkeit verloren gegangen war. Auf Grund des um 200 auf 2400 mm reduzierten Radstands war er kürzer und zugleich eine Idee niedriger und breiter über einem Zuwachs von Spur vorn und

vents behind the front wheels. The changeover to Dunlop disk brakes was made at the end of 1959. The spark plugs were repositioned outside the cylinder banks of the V12, as on the Testa Rossa.

The first example of the second series at the 1960 Geneva Motor Show proved to be a derivative of the Berlinetta SWB, although any similarity was hard to find. The wheelbase had been reduced by eight inches (200 mm) to 7 feet 10 inches (2400 mm), while at the same time the front and rear track had been increased, making it look

The 250 GT California Spyder owes its existence to the initiative of American Ferrari dealers. With its unity of form, it is today still considered one of the Pinin Farina design icons.

hinten - und noch schöner. Einstellbare Teleskopdämpfer fanden sich statt der Houdaille-Drehstäbe, und neue Zylinderköpfe sorgten für mehr Kraft, die im Laufe der Zeit von 250 auf 280 PS stieg.

Im Februar 1963 wurden die letzten Exemplare in die USA ausgeliefert. Einige Versionen waren ganz aus Aluminium, andere hatten reine Rennmotoren oder beides, und einer wurde 1959 in Le Mans sogar Fünfter.

shorter and a touch lower and wider—and more beautiful. Adjustable telescopic dampers had replaced the Houdaille torsion bars, and new cylinder heads gave an increase in power, which rose over time from 250 to 280 bhp.

The final units were delivered to the USA in February 1963. Some versions were built entirely of aluminum while others had genuine racing engines; some had both, and one even came fifth at Le Mans in 1959.

Sieben Instrumente dienen der Fahrerinformation, ansonsten bietet das Cockpit keinerlei optische Höhepunkte. Mit dem kräftigen Schalthebel sortiert der 250-GT-Pilot vier Vorwärtsgänge.

Apart from the seven instruments providing information, the cockpit offers no optical highlight. Four forward gears can be engaged by the 250 GT pilot using the hefty gear lever.

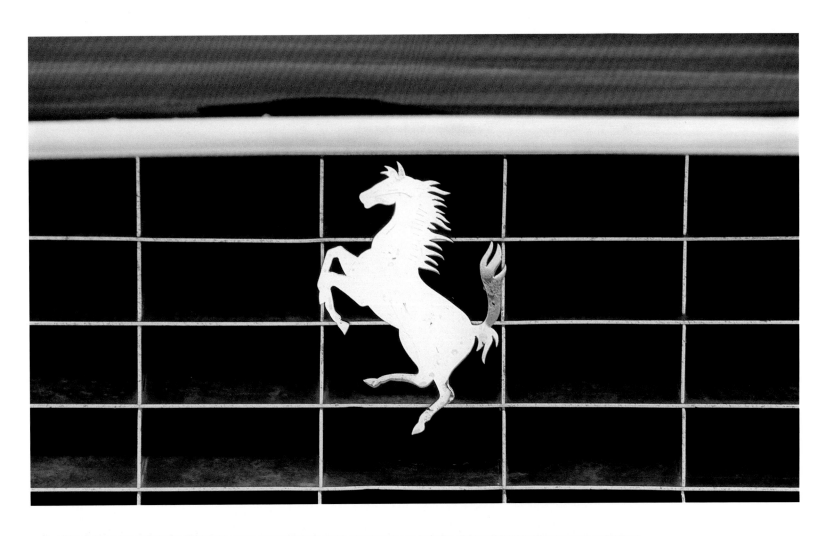

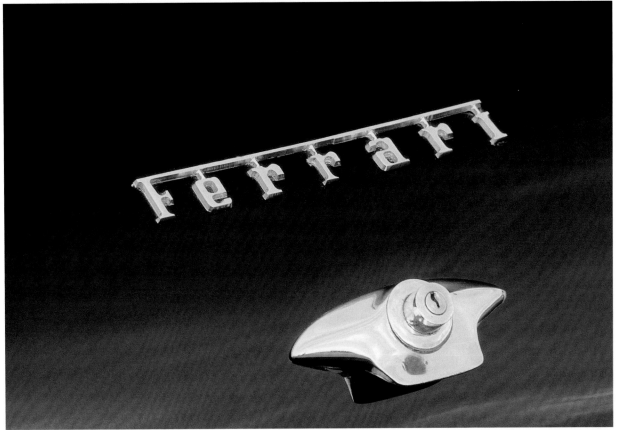

Die Silhouette des California Spyder betört aus jedem Blickwinkel, auch unter der Haube offeriert das Dreiliter-Aggregat mit seinen drei Weber-Doppelvergasern einen visuellen Genuss.

The California Spyder silhouette bewitches from every point of view, while, under the hood, the three-liter engine with its three double Weber carburetors provides a feast for the eyes.

Je nach Kundenwunsch variierte die Gestaltung der Frontpartie. Bei dieser Version mit großen Stoßstangen verbargen sich die Marchal-Hauptscheinwerfer hinter Plexiglasabdeckungen.

The layout of the front is variable according to customer wishes. In this model with its large fenders, the Marchal main headlights are concealed behind plexiglas covers.

250 GT Coupé Pinin Farina

Im Juni 1958 der Presse in Mailand präsentiert, hob sich der 250 GT eher ab von seinem Vorgänger, dem Coupé von Boano und Ellena, als dass er dessen Philosophie fortführte: Vergleichsweise niedrig war seine Gürtellinie, relativ hoch seine Fensterfläche, ungewöhnlich prononciert die Waagerechte.

Bevor sich eine größere Öffentlichkeit auf der Pariser Ausstellung daran erfreuen durfte, wurde der Neue klammheimlich auf einem *Concours d'Élégance* in Antibes eingeschleust, wo allerdings sein Inkognito angesichts des magischen Kennzeichens PROVA MO 58 rasch zerbröckelte. Das 250 GT Coupé entstammte bereits den neuen Farina-Werkanlagen in Grugliasco und teilte seine Geburtsstätte folglich mit dem Cabriolet sowie den Traumwagen für die Bezieher mittlerer Einkommen wie dem Alfa Romeo Giulietta Spider und dem Lancia B 24.

Da lag die Möglichkeit einer Serie natürlich nahe, und tatsächlich brachte es der gewichtige Zweisitzer auf die bislang nie erreichte Auflage von 343 Exemplaren.

Im Jahr des Umbruchs 1959 gab es die üblichen Novitäten: elektrischer Overdrive von Laycock de Normanville, Teleskopstoßdämpfer, das Triebwerk vom Typ 128 DF, dessen Zündkerzen über den Auspuffkrümmern eingeschraubt waren, und Scheibenbremsen von Dunlop. Die waren auch dringend notwendig, denn selbst versierte Ferrari-Eigner benötigten eine Dreiviertelstunde zum Kerzenwechsel, und die Wirkung der Trommelbremsen galt als matt, solange sie nicht heiß waren.

Rather than continuing the philosophy of its predecessor, the Coupé by Boano and Ellena, the 250 GT was quite different. Presented to the press in Milan in June 1958, the car's waistline was comparatively low, the windows taller, the horizontal lines extremely pronounced.

Before its public launch at the Paris Salon, it was secretly entered in a *Concours d'élégance* in Antibes, although its cover was quickly blown by its license plate: PROVA MO 58. The 250 GT came from the new Farina factory in Grugliasco, and so shared its birthplace with the Cabriolet and dream cars destined for more modest budgets, such as the Alfa Romeo Giulietta Spider and the Lancia B 24.

It was possible to think in terms of a production run, and indeed a record 343 units were produced of the weighty two-seater.

In 1959 the usual novelties were introduced: electric overdrive by Laycock de Normanville; telescopic dampers; the type 128 DF engine with spark plugs above the exhaust manifolds; and Dunlop disk brakes. These last two were essential, as even the most accomplished Ferrari owner needed 45 minutes to change the plugs, while the performance of the drum brakes left something to be desired unless they were hot.

Im Juni 1958 präsentierte Ferrari mit dem 250 GT Pinin Farina für den Connaisseur ein Coupé mit schlichtem Understatement und großzügig verglastem Pavillon.

In June 1958, Ferrari presented a coupé with a simple understatement and a generously glazed pavilion—the 250 GT Pinin Farina. A coupé for the connoisseur.

Für zwei Personen und Gepäck präsentierte sich das Coupé als idealer Reisewagen. Die Front mit dem flachen Kühlergrill ließ das Coupé breiter wirken als es tatsächlich war. Ein Ferrari-Schriftzug am Heck und die beiden dezenten Pinin-Farina-Wappen an den Flanken identifizierten das rassige Coupé als Pferd aus bestem Stall. Für die betuchte Klientel von der britischen Insel gab es natürlich auch eine Version mit Rechtslenkung.

The coupé presented itself as the ideal touring vehicle for two people and their luggage. The front with its flat radiator grille lent the coupé a wider appearance than was actually the case. The Ferrari name on the rear and the discreet Pinin Farina arms on both flanks identify this racy coupé as a steed from the very best of stables. Of course, it was also available with right-hand drive for well-off customers from the British Isles.

250 GT Berlinetta SWB

Der 250 GT Berlinetta SWB lässt bereits im Stand seine Potenz erkennen, was seiner Schönheit keinen Abbruch tut.

Er war gefügig auf der Straße und gefürchtet auf der Piste, Jekyll und Hyde in der Doppel-Tradition der Berlinettas aus Maranello, nur noch ein bisschen mehr so.

Ein Interimstyp im Juni 1959 hatte noch das bisherige lange Chassis und schon die zukünftige Form, abgesehen von ein wenig unbeholfen hingestylten Fensterchen hinter den Seitenscheiben. Die waren weg, als Ferrari und Farina den 250 GT im Oktober 1959 in Paris mit dem kurzen Radstand von 2400 mm vorstellten. Da stimmte plötzlich alles,

It was responsive on the road and feared on the track; Jekyll and Hyde in the purest tradition of the Maranello Berlinettas, but with a little something extra.

An intermediate version of June 1959 had the existing long chassis but the shape of the future, with the exception of a small glass area behind the side windows. This had gone by the time Ferrari and Farina presented the 250 GT with the short wheelbase of 7 feet 10 inches (2400 mm) at the Paris Salon of October 1959. Suddenly everything

und die technische Information *Short Wheelbase* (kurzer Radstand) wurde fortan zum Kultbegriff unter den Jüngern der Marke. Im Lauf der nächsten Monate brach man sein glattes Kleid hinter den Rädern und über der Heckscheibe mit fünf Auslässen auf, damit er sich und seinen Insassen Luft machen konnte. Zu ungefähr gleichen Teilen wurde er als Lusso - mit 240 PS und rund 110 kg mehr auf Grund von elementarem Luxus - und als Wettbewerbs-Version mit 280 PS oder gar den 293 PS des Testa-

was in perfect harmony, and the technical information "SWB"—short wheelbase—became the accepted shorthand for a legend in the history of the marque. Over the course of the next few months, five vents appeared behind the wheels and above the rear window to improve the air circulation and passenger comfort. Roughly equal numbers were produced of the Lusso version with 240 bhp and weighing approximately 240 pounds (110 kg) more; the competition version with 280 bhp; and the Testa Rossa

The power of the 250 GT Berlinetta is evident even when it is standing still— and in no way detracts from its beauty.

Der V12 machte auch visuell eine gute Figur, akustisch ohnehin. Hinter den Borrani-Speichenrädern warteten auch achtern Scheibenbremsen auf ihren Einsatz, heiße Luft entwich durch seitliche Schlitze.

The V12 looked every bit as good as it sounded. The Borrani spoke wheels also concealed disk brakes at the rear; hot air escaped through the side vents.

Rossa-Triebwerks angeboten, mit Türen und Deckeln aus Leichtmetall oder einem Aufbau ganz aus Aluminium.

Schier endlos war die Liste seiner Erfolge im Sport, denen die *Motor Revue* ein bisschen auf die Spur kam, als Redakteur Heinz-Ulrich Wieselmann 1960 mit dem schwarzen Exemplar des Düsseldorfers Wolfgang Seidel bare 22 Sekunden maß für die Beschleunigung auf Tempo 160 und wieder zurück bis zum Stillstand ...

with 293 bhp, with doors and hood in light alloy—in some cases the entire body was made of aluminum.

Its list of racing successes was endless—and another feat, albeit on a smaller scale, was achieved by *Motor Revue* editor Heinz-Ulrich Wieselmann. He borrowed the black version belonging to Wolfgang Seidel of Düsseldorf and accelerated from zero to 100 mph (160 kph) and back to a standstill in just 22 seconds ...

Der Berlinetta SWB war gefügig auf der Straße und gefürchtet auf der Piste – da blieb manchem Gegner nur übrig, sich an seiner sinnlichen Heckpartie zu erfreuen.

The Berlinetta SWB was responsive on the road and feared on the track – but at least its opponents could enjoy its wonderful rear.

400 Superamerica

In einer Auflage von 45 Exemplaren, jedes anders als die anderen, war er adressiert an Nonkonformisten, die auf mehr Leistung, mehr Luxus und mehr Prestige aus waren. Die Konstanten: die jüngste großkalibrige Version des Colombo-Triebwerks mit außen angebrachten Zündkerzen und 3967 cm³, mit den 400 PS, die dem Modell den Namen gaben (gemessen wurden 340 PS), oder das Chassis mit 2420 mm Radstand, das ab Herbst 1962 gleichwohl zu den 2600 der letzten 410 Superamerica zurückkehrte. Dazu Scheibenbremsen von Dunlop, Teleskopdämpfer von Koni und der elektrische Overdrive von Laycock de Normanville. Alle wurden sie bei Farina gefertigt.

Der Wachwechsel mit dem 410 Superamerica vollzog sich diskret, eingeleitet vermutlich von einem kantigen Coupé sowie sechs offenen Spielarten, die ihre Nähe zum 250 GT Cabriolet nicht verhehlen mochten. An den Gelenkstellen der Baureihe deuteten vier Coupés jeweils die zukünftige Richtung an, der Superfast 2 auf der

Just 45 versions were built, each one different from the others, and aimed at nonconformists who wanted more performance, more luxury, and more prestige. The constants: the most recent large-caliber Colombo engine with spark plugs on the outside and 3967 cc; the 400 bhp that gave the car its name (although it measured 340 on the test bed); and the chassis with the 7'11"- (2420 mm-) wheelbase, although that reverted to the 8 feet 6 inches (2600 mm) of the last 410 Superamerica in the fall of 1962. Added to this were Dunlop disk brakes, Koni telescopic dampers, and the electric overdrive by Laycock de Normanville. They were all made by Farina.

The changing of the guard from the 410 Superamerica was done discreetly, by way of an angular coupé and six convertible models with obvious links to the 250 GT Cabriolet. At the critical points in the development of the model were four coupés that pointed the way forward for

Die schlichten Rückleuchten des 400 Superamerica waren eingebettet in massive Chromrahmen. Das nahm ihnen die Eleganz und optische Klarheit.

The simple rear lights of the 400 Superamerica were embedded in massive chrome frames. This took away their elegance and optical clarity.

Turiner Show 1960, glatt wie junge Haut, offensichtlich inspiriert vom Profil eines Flugzeugflügels, das Coupé Special Aerodinamico in Genf 1961 mit einer Hutze auf der Motorhaube, Ausstellfensterchen und offenen Scheinwerfern, der Superfast 3 ein Jahr später wieder in Genf mit einem filigranen Dachpavillon mit viel Glas über einem vergleichsweise zerklüfteten und durchfurchten Rumpf, schließlich der Superfast 4, mit Scheinwerfern, die der Mode folgend als Zwillinge aus den Enden der Kotflügel sprossen. Der Vorreiter der letzten Generation erschien auf der Londoner Show 1962.

the future: the Superfast 2, shown at the Turin Show in 1960, smooth as baby's skin, obviously inspired by the profile of an aircraft wing; the Coupé Special Aerodinamico, launched at the Geneva Show in 1961, with an air intake on the hood, windows with quarter lights, and open headlights; the Superfast 3 a year later, again in Geneva, with narrow roof pillars and large glass areas over a comparatively clumpy rear; and finally, the Superfast 4 with headlights that, following the fashion of the time, were mounted on the ends of the fenders. The final generation was previewed in London in 1962.

Fließende Formen und ein filigraner Dachaufbau charakterisieren die Linie des Coupés Aerodinamico.

The lines of the Coupé Aerodinamico were characterized by flowing forms and a filigree roof construction.

Als Ferrari-Fahrer noch rauchten: Der zierliche Aschenbecher, platziert auf der mit Leder verkleideten Mittelkonsole, zeigt die Liebe zum Detail. Drei Weber-Doppelvergaser thronten auf dem Zwölfzylinder, der angeblich 400 PS leistete.

From a time when Ferrari drivers still smoked: the dainty ashtray placed on the leather bound central console, shows a love of detail. Three double Weber carburetors crowned the twelve-cylinder engine and its allegedly 400 bhp.

250 GTE Coupé 2+2

Sein dezentes Debüt gab der 250 GTE 1960 in Le Mans als Einsatzfahrzeug der Rennleitung. Mit Bravour hatte Farina auf dem Chassis von 2600 mm Radstand, um 200 mm in Fahrtrichtung verschoben, den Dreiliter-V12 in seiner mildesten Form von 240 PS und Lebensraum für bis zu vier Passagiere untergebracht.

Auf dem Pariser Salon im Oktober des Jahres wurde er der Weltöffentlichkeit vorgestellt. Viel Vorarbeit war im Windkanal geleistet worden. Eine schmale horizontale Sicke brach das gewichtige Erscheinungsbild des Coupés auf. Die seitlichen Entlüftungsschlitze, mit Ausnahme des glatten Prototyps von Le Mans unmittelbar in die Karosserien der Prototypen gekehlt, fanden sich nun in ein gesondertes Teil eingegraben. Ein Overdrive, von einem handlichen Hebelchen an der Lenksäule aus zu bedienen, wurde mit der kürzeren der beiden angebotenen Übersetzungen geliefert.

Ein komfortabler und majestätischer Reisewagen, ließ der 250 GTE dennoch an Behändigkeit nichts zu wünschen übrig. Ab Genf 1963 gab es ihn gelinde retuschiert. Seine Nebellampen, bislang

The 250 GTE made its elegant debut at Le Mans in 1960, when it was used as the race director's car. In a daring move, Farina shifted the chassis with a wheelbase of 8 feet 6 inches (2600 mm) 8 inches (200 mm) in the drive direction, grafted on the three-liter V12 in its most modest guise of 240 bhp, and provided space for up to four passengers.

It had its world premiere at the Paris Salon in the October of that year. A great deal of preparatory work had been carried out in the wind tunnel. A thin horizontal molding softened the lines of this imposing coupé. Apart from the version that ran at Le Mans, which had smooth sides, the first prototypes had side air vents built into the bodywork, while on the production model they were fitted to an additional panel. An overdrive operated by a lever on the steering column was available with the shorter of the two drive ratios.

A comfortable and prestigious tourer, the 250 GTE left nothing to be desired in the way of agility. After the Geneva Show of 1963, it was given some small modifications. The fog lights, previously fitted on the edges of the radiator grille, were now

Zu einem Ensemble vereint in einem Chromrahmen zierten die Rückleuchten das elegante Heck des 250 GTE, der auf dem Pariser Salon 1960 debütierte.

The rear lights, brought together as an ensemble in a chrome frame, adorned the elegant rear of the 250 GTE, which had its debut at the 1960 Paris Show.

Den formal überaus
gelungenen 250 GTE benutzte
Commendatore Enzo Ferrari
bevorzugt für seine privaten
Reisen. Die horizontale Sicke
verlieh der Pinin-Farina-
Kreation eine willkommene
Leichtigkeit.

Commendatore Enzo Ferrari
preferred using the 250 GTE,
with its most successfully
designed form, for his private
journeys. The horizontal
beading lent the Pinin Farina
creation a welcome lightness
of form.

in den Winkeln der Kühleröffnung, lugten jetzt unter den in Chromringen eingefassten Hauptscheinwerfern hervor. Die Rückleuchten, die einzeln aus den Kotflügeln wuchsen, waren in senkrechten Ensembles versammelt, während die hinteren Kanten selbst steiler abfielen als bisher. Die Borrani-Räder waren breiter, die Stoßdämpfer hinten mit Schraubenfedern kombiniert. So ging das Coupé Ende des Jahres 1963 in ungefähr 49 Exemplaren in die letzte Phase seines Daseins, 330 America geheißen und mit einer Vierliter-Maschine.

mounted under the main lights, which had chrome rings. The rear lights were all grouped together vertically, while the rear of the car now had a steeper slope. The Borrani rims were wider, the rear dampers combined with helical springs. Toward the end of 1963, in its last phase, about 40 units of the coupé were produced to this specification; it was called the 330 America, and had a four-liter engine.

Insgesamt acht Instrumente informierten den Fahrer über das Wohlbefinden des 240 PS leistenden Zwölfzylinders mit drei Litern Hubraum. Genug für eine Höchstgeschwindigkeit von 220 km/h.

A total of eight instruments informed the driver of the well-being of the twelve-cylinder, 240 bhp engine with its three-liter capacity. Enough to provide a top speed of 137 mph (220 kph).

Dino 246 SP
Dino 196 SP
Dino 286 SP
Dino 248 SP
Dino 268 SP

Auf einer Pressekonferenz im Februar 1961 zeigte Enzo Ferrari den 156 F1 Seite an Seite mit dem zweisitzigen Dino 246 SP, mit einem nach hinten verpflanzten V6 wie jener. Beide verrieten die Handschrift des gewichtigen Projektleiters Carlo Chiti, aus dessen Schatzkästlein auch das Doppelnüstern-Layout der Kühleröffnung sowie die Einbindung des Windkanals stammten. Auf das Niveau des Überrollbügels hochgezogen war die Heckpartie, auf deren Höhe ein umlaufender Scheibentrakt. Über dem Kamm-Heck warf sich keck eine Spoilerlippe auf.

Enzo Ferrari presented the 156 F1 side by side with the two-seater Dino 246 SP at a press conference in February 1961; both had a V6 located at the rear. Both bore the signature of project leader Carlo Chiti, who was also responsible for the radiator intake and the testing in the wind tunnel. The rear bodywork went all the way up to the rollover bar, with a windshield wrapping around to the side windows. A rear lip curled up cheekily, rather like a spoiler.

Everywhere it was seen that year, the 246 SP demonstrated just what was hidden away inside it, but it had to be

Wie das Kürzel 268 SP besagte, war dieser Dino von 1962 ein Sport-Prototyp mit einem V8 von 2,6 Litern.

This 1962 Dino 268 SP had a V8 engine with 2.6 liters; "SP" was short for "sports prototype."

Überall zeigte der 246 SP, was in ihm schlummerte, musste sich indessen mit einem Sieg bei der 45. Targa Florio unter Graf Berghe von Trips und Olivier Gendebien begnügen. 1962 gewann ein 246 SP erneut die Targa, mit Ricardo Rodriguez, Willy Mairesse und Olivier Gendebien am Volant, der mit dem gleichen Auto, aber Phil Hill als Partner, auch beim 1000-km-Rennen am Nürburgring siegte.

Auf der Pressekonferenz Ende Februar 1962 war noch eine ganze Dino-Armada aufgezogen, der 196 SP, der 286 SP sowie der Achtzylinder 248 SP, dem bald der 268 SP mit einem auf 2644,9 cm³ vergrößerten V8-Triebwerk folgte. Sie waren alle fast identisch mit einer abgesenkten Rückenpartie und Kerben hinter den Türen zur Ventilation der Scheibenbremsen. Der erhoffte Erfolg blieb aus, abgesehen von der Europa-Bergmeisterschaft, die sich Ludovico Scarfiotti mit dem flinken 196 SP sicherte.

content with one win: at the 45th Targa Florio in the expert hands of Count Berghe von Trips and Olivier Gendebien. A 246 SP again won the Targa in 1962, this time with Ricardo Rodriguez, Willy Mairesse and Olivier Gendebien; the latter also won the 1000-kilometer race at the Nürburgring in the same car, but this time with Phil Hill as his partner.

A whole fleet of Dinos was unveiled at the press conference at the end of February 1962: the 196 SP, the 286 SP, and the eight-cylinder 248 SP, which was soon followed by the 268 SP with a V8 engine bored out to 2644.9 cc. They were almost all identical, with a lower rear end and openings behind the doors to improve the brake cooling. However, for a variety of reasons the hoped-for success did not materialize, with the exception of the European Hillclimb Championship, which was won by Ludovico Scarfiotti with the agile 196 SP.

Die Spoilerlippe über dem Kamm-Heck sollte erst nur verhindern, dass Auspuffgase ins Cockpit zurückschlugen, entpuppte sich dann aber als willkommene aerodynamische Hilfe.

The spoiler lip at the rear was intended to prevent exhaust gases from getting into the cockpit, but then turned out to be a welcome aerodynamic aid.

250 GTO Series I
250 GTO Series II

Das Championat 1962 war ausgeschrieben für GT Wagen. Man brauche, trug Enzo Ferrari seinem Versuchsleiter Giotto Bizzarrini und Scaglietti-Chef Sergio Scaglietti vor, ein Auto, das klein sei und leicht, auf der Basis des Berlinetta. Also versteifte Bizzarrini das vorhandene Chassis mit dem kurzen Radstand von 2400 mm zu einer ungemein rigiden Struktur und nahm die Colombo-Maschine weit an die Fahrgastzelle heran, so dass ihre Hitze in zwei (am Ende drei) seitlichen Kiemen abgeführt werden musste. Er hatte sie aufgerüstet mit größeren Ventilen, schärferen Nockenwellen und neuen Auspuffkrümmern, und zwischen den Schenkeln des V12 spendeten sechs Weber-Doppelvergaser das Ihre zu fast 300 PS.

Die Form hatte der Commendatore selbst roh vorgegeben. Die drei markanten Halbrunde, die den Triebwerkstrakt von vorne beatmeten, gliederten sich ebenso gefällig ins schöne Erscheinungsbild ein wie die kühn geschürzte Spoilerkante hinten, beim ersten Rennen des

The 1962 World Championship was for GT cars. Enzo Ferrari told his chief engineer Giotto Bizzarrini and Scaglietti boss Sergio Scaglietti that he needed a small, light car based on the Berlinetta. Bizzarrini set to, strengthening the existing chassis with the short wheelbase of 7 feet 10 inches (2400 mm) to the maximum, and moving the Colombo engine closer to the passenger cell so that the heat from it had to be discharged from two (later three) vents on the side. He improved the engine by giving it bigger valves, higher profile camshafts, and new exhaust manifolds, and between the V of the twelve-cylinder engine, six double-bodied Weber Type 38 DCNs gave their all at almost 300 bhp.

The Commendatore himself had stipulated the basics of the form. The three striking half-moon shaped openings in the front end that allowed the engine to breathe highlighted the powerful nature of the car, as did the spoiler lip on the rear of the tail; the latter was used in the GTO's

Der GTO war der König unter den Gran Turismo der frühen sechziger Jahre. Er gewann für das Unternehmen aus Maranello drei Marken-Weltmeisterschaften.

The GTO was the king of the Gran Turismos of the early 1960s. It won three constructor's world championships for the company from Maranello.

GTO in Sebring 1962 noch einfach aufgesetzt, später ganz integriert.

Auf Enzo Ferraris Pressekonferenz am 24. Februar 1962 wurde der GTO (das O steht für *omologata*, homologiert), einer respektvoll ergriffenen Öffentlichkeit vorgestellt, der König unter den GT der Sechziger: Auf sein Konto gingen die drei Championate 1962 bis 1964 sowie unzählige Rennsiege. Es gab ein paar Vierliter-Modelle mit dem modifizierten Motor des Superamerica, etliche wunderliche Mutanten, und der knappen Restauflage für 1964 (drei neue Wagen, vier frühere neu karossiert) hatte man ein bisschen das gewisse Etwas geraubt.

first race at Sebring in 1962, and later fully integrated into the design.

At Enzo Ferrari's press conference on February 24, 1962, the GTO (the O stood for *omologata*, homologated) was shown to a respectful audience; the King of the Sixties GTs took three world titles from 1962 to 1964 and won numerous races. There were a few four-liter models with the modified engine from the Superamerica, countless strange hybrids, and the small series for 1964 (three new cars, four earlier ones with new bodywork) which had been robbed of a little of that "certain something."

Die Aluminiumbleche für den GTO wurden im Scaglietti-Atelier in Modena in je einwöchiger Arbeit skulptiert.

The aluminum panels for the GTO were sculpted at the Scaglietti studio in Modena; each one took a week to complete.

Sechs Weber-Doppelvergaser versorgten den Zwölfzylinder mit dem optimalen Gemisch. Die Fahrer hatten den zentral eingebauten Drehzahlmesser stets im Blick, schließlich drehte das fast 300 PS leistende Triebwerk rund 7500/min.

Six Weber double carburetors provided the twelve-cylinder engine with an optimal mixture. The driver kept the built-in rev counter constantly in view, for the 300 bhp strong engine produced around 7500 rpm.

*Die letzte Version
des GTO präsentierte
sich mit einer stark
modifizierten Karosserie,
die noch intensiver auf
Erfordernisse des Rennsports
zugeschnitten war.*

*The last version of the
GTO presented itself with
a strongly modified body,
which had been more
intensely tailored to the
requirements of racing sport.*

Der GTO von 1964 hatte viel
von seinem ursprünglichen
Charme verloren, seine
Form läutete jedoch bereits
die künftigen Heckmotor-
Generationen ein.

Although the 1964 GTO
had lost much of its
original charm, its shape
already heralded the
future generation of rear-
engined cars.

250 GT Lusso

Der 250 GT Lusso war das automobile Schönheits-ideal der frühen Sechziger - natürlich von Pininfarina gezeichnet.

Luxus - den Namen Lusso gaben ihm Verehrer der Marke - war eher rar, unbestritten aber seine Schönheit, gleitende, fließende Linien, harmonisches Widerspiel von Gerade und Rundung, viel Glas, mit einem filigranen Steg zwischen den hinteren Dreieckfensterchen und der großen Heckscheibe. Als 1975 Juroren die 60 attraktivsten Autos seit 1903 kürten für

Luxury—it was named Lusso by admirers of the marque—was perhaps not so much in evidence, but its beauty was undeniable: light, flowing lines that successfully combined straights and curves, and lots of glass with just a narrow pillar between the rear side windows and the large rear window. In 1975, when a jury was tasked with choosing the 60 most beautiful cars built since 1903 for an

eine Ausstellung im kalifornischen Newport Harbor Art Museum, blieb der Kandidat Ferrari 250 GT/L
ohne Gegenstimmen.

Bei seiner Premiere beim Pariser Salon 1962 erschien er
zu spät, begleitet von Battista Pininfarina – 1961 hatte man
Spott- (*pinin* heißt Zwerg) und den Familiennamen des
Alten von Grugliasco zum Künstlernamen verschnitten.

exhibition at the New Harbor Art museum in California,
the Ferrari 250 GT/L was the outright winner.

This great lady of the car world could permit herself to
arrive late at the 1962 Paris Salon, accompanied by Battista
Pininfarina, the master of Grugliasco—in 1961 his nickname *pinin* (which means "dwarf" in Italian) and his sur-
name were combined to form his working name.

*The 250 GT Lusso was the
ideal of automobile beauty in
the early sixties—designed by
Pininfarina, of course.*

Tachometer und Drehzahlmesser waren zentral im Armaturenbrett platziert, was nicht von allen Käufern goutiert wurde. Leder und Holz sorgten für ein Ferrari-adäquates Ambiente im Interieur.

The speedometer and rev counter were placed centrally on the dashboard, which was not well appreciated by all buyers. Leather and wood provided an adequate Ferrari ambience for the interior.

Komponiert im eigentlichen Sinne des Begriffs war auch der Lusso. Vom Berlinetta SWB hatte er das Chassis, mit Rohren schmaleren Querschnitts, auf dem der Motor nach vorn verpflanzt worden war, vom GTO kam das Wattgestänge, welches das Differentialgehäuse mit dem Fahrwerk verband. Und das Triebwerk setzte Tendenzen aus dem Berlinetta SWB und dem GT 2+2 fort.

Die Instrumentierung des Lusso wich etwas verspielt von der Norm ab: Tachometer und Drehzahlmesser waren nach rechts oberhalb des Schaltstocks ausgelagert und leicht angewinkelt zum Piloten, in dessen bestem Blickfeld fünf Rundührchen von eher sekundärer Bedeutung hinter dem fast senkrecht stehenden Nardi-Lenkrad.

The Lusso was created in much the same way as earlier cars. It had the chassis of the Berlinetta (although the tubing had a narrower cross-section); the engine had been moved forward to give the occupants more room; and it had the GTO's Watt linkage from the differential casing to the front axle. The engine characteristics were similar to those of the Berlinetta SWB and the GT 2+2.

The layout of the Lusso's instruments was somewhat unusual: The speedometer and rev counter were slightly to the right above the gear lever, angled towards the driver, and five round dials, of secondary importance, were situated just behind the almost vertical Nardi steering wheel.

Gleitende Linien in einem harmonischen Zusammenspiel aus Geraden und Rundungen sowie viel Glas charakterisierten das schöne Coupé mit den Borrani-Speichenrädern.

Gliding lines in a harmonious interaction of straights and curves with a lot of glass characterized the beautiful form of this coupé with Borrani spoke wheels.

250 LM

Er war wirklich ein Dreiliter, der erste 250 LM (wie Le Mans), der auf der Pariser Ausstellung im November 1963 seine Aufwartung machte. Dann aber diente das Sigel nur noch zur Tarnung:

Shown at the Paris Salon in November 1963, the first 250 LM (Le Mans) actually had a three-liter engine. However, the model number was only a disguise: the other 31 had 3.3-liter engines and so,

Die restlichen 31 hatten Maschinen von 3,3 Liter Volumen, waren also, in Ferrari-Sprache übersetzt, 275 LM. Der listige Commendatore wollte nämlich die Homologation des Neuen als Gran Turismo translated into Ferrari-speak, they were in fact 275 LMs. The wily Commendatore did not want to jeopardize the new car's homologation as a Gran Turismo, and so decreed that the original name should be

Der 250 LM, Le-Mans-Sieger 1965, war der erste käufliche Mittelmotor-Ferrari.

The 250 LM, winner of the 1965 Le Mans, was the first mid-engine Ferrari available for purchase.

nicht gefährden und gab deshalb Order, die ursprüngliche Bezeichnung beizubehalten. Die FIA indessen reagierte bürokratisch-dickfellig und gab seinem Antrag erst am 19. Februar 1966 statt – da hatte Scaglietti die Produktion bereits wieder eingestellt.

Der 250 LM, Design Pininfarina, war der erste käufliche Ferrari mit Mittelmotor. Windschutzscheibe, Seitenfenster und Dach entsprachen jenen des GTO der zweiten Serie. Unmittelbar hinter der Frontöffnung verbargen sich

retained. In the end, the FIA acted bureaucratically—and stubbornly—and delayed approving his application until 19 February 1966, by which time Scaglietti had already stopped the production run.

The 250 LM, designed by Pininfarina, was the first commercially available mid-engined Ferrari. The windshield, side windows, and roof were the same as those of the second series GTO. Just behind the grille were the oil cooler and radiator and the tank for the dry sump lubrication.

Von vorn erinnerte der 250 LM an den GTO, ansonsten aber war
dieser Ferrari kompromisslos für den Einsatz auf der Rennstrecke
konzipiert. Graham Hill und Jochen Rindt zählen zu den
erfolgreichen 250-LM-Fahrern.

The 250 LM is reminiscent of the GTO from the front view; otherwise,
this Ferrari was conceived without compromise for action on the
racetrack. Graham Hill and Jochen Rindt were among the most
successful 250 LM drivers.

Der als Mittelmotor installierte Zwölfzylinder arbeitete mit einem Hubraum von 3,3 Litern und leistete 320 PS. Damit erreichte man eine Höchstgeschwindigkeit von 287 km/h.

The mid-mounted twelve-cylinder engine operated with a capacity of 3.3 liters producing 320 bhp. This powerhouse achieved a top speed of 178 mph (287 kph).

die Kühler für Öl und Wasser sowie das Reservoir für die Trockensumpfschmierung. Der Kofferraum fand sich im Bug, das Reserverad hinten, und die Sitzposition hatte sich gewöhnungsbedürftig nach vorn verlagert.

Am Ende der Saison 1964 hatte der 250 LM zehn große Veranstaltungen gewonnen. 1965 verließ sich Ferrari auf seine Kunden und ließ siegen, in Le Mans zum Beispiel am 19. und 20. Juni, als sich der LM des North American Racing Teams mit Jochen Rindt und Masten Gregory durchsetzte.

The trunk was at the front, the spare wheel in the back, and the driving position was moved forward.

At the end of the 1964 season, the 250 LM had won ten major events. In 1965 Ferrari relied on its customers and had wins in Le Mans—for example, on 19 and 20 June, with the LM of the North American Racing Team in the hands of Jochen Rindt and Masten Gregory.

330 GT 2+2

Gelegentlich befremdeten Pininfarina-Designs, vor allem, wenn der Hexer von Grugliasco das Prinzip der edlen Simplizität auf den Altären der Mode schlachtete wie beim 330 GT 2+2, auf dem Brüsseler Salon 1964 präsentiert. Da glotzten den Betrachter unförmige Doppelscheinwerfer an, und auch die hölzernen Applikationen im Inneren gefielen nicht jedermann.

Ansonsten war kein Superlativ zu hoch gegriffen für den Viersitzer aus Maranello. Sein Vierliter, aus dem V12 des Superamerica sublimiert, gab seine Spitzenleistung von 300 PS turbinengleich mit wuchtigem Drehmoment schon viel früher ab als die vergleichsweise rassig-nervösen 250 GT-Triebwerke der Aufbaujahre. Der Auspuffanlage entströmten Klänge von aufreizender Melodik, kraftvoll und dennoch einschmeichelnd. Der Radstand

Just occasionally, Pininfarina got it wrong with a design, and no less so than when the wizard of Grugliasco abandoned his philosophy of elegant simplicity to follow the whims of a passing fashion—as when he presented the 220 GT 2+2 at the Brussels Motor Show in 1964. Some onlookers could not believe their eyes when they saw the strange protuberances that were the headlights, and nor was the wood veneer to everyone's taste.

Apart from that, though, there were not enough superlatives to describe the four-seater from Maranello. The four-liter engine, based on the V12 of the Superamerica and claimed by the factory to be 300 bhp, had tremendous torque and was a great improvement on the nervous performance of the 250 GTs in their development years. The sounds from the exhaust were wonderfully melodic,

Der 330 GT trug als erster Ferrari Doppelscheinwerfer, noch dazu mit unterschiedlicher Größe. Diese Lösung fand nicht überall Beifall.

The 330 GT was the first Ferrari to carry double headlights, and those being of different sizes. Not everyone greeted this solution with applause.

In der Seitenansicht überzeugte der 330 GT auch seine stärksten Kritiker. Mit seinem Radstand von 2,56 Metern war er ein echter 2+2-Sitzer von guter Übersichtlichkeit.

war um 50 auf 2650 mm verlängert worden, mithin die hintere Kniefreiheit um 100 mm gegenüber dem Vorgänger 250 GT 2+2, das Fahrwerk straff, aber keineswegs von übertriebener Härte.

An der zweiten Generation des 330 GT ab Mitte 1965 schmückten Einzelscheinwerfer die Front und drei Luftschächte hinter den Vorderrädern die Flanken, die bislang

strong and seductive. The chassis had been stretched by two inches (50 mm) to 8 feet 8 inches (2650 mm), which resulted in a 4-inch (10-cm) increase in rear legroom over the 250 GT 2+2; the chassis was more taut, but by no means over-hard.

From mid-1965, single headlights adorned the front of the second generation 330 GT, and three large openings

von Schlitzen im unruhigen Muster 4/3/4 aufgebrochen wurden. Leichtmetallfelgen hatten die traditionellen Borrani-Speichenräder ersetzt, die nur noch auf Wunsch erhältlich waren. Und an der Stelle der Viergang-Box mit dem Overdrive von Laycock de Normanville fand sich ein weit gespreiztes Fünfganggetriebe, ohne dass dies die Spitzengeschwindigkeit von 245 km/h beeinflusst hätte.

behind the front wheels replaced the previous slits that had been spaced in the traditional 4/3/4 design. Steel wheels replaced the traditional Borrani wire rims, which were now only available by request. And instead of the four-gear box with Laycock de Normanville overdrive there was now a new five-speed all-synchromesh box; the top speed of 152 mph (245 kph) was unaffected.

The side view of the 330 GT could persuade even its strongest critics. With its 8'5" - (2.56-meter) wheelbase, it was a well laid out, real 2+2 seater.

*Das Vierliter-Kraftwerk
mit 300 PS verwöhnte mit
wuchtigem Drehmoment,
während bequeme Fauteuils
für kommodes Reisen sorgten.*

*The four-liter engine with
300 bhp indulged the owners
with its hefty torque, while
comfortable seating made
sure they traveled in luxury.*

500 Superfast

Die 500 stand für das Gesamtvolumen des Motors, für den man urige 400 PS verhieß. Zum ersten Mal erregte er die Phantasie und die Gemüter auf der Genfer Show 1964. Das Coupé Aerodinamico von 1961 ließ grüßen, nur dass das Heck vorzeitig jäh abriss. Flächig waren seine Flanken, weit nach vorn gespitzt sein Kühlermund, durch Stoßstänglein von eher symbolischem Wert gesäumt. Das Fahrgestell entsprach dem des 330 GT, mit effizienteren Dunlop-Disks und zwei getrennten Bremskreisen nebst Servohilfe, einstellbaren Koni-Dämpfern und Blattfedern hinten, unterstützt durch Schraubenfedern.

Drinnen aber herrschte das vornehme Kolorit eines fürstlichen Boudoirs, mit kostbarem Holz und mit edelstem Leder bespannten Fauteuils. Zwischen Oktober 1963 und August 1966 wurde dieses Prestigeobjekt der Reichen und Schönen in 37 Exemplaren bei Pininfarina mit

The 500 referred to the size of the engine, which provided a rich 400 bhp. It first caught the eye of the general public at the Geneva Motor Show of 1964. The Coupé Aerodinamico of 1961 had an obvious influence on its lines, although the rear ended abruptly. With its flat sides and pointed radiator grille, its fenders were basically decorative. The rolling chassis was much the same as that of the 330 GT, but it had more efficient Dunlop disks with a dual circuit and a servo, adjustable Koni dampers, and leaf springs supported by helical springs at the rear.

The interior, though, had all the elegance and style of a royal boudoir with elegant woods and the very best leather for the seats. Between October 1963 and August 1966, 37 examples of this Pininfarina masterpiece for the rich and beautiful were produced with the utmost care and skill. Twenty-nine were left-hand, the other eight right-hand

Der Schah von Persien, Playboy Gunter Sachs und Prinz Bernhard der Niederlande zählten zu den insgesamt 37 Käufern eines Ferrari 500 Superfast. Die seitlichen Kiemen sorgten für Wärmeabfuhr aus dem Motorraum.

The Shah of Iran, playboy Gunter Sachs, and Prince Bernhard of the Netherlands were among the 37 buyers of a Ferrari 500 Superfast. The side grills ensured a good dispersion of engine room heat.

höchster handwerklicher Sorgfalt erzeugt. 29 hatten Links-, die restlichen acht Rechtslenkung. Eine erste Serie umspannte 25, eine zweite ab Dezember 1965 die zwölf übrigen Wagen. Wie bereits der 330 GT 2+2 vor ihnen hatten sie fünf Gänge anstatt wie bislang vier zuzüglich des Overdrives von Laycock, hängende Pedale, und drei große seitliche Lamellen ventilierten den Maschinenraum anstelle der bisherigen elf kleinen.

drive. The first series consisted of 25 cars, while the other 12 were built in the second batch from December 1965. They benefited from the improvements already made to the 330 GT 2+2: a five-speed mechanical gearbox in place of the Laycock overdrive; suspended pedals; and three large side vents to cool the engine compartment instead of the eleven little slits.

Flächige Flanken und ein langer vorderer Überhang ließen den
Superfast größer wirken als er tatsächlich war. Gleichwohl ein
Wagen für die große Reise mit bequemen Sitzen und viel Komfort
im Innenraum.

Plane flanks and a long front overhang let the Superfast appear
bigger than it actually was. Nevertheless, it remained a vehicle for
long distances with comfortable seating and many interior comforts.

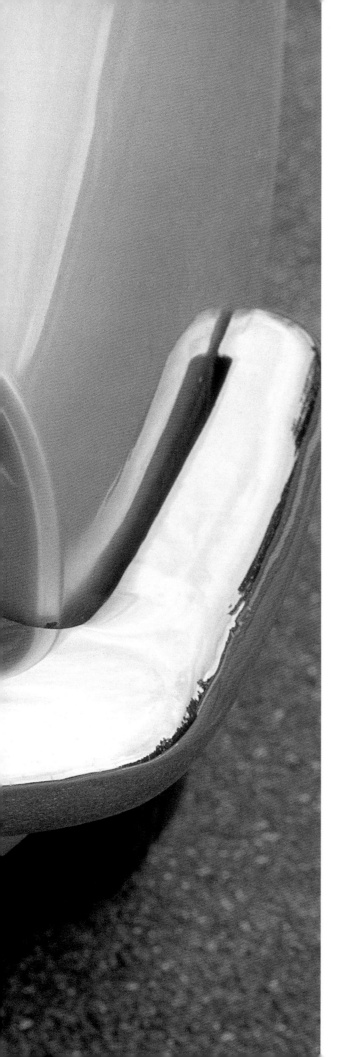

Vorn wie hinten zierten den Superfast zierliche Stoßstangenecken, denen eher Alibi- als eine reale Schutzfunktion zukam, selbst bei leichten Fremdkontakten.

The Superfast had only small fender corners at the front and rear that played more of a cosmetic role rather than offering genuine protection in the event of even slight contact.

275 GTB
275 GTS
275 GTB/4
Spider NART

Im 275 GTB, beim Pariser Salon 1964 Seite an Seite mit dem GTS (S für Spider), verquickten sich Motive aus den GTO der ersten und der zweiten Serie mit Zitaten aus dem GT/L, den er ablöste. 280 PS schöpfte das Triebwerk aus 3,3 Litern, Differential und Fünfganggetriebe waren miteinander verblockt, die Räder einzeln aufgehängt. Ein Jahr später, gleicher Schauplatz: Da hatte man die Heckscheibe vergrößert und die Scharniere des Kofferraumdeckels nach

The 275 GTB, displayed at the Paris Show in 1964 together with its sister the 275 GTS (S for Spider), combined details from the first- and second-series GTO with touches from the GT/L that it replaced. The 3.3-liter engine produced 280 bhp; the differential was attached to the five-speed gearbox; and the wheels were suspended independently. Same place, a year later the rear window was bigger, and the hinges for the trunk had

Der üppige Hüftschwung des 275 GTB kontrastiert apart mit den grafisch anmutenden Entlüftungsschlitzen für den Innenraum.

The generously curving hips of the 275 GTB contrasted stylishly with the graphically striking ventilation slits for the interior.

außen verbannt. Auf der Show in Brüssel 1966 zeigte sich der GTB erneut überarbeitet, durch eine Kühleröffnung weiter vorn sowie Campagnolo-Felgen ähnlich denen des P2 von 1965 und das starre Rohr um die Antriebswelle zwischen Motor und der Differential-Getriebeeinheit.

Zwischen Mai und August 1966 entstanden zwölf 275 GTB/C (C für Competition), rennfähig mit viel Plexiglas, breiteren Felgen, Trockensumpfschmierung sowie einer deftig erleichterten Maschine, von 300 PS wie die des GTB-Thronfolgers GTB/4 mit oben liegenden Nockenwellen, im Oktober 1966 wiederum in Paris vorgestellt. Ein sanfter Buckel auf der Fronthaube unterschied ihn nach außen hin vom Vorgänger. Den Spider NART, ein Derivat des GTB/4, bestellte der rührige amerikanische Ferrari-Händler Luigi Chinetti in zehn Exemplaren bei Scaglietti in Modena. Der Serien-GTS, zwischen November 1964 und Mai 1966 bei Pininfarina in 200 Exemplaren gefertigt, war dem alten Rennsoldaten einfach zu schlapp.

been moved to the outside. Further modifications were revealed at the Brussels Show in 1966: the radiator grille had been moved forward; the Campagnolo wheels were reminiscent of those on the 1965 P2; and a rigid housing enclosed the drive shaft from the engine to the differential gearbox unit.

Twelve 275 GTB/Cs (C for Competition) were built between May and August 1966; ready for racing with lots of Perspex, wider rims, dry sump lubrication, and a much lighter 300-bhp engine—like the GTB's heir the GTB/4 it had overhead camshafts, it was again presented at the Paris Show, this time in October 1966. A gentle bulge on the hood distinguished it externally from its predecessor. Luigi Chinetti, the dynamic American Ferrari dealer, ordered ten Spider NARTs based on the GTB/4 from Scaglietti in Modena. The standard GTS, 200 of which were built by Pininfarina between November 1964 and May 1966, were just not strong enough for the racing veteran.

Der 275 GTS rollte mit seinen 260 PS gezähmter auf die Straße, spielte eher die Rolle des sanften Beaus. Von ihm fertigte Pininfarina exakt 200 Exemplare.

The 275 GTS with its 260 bhp behaved in a tamer manner on the road, playing more the role of the gentle beau. Exactly 200 examples were produced by Pininfarina in Turin.

*Aus der Form - lange Haube, hohe Gürtellinie, kurzes Heck -
sprach seine Kraft: 280 PS aus 3,3 Litern Hubraum sorgten im
275 GTB für stolze 260 km/h Höchstgeschwindigkeit.*

*The form of the 275 GTB – long hood, high waistline, short rear –
mirrored its power: 280 bhp and 3.3-liter capacity ensure an
impressive top speed of 162 mph (260 kph).*

Serienmäßig stand der 275 GTB auf Leichtmetallrädern von Formel-1-Lieferant Campagnolo. Die Speichenräder von Borrani gab es nur noch auf Wunsch.

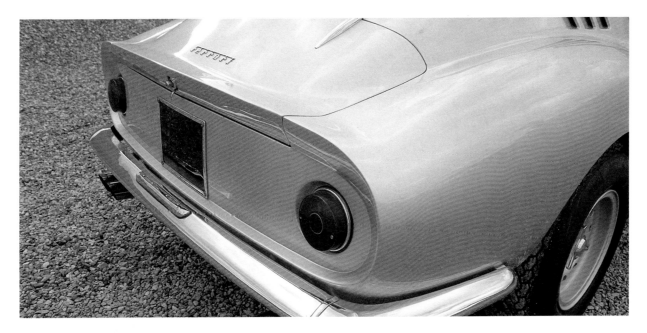

Alloy wheels from Formula 1 supplier Campagnolo were fitted to the 275 GTB as standard. Borrani spoke wheels were only available on request.

*Formal völlig eigenständig
präsentierte sich der Spider
NART, den der amerikanische
Ferrari-Importeur Luigi
Chinetti in einer Auflage
von zehn Exemplaren bei
Scaglietti in Auftrag gab.*

*The Spider NART ordered by
the American Ferrari importer
Luigi Chinetti from Scaglietti
as a batch of ten, presented
itself totally independent in
its form.*

275/330 P
275/330 P2
330 P3
330 P4

Der P2 von 1965 nahm eine Architektur wieder auf, die seit dem 335 S von 1957 auf Eis lag: vier oben liegende Nockenwellen. Hektische Evolution folgte: Es gab die P-Modelle offen und geschlossen, Interimsversionen wie den P2/3, und schon im ersten Jahr verwirrten drei Maschinen von 3,3, 4 und 4,4 Litern – letztere nur für Kunden – den Chronisten. Viel Technik kam aus der Formel 1, etwa das Halbmonocoque. Die Form des P2 hatte man im Windkanal selbst gestaltet. Der Aufbau entstand bei Piero Drogos Carrozzeria Sports Cars in Modena. Der P3 anno 1966 war kürzer, breiter, niedriger und leichter, und der Spider schaute aus wie ein Berlinetta ohne Dachteil.

Im Umkreis des Chassis hatte Fiberglas als Werkstoff Einzug gehalten. Die sechs Weber-Vergaser hatten einer

The P2 of 1965 used a configuration that had not been seen since the 335 S of 1957: four overhead camshafts. Rapid evolution followed: open and closed P models were available; interim versions such as the P2/3, and in the first year alone, three power units of 3.3, 4, and 4.4 liters (the latter only for customers) caused chaos for historians. Much of the technology, such as the monocoque structure, came from Formula 1. The shape of the P2 had been tested in a wind tunnel. The cars were built by Piero Drogos Carrozzeria Sports Cars in Modena. The P3 of 1966 was shorter, wider, lower, and lighter, and the Spider looked like a Berlinetta without the roof.

Fiberglass was the material of choice for the chassis. The six Weber carburetors had been ripped out and replaced

Dieser Tankdeckel gehört zum Ferrari 330 P, jenem Mittelmotor-Rennsportwagen von Ferrari, mit dem man 1965 einige Rennen zur Markenweltmeisterschaft gewinnen konnte.

This tank cap belongs to a Ferrari 330 P, the Ferrari mid-motor racing sports car which won several constructors' world championship races in 1965.

Ein einsatzfähiges Reserverad war vorgeschrieben. Ob 275 P von 1963 (oben) oder 330 P von 1964 – der Baureihe waren unzählige Siege und eine lange Verweildauer beschieden.

A ready-to-use spare wheel was required. Whether the 275 P (above) or the 330 P of 1964, this range achieved very many wins, and remained in action for a remarkably long time.

330 GTC
330 GTS
365 GTC
365 GTS

Der 330 GTC besetzte vom Genfer Salon 1966 an eine Leerstelle, die man zwischen dem 275 GTB und dem 330 GT 2+2 geortet hatte. Wieder verschnitt man Bekanntes miteinander: Pininfarina-Motive aus dem 500 Superfast (vorn) und dem 275 GTS (hinten), gekrönt von einem Dachaufbau mit viel Glas, und von Ferrari das Kurzchassis mit 2400 mm Radstand, einzeln aufgehängten Rädern und das Triebwerk des 330 GT 2+2. Der 300 PS starke Vierliter hatte leicht modifiziert werden müssen, da er mit der Einheit von Getriebe und Differential an der Hinterachse fest verbunden war

The 330 GTC filled a gap that had been left between the 275 GTB and the 330 GT 2+2. Once again, familiar ingredients had been brought together: there were obvious touches of Pininfarina's 500 Superfast at the front and the 275 GTS at the rear, the whole topped off with a roof that rested on large windows; the chassis was a 7'10" (2400 mm) short wheelbase with independent suspension, and it had the 330 GT 2+2 engine. The 300 bhp 4-liter had been slightly modified, since it was now linked to the gearbox and rear

Der 365 GTS bestach nicht nur mit der flüssigen Eleganz seiner Linienführung, sondern schüttelte auch mit seinen 320 PS bei Bedarf lässige Leistung aus dem Ärmel.

The 365 GTS appealed not only for the fluidity of its lines, but its 320 bhp also provided the performance—with ease and elegance—when required.

durch ein massives Rohr, in dem die Antriebswelle rotierte.

Bequeme Ledersessel, elektrische Fensterheber, heizbare Heckscheibe und Klimaanlage als Extras rundeten den Eindruck ab, dieser Ferrari verwöhne nicht nur durch Leistung und glänzende Straßenlage. Mit dem 365 GTC sattelte man 1968 auf der Pariser Show 400 cm^3 und 20 PS drauf, was dem Verlauf der Drehmomentkurve gut tat, ohne dass es die Spitzengeschwindigkeit angehoben hätte. Die Öffnungen für die Ventilation

axle unit by a massive housing which contained the prop shaft.

Comfortable leather-trimmed seats, electric windows, a heated rear windshield, and air conditioning were options that completed the impression that this Ferrari was designed to pamper the driver on various levels—not just with its performance and fabulous road holding. The 365 GTC appeared at the Paris Salon in 1968 with an engine that had an added 400 cc and 20 bhp, which improved the torque but had no effect on the maximum

des Motorraums waren von der Seite umgesiedelt worden auf die Haube nahe der Windschutzscheibe.

Der 330 GTS folgte dem Coupé auf dem Pariser Salon 1966. Er nahm die Linie des 275 GTS auf, bis auf die längere Frontpartie wie auch die geschlossene Version. Bis zum März 1968 wurden 100 Spider gebaut, 20 weitere vom Typ 365 GTS folgten zwischen Januar und April 1969, in den USA angesichts der strikten Paragraphen hinsichtlich Emission und Sicherheit bereits eine bedrohte Spezies.

speed. The air intakes for ventilating the engine had been moved from the sides to the hood, near the windshield.

After a short wait, the 330 GTS appeared at the Paris Salon in 1966. It reprised the shape of the 275 GTS apart from a longer frontal area, which it shared with the hard-top version. By March 1968, 100 Spiders had been built, followed by 20 365 GTSs between January and April 1969—although they were now an endangered species thanks to strict US regulations governing emissions and safety.

Der 365 GTS begeisterte auch
mit seiner klar gezeichneten
Heckpartie. Hausdesigner
Sergio Pininfarina
hatte wieder einmal ein
Meisterwerk auf die Borrani-
Räder gestellt.

The 365 GTS inspired
with its clearly designed
rear. Company designer
Sergio Pininfarina once
again set a masterpiece on
Borrani wheels.

330 GTC · 330 GTS · 365 GTC · 365 GTS

Der grazil wirkende Dachaufbau mit viel Glas verlieh dem Coupé eine optische Leichtigkeit, das schlichte Nardi-Holzlenkrad setzte diesen Akzent innen fort.

The delicate appearance of the greenhouse with its large amount of glass lends the coupé an optical lightness carried into the interior by the simple Nardi wooden steering wheel.

365 California

*Vom luxuriösen
365 California, den es
nur als Cabriolet gab,
entstanden 1966 und
1967 bei Pininfarina
lediglich 14 Exemplare.*

Der 365 California, Premiere 1966 in Genf, löste den 500 Superfast ab und ließ diesen, allerdings oben offen, im Geiste wieder aufleben: Motorisierung auf höchster Ebene, horrend teuer zumal.

Zugleich zitierte ihn Pininfarina, wie etwa mit der langen und geduckten Frontpartie, in die sich Scheinwerfer hinter Plexiglasabdeckungen flüssig eingliederten. Zwei

The 365 California, premiered at the Geneva Show in 1966, replaced the Superfast and also brought its spirit back to life—albeit with an open top. It was the ultimate in engine power, and staggeringly expensive.

So that its links with the Superfast could never be in doubt, Pininfarina did not hesitate in borrowing certain elements, such as the long, curved hood set between

weitere Lampen innen neben ihnen wurden bei Bedarf emporgestülpt. Tief eingekehlt wie beim 206 Dino von 1965: die mit den Türgriffen kombinierten seitlichen Lufteinlässe, schier endlos lang das Heck, endend in einer vertikalen Kante von bizarrer, fast kubistischer Geometrie. Servolenkung und Speichenräder von Borrani waren Standard. Der Motor von 4390 cm³ und 320 PS entsprach

wings that housed the headlamps behind Perspex protectors. Two further retractable lights were fitted beside them. As with the Dino of 1965, the door handles were combined with the side air intakes; the rear seemed endlessly long, and ended in a vertical drop of bizarre, almost Cubist geometry. Power steering and Borrani rims were standard. The 4390 cc engine provided 320 bhp, and matched

Only 14 examples of the luxurious 365 California, which was only available as a cabriolet, were produced at the Pininfarina works between 1966 and 1967.

Charakteristisch für den 365 California waren das noble Interieur sowie die zu einem Trapez geformte Rückleuchten-Einheit, bestehend aus drei runden Einzelleuchten und dem sichelförmigen Blinkerglas.

Characteristic for the 365 California was the noble interior as well as the trapezoidal rear light unit consisting of three round individual lights and the crescent-shaped indicator.

Mit dem klangvollen Appendix wollte man vor allem die gut betuchte Kundschaft jenseits des großen Teiches ansprechen. Schließlich kostete das Cabriolet im Deutschland des Jahres 1967 stolze 76 000 DM.

dem des 365 P2 der Saison 1965 und war, verblockt mit einem Fünfganggetriebe, in das Chassis von 2650 mm Radstand implantiert. So wurden hinter den Frontsitzen zwei Notunterkünfte frei.

Bis zum Juli 1967 fertigte man in Grugliasco 14 California, Handarbeit je Exemplar: neun Monate.

the 365 P2 of 1965. Linked to a five-speed gearbox, it was fitted in a chassis with an 8'8" (2650 mm) wheelbase. This freed enough space behind the front seats for two additional passengers.

By the end of July 1967, 14 California Cabriolets had been made in Grugliasco, each one by hand and taking nine months.

The sonorous appendix was designed to attract well-situated customers from across the Atlantic. After all, in Germany the cabriolet was priced at a proud 76,000 marks in 1967.

Dino 206 S

Klein, leicht, schnell – so lässt sich der Dino 206 S am besten charakterisieren. Besonders auf kurvenreichen Kursen wie der Targa Florio oder dem Nürburgring konnte der formschöne Rennwagen überzeugen.

Als beim 1000-km-Rennen des ADAC im Mai 1965 Lorenzo Bandini und Nino Vaccarella zeitweise Dritte waren mitten zwischen den Großen und am Ende Vierte mit dem Prototyp 166 SP, wurde Häme laut: der sei lediglich ein verkappter Grand-Prix-Wagen und habe gewiss mehr als nur 1,6 Liter. Teamchef Eugenio Dragoni ließ den Motor unter Aufsicht obduzieren, und zum Vorschein kamen in der Tat die angegebenen 1593 cm³. Klein, leicht und immens handlich, hieß der 166 P nicht nur Dino,

After the ADAC 1000-kilometer race at the Nürburgring, where Lorenzo Bandini and Nino Vaccarella held down third place for some time before finally finishing fourth, there was much ill-natured muttering: it could only be a thinly disguised Grand Prix car, and undoubtedly had a greater capacity than the claimed 1.6 liters. Team boss Eugenio Dragonio remained calm; he had the engine dismantled under official control, and it did indeed have only the stated capacity of 1593 cc. Compact, light, and

sondern ein Logo wies ihn als Produkt eines Ferrari-Sub-unternehmens mit diesem Namen aus.

Mit der europäischen Bergmeisterschaft 1965 entriss er Porsche eine sicher gewähnte Domäne. Beim vierten Lauf in Cesana-Sestriere lenkte Champion Ludovico Scarfiotti bereits den offenen 206 P, mit Franco Rocchis kompak-tem V6 von 1987 cm³, der in sanfterer Form ab 1966 im Fiat Dino und 1967 in Ferraris Dino 206 GT Einzug hielt. Auf dem Bergspider fußte der 206 S von 1966, 50 Kilo leichter

incredibly easy to handle, the 166 P was not simply called Dino, but a badge showed that it was in fact produced by a Ferrari affiliate of that name.

In 1965, it struck a blow against Porsche by winning the European Hillclimb Championship. In the fourth round at Cesana-Sestriere, champion Ludovico Scarfiotti was already driving the open 206 P, a car that was powered by Franco Rocchi's compact V6 of 1987 cc—a watered-down version of the engine that was fitted to the 1966 Fiat Dino,

Small, light, fast—that is how the Dino 206 S can best be characterized. This beautifully shaped racing car performed convincingly on those courses rich in curves such as Targa Florio or the Nürburgring.

Benannt nach dem 1956 verstorbenen Sohn Enzo Ferraris wurde der Dino 206 S von einem kompakten V6 mit bloßen 1987 cm³ angetrieben. Die Ähnlichkeit zu den großen Prototypen der Marke wie dem P3 war unverkennbar.

mit seinem ansehnlichen Gewand aus Leichtmetall, das ein filigranes Chassis aus Rohren kleinen Querschnitts mit einer Bodenplatte aus Fiberglas bekleidete. Eine Auflage von 50 war geplant, damit ihm der Segen der CSI als Sportwagen zuteil werde. Aber nach 16 Exemplaren, drei davon geschlossen, riss die Produktion in der Carrozzeria Sports Cars in Modena ab. Der Dino musste als Prototyp starten, mit Vergasern oder Einspritzung, zwei oder drei Ventilen sowie ein und zwei Zündkerzen je Zylinder.

Named after Enzo Ferrari's young son, who died in 1956, the Dino 206 S was powered by a compact V6 with only 1987 cc. The resemblance to the marque's big prototypes such as the P3 was undeniable.

and to Ferrari's Dino 206 GT in 1967. The 1966 206 S was based on the hillclimb Spider, although it was 110 pounds (50 kg) lighter and its appealing light alloy body rested on a tubular chassis of small-diameter sections, with a fiberglass belly pan. The plan was to build 50 so that the CSI would homologate it as a sports car. But after 16 had been built, three of them hard-top versions, Carrozzeria Sports Cars in Modena discontinued production. The Dino had to race as a prototype, with injection and double ignition, two or three valves, and one or two spark plugs per cylinder.

350 CanAm
612 CanAm
712 CanAm

Um ihn dort technisch und visuell auf die sechs CanAm-Läufe im Herbst 1967 einzustimmen, verfrachtete Luigi Chinetti den P3/4 des North American Racing Team nach Maranello. Hinter den Häuptern von Fahrer und gedachtem Beifahrer ragte nun ein kahler Sturzbügel. Niedriger und leichter war der gesamte Aufbau, flacher und glatter die Fronthaube, aus der zwei Scheinwerfer blickten, erheblich geschrumpft die Windschutzscheibe, auf der ein winziger Rückspiegel hockte.

Vom vierten Lauf an erschienen zwei ausgebeinte P4 mit Karosserien aus Fiberglas, weiteren Einsparungen an der Frontscheibe, einem großen Spoiler hinten, föhnförmigen Vorkehrungen zur Beatmung ihrer V12 von 4,2 Litern sowie einer NACA-Öffnung vorn rechts und ohne Scheinwerfer, peinlich unterlegen auch sie. Für die kommende Saison setzte Mauro Forghieri folglich eine technische und optische Leckerei ein mit 6222 cm^3 Hubraum, 48 Ventilen und 620 PS sowie

In 1967, Luigi Chinetti sent the North American Racing Team's P3/4 to Maranello to have it fine-tuned mechanically and visually for the six CanAm races in the fall. There was now a naked roll-over bar between the heads of the driver and his hypothetical passenger. The whole car was lower and lighter; the hood flatter and smoother with two headlights rising up out of it; the windshield much smaller and with a tiny rear-view mirror.

For the fourth race, two P4s appeared with fibreglass bodies; additional changes to the windshield; a large rear spoiler; contraptions shaped like a hairdryer to allow the 4.2-liter V12 to breathe; plus a NACA vent on the front right side. This time there were no headlamps. For the following season, Mauro Forghiere produced a technical and visual delight of 6222 cc with 48 valves, providing 620 bhp, plus a huge wing and aerodynamic brakes at the front controlled by a complex hydraulic system; however, at 1700 pounds (770 kg), it was just too heavy. Bad

Der Ferrari 712 CanAm reckte seinen Rückspiegel hoch in den Fahrtwind, um seinem Piloten freie Sicht nach hinten zu ermöglichen.

The rear-view mirror on the 712 CanAm reached high up into the air to give the pilot a clear view to the rear.

einem riesigen Heckflügel und Luftbremsen vorn, von einer komplizierten Hydraulik aktiviert, mit 770 kg allerdings zu schwer. Skurrile Pointe: Ausfall für Chris Amon in der ersten Kurve in der ersten Runde des Finales in Las Vegas.

1969 kehrte der Neuseeländer mit einem weiteren 612 zurück, kürzer und leichter und ohne die aufwändige Bedienung der Spoiler. Selbst ein brandneuer Kurzhuber von 6,9 Litern beim vorletzten Lauf in Riverside schuf keine Abhilfe. Magere Ausbeute auch bei den Rückzugsscharmützeln der Marke 1971 und 1972: zwei vierte Plätze für Mario Andretti und Jean-Pierre Jarier.

luck followed, with Chris Amon having to retire at the first corner on the first lap in the finale at Las Vegas.

In 1969 the New Zealander was again in the running with a new 612, which was shorter and lighter and no longer had the complicated rear wing. Even a new, longer stroke 6.9-liter engine that appeared for the penultimate race at Riverside failed to make it competitive. The results were no better when the last shots were fired in 1971 and 1972: two fourth places for Mario Andretti and Jean-Pierre Jarier.

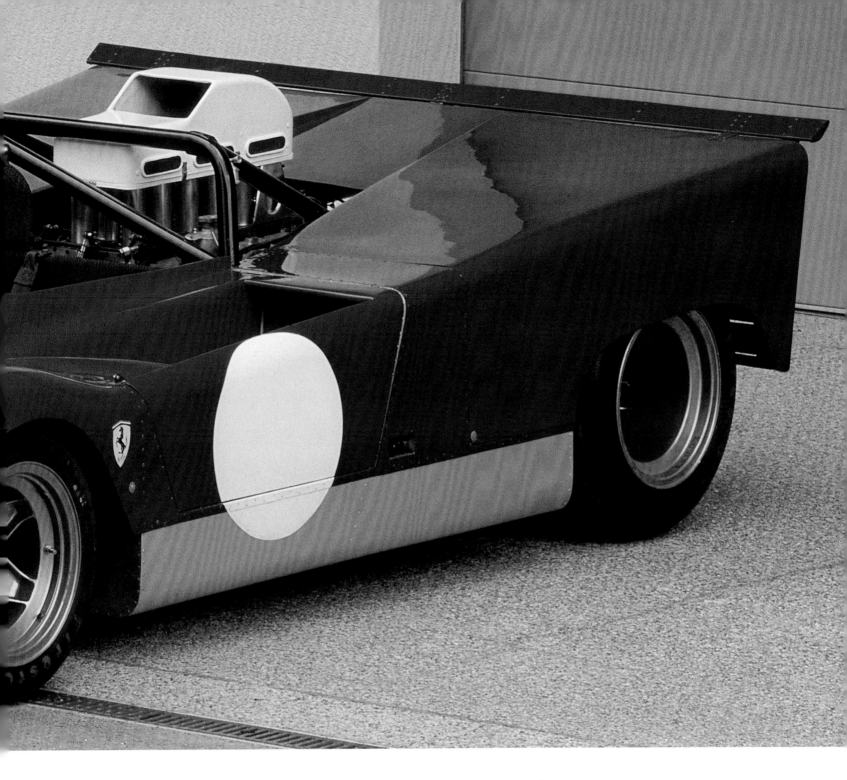

Direkt hinter dem mit einem Vierpunktgurt gesicherten Fahrer
platziert, sorgte der 6,9-Liter-V12 mit 620 PS für wuchtigen
Vortrieb. Es reichte dennoch nicht.

The 6.2-liter engine with its 620 bhp was the source of gutsy
acceleration, while the pilot was secured by a four-point safety belt.
But it still wasn't enough.

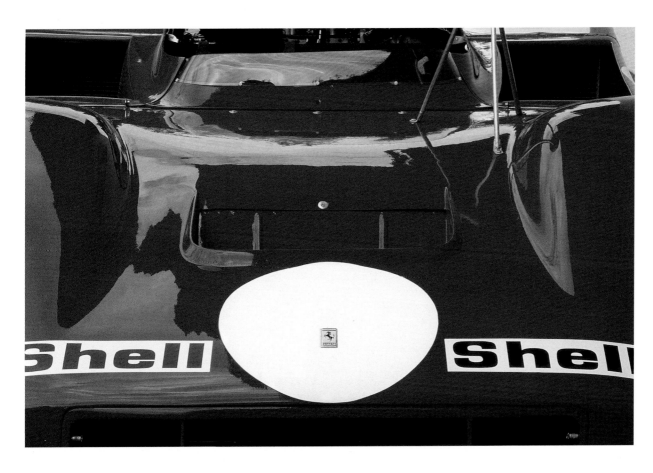

Mit dem einstellbaren
Heckspoiler konnte man
den Anpressdruck auf die
Hinterachse variieren.
Mächtige Slicks von Firestone
stellten den Kontakt zur
Piste her.

Tread pressure on the rear
axle could be varied by
the adjustable rear spoiler.
Powerful Firestone slicks
provided the ground contact.

365 GT 2+2

Der 365 GT 2+2, vorgestellt 1967 im Pariser Grand Palais, war der erste viersitzige Ferrari mit unabhängig aufgehängten Rädern, zunächst mit Lochfelgen, später im Fünfzack-Design des Daytona. Wieder hatte sich Pininfarina vom 500 Superfast inspirieren lassen: Lang und geduckt schmiegte sich der 365 GT vorn in den Fahrtwind, lange ließ er sich Zeit vor dem Absturz des Kamm-Hecks. Die guten Manieren des fast fünf Meter langen und voll getankt 1825 kg schweren Coupés begannen mit exemplarischer Laufruhe: Sein V12 mit 4,4 Litern war verblockt mit dem Fünfganggetriebe. Ein massives Rohr umschloss die Antriebswelle und stellte eine feste Verbindung mit dem Differential an der Hinterachse her.

Dieses Ensemble war an je zwei Punkten vorn und hinten über dicke Gummipuffer mit dem Fahrgestell verschraubt. Die Bewegungen des Fahrzeugs aktivierten eine Pumpe für den Niveauausgleich. Michelin-Pneus mit Stahlgürteln ersetzten die relativ kurzlebigen Reifen

The 365 GT 2+2, first presented at the Paris Grand Palais in 1967, was the first four-seat Ferrari with independent suspensions, initially with drilled rims, although they were later replaced with the five spoke design of the Daytona. Once again, Pininfarina had been inspired by the 500 Superfast. The hood was long and raked for improved aerodynamics, and the rear was also long and gently sloping until it was abruptly cut off to improve airflow. The good manners of this more than 16-foot (almost 5-meter) long coupé that weighed 4015 pounds (1825 kg) with a full tank, began with its exemplary silence. Its 4.4-liter V12 was partnered by a five-speed gearbox. A solid tube encased the drive shaft and created a firm connection to the differential of the rear axle.

The whole was fixed to the chassis with two thick silent blocks at the front and two at the rear. A pneumatic system kept the vehicle level irrespective of the load. Steel-belted Michelins had replaced the Firestones, which

Der 365 GT 2+2 war wieder ein klassischer Gran Turismo, mit viel Platz für zwei und Gepäck. Auf kurzen Strecken konnten zwei weitere Passagiere die Faszination Ferrari genießen.

The 365 GT 2+2 was another classic Gran Turismo with lots of room for two people and their baggage. On short distances, two more passengers could share the enjoyment provided by Ferrari.

von Firestone und vermittelten einen Kontakt zur Straße, den man spürte und hörte. Sogar die Ausstellfenster vorn wurden von schnurrenden Elektromotoren bewegt. Die Frontsitze waren tief und komfortabel und konnten selbst für lange Beine ausreichend zurückgestellt werden. Der linke Fuß des Piloten ruhte bequem auf einer Stütze neben dem Kupplungspedal. Eine Servohilfe erleichterte seine Arbeit am Lenkrad, den Puristen ein Dorn im Auge wie die Klimaanlage, die sich im Motorraum ganz schön breit machte und mit einem Zentner zu Buche schlug.

tended to be shorter-lived, and created contact with the road that could be felt and heard. Even the quarter lights were controlled by purring electric motors. The front seats were deep and comfortable, and would move back far enough to accommodate even the tallest passenger. The driver's left foot rested comfortably on a footrest beside the clutch. Power-assisted steering made driving easier, although the air-conditioning upset purists because of the amount of space it took up under the hood, and it added to its weight.

Das große Coupé galt als der bis dato kultivierteste Ferrari.

The large coupé was considered the most refined Ferrari to date.

Dino 206 GT
Dino 246 GT
Dino 246 GTS

Am Anfang war ein tastender Dreischritt: die Stilstudie 206 GT Speciale auf dem Pariser Salon 1965, der Dino Berlinetta GT 1966 in Turin, der Dino 206 GT, 1967 wiederum in Turin ausgestellt. Er war bereits fast identisch mit dem Serienwagen, dessen Produktion wenig später Scaglietti aufnahm. Sein Triebwerk von 1987 cm³, 180 PS stark, war die Frucht der Liaison mit Fiat. Franco Rocchis kompakter V6, mit dem Fünfganggetriebe und dem Differential zu einer Einheit verquickt, kauerte quer vor der Hinterachse. So schuf man Platz für ein Kofferabteil von 300 Litern unter einer von drei vorn angelenkten Hauben. Scaglietti kleidete den Dino in Aluminium ein, entfernte die Plexiglasschalen über den Scheinwerfern des Prototyps und fügte seitliche Ausstellfenster vorn hinzu.

It went through three careful stages: the styling exercise that was the 206 GT Speciale at the Paris Salon in 1965; the Dino Berlinetta GT 1966 in Turin; and the Dino 206 GT of 1967, also shown at Turin. This was almost identical to the production car that Scaglietti would build a short time later. Its 1987 cc, 180 bhp engine was the fruit of a collaboration with Fiat. Franco Rocchi's compact V6, connected to the five-speed box and differential to form a single unit, lay diagonally in front of the rear axle. This allowed 10½ cubic feet (300 liters) of trunk space in one of three compartments under the hood. Scaglietti re-bodied the Dino in aluminum, removed the Perspex covers over the prototype's headlights, and added quarter lights to the front side windows.

Hinter dem Label Dino verbirgt sich ein kleiner, aber feiner Ferrari, nur dass er diesen glorreichen Namen nie tragen durfte.

One of the most beautiful Ferraris hides behind the simple notation "Dino," although it never actually bore that glorious name.

Nach 152 Exemplaren löste den 206 GT auf dem Genfer Salon 1969 gleichwohl der 246 GT ab, mit 2,4 Litern über mehr Bohrung und mehr Hub. Er wog 150 kg mehr, vor allem, da sein Triebwerk aus Gusseisen und nicht mehr aus Silumin bestand. Aber 15 weitere PS wurden damit spielend fertig. Der Radstand war von 2280 auf die 2340 mm der Vorserienwagen angewachsen,

After a run of 152, the 206 GT was replaced at the 1969 Geneva Show by the 2.4-liter 246 GT with an increased bore and stroke. It weighed 330 pounds (150 kg) more, since its engine was made of cast iron rather than silumin. However, this was not a problem because it had an additional 15 bhp. The wheelbase had been increased from 7'6" (2280 mm) to the 7'8" (2340 mm) of the pre-production

Vollendete Pininfarina-Eleganz in Blau und Rot: Neben dem Coupé erschien 1972 der Spider genannte GTS mit einem abnehmbaren Dachteil. Die Sitzposition hinter dem etwas zu flach stehenden Lenkrad war gewöhnungsbedürftig. Dafür entschädigte der Mittelmotor-Zweisitzer mit überaus agilem Handling.

der Tankdeckel in der linken Verlängerung des Dachs untergebracht. 1970 wichen die Schnellverschlüsse von Rudge fünf Bolzen. Und seit der Genfer Ausstellung 1972 krönte die Baureihe in 1274 Exemplaren der GTS mit einer abnehmbaren Dachplanke vor dem Überrollbügel und ohne Dreieckfensterchen. Pininfarina zählte den Dino zu seinen gelungensten Entwürfen.

vehicles, and the fuel filler was now under a flap on the left-side extension of the roof. In 1970, the Rudge wheels were replaced by five stud-fixing wheels. It was at the 1972 Geneva Show that the GTS, a version with a removable roof fitted forward of a roll-over hoop but without the triangular side windows, made its first appearance. Pininfarina counted the Dino amongst his greatest successes.

Perfect Pininfarina elegance in blue and red: a Spider version with a detachable roof appeared in 1972 alongside the coupé. The seating position behind the rather low steering wheel took some getting used to. However, the mid-engine two-seater compensated for this with exceedingly agile handling.

365 GTB/4 Daytona
365 GTS/4 Daytona

Mit ihm wurde das Prinzip des Frontmotor-Sport-
wagens auf die Spitze getrieben: Der Trakt für seinen V12 erstreckte sich über die Hälfte seiner Länge bis
zum Ansatz der A-Säulen, gefolgt von einem knappen
Kämmerchen und einem karg bemessenen Kofferraum.
Auf der Pariser Show 1968 wurde der 365 GTB, von jedermann Daytona geheißen zum Gedenken an den Ferrari-
Dreifachsieg 1967 bei dem amerikanischen Klassiker, in
ein sich wandelndes Umfeld hineinplatziert. Einige Kon-
kurrenten wie der Lamborghini Miura und der De Tomaso
Mangusta hatten bereits Mittelmotoren, Maserati hielt
vorerst mit dem Ghibli noch an der klassischen Auslegung
fest, auf der lediglich Aston Martin unbeirrbar beharrte.

Der Daytona schlug sie alle, allein schon in puncto
schiere Geschwindigkeit: Er lief 275, der Miura 273, der
Ghibli 257, der Mangusta 242 und der Aston Martin DBS
238 km/h. Von Pininfarina konzipiert, wurde er in Modena
hergestellt, wo Scaglietti zunächst die Leuchteneinheit
vorn hinter einer durchgehenden Perspex-Abdeckung

It was the supreme incarnation of the front-engined
sports cars. The section that contained its V12 extended
for almost half the length of the car, to the A-pillars,
followed by a short cockpit and a minimal trunk. The
365 GTB, called the Daytona in memory of Ferrari's 1967
triple success at this classic American 24-hour event, took
center stage at the 1968 Paris Salon. Some of its competitors, such as the Lamborghini Miura and the De Tomaso
Mangusta, already had a centrally mounted engine;
Maserati persisted for a while with the classic configuration in the Ghibli, as did Aston Martin.

The Daytona was the best of the bunch, in pure speed
alone. It could reach 171 mph (275 kph); the Miura 170
(273); the Ghibli 160 (257); the Mangusta 150 (242), and the
Aston Martin 148 (238). Designed by Pininfarina, it was
built in Modena, where Scaglietti adopted the idea from

*Bei seinem Debüt im Herbst 1968 leuchteten die Scheinwerfer des Ferrari 365 GTB noch
durch Plexiglas - spätere Versionen hatten profane Klappscheinwerfer.*

*While the headlights of the Ferrari 365 GTB were hidden behind plexiglas at its debut in
the fall of 1968, later versions had profane pop-up headlights.*

vom ursprünglichen Entwurf übernahm und nach den Werksferien 1971 durch Klappscheinwerfer ersetzte.

Seit der Frankfurter Ausstellung im September 1969 stand dem Berlinetta der Daytona Spider zur Seite, auf Speichenrädern von Borrani, schön und von männlicher Ausstrahlung wie jener. Mit 124 Exemplaren blieb er vergleichsweise rar, so dass später mancher zur Selbsthilfe schritt und der geschlossenen Version kurzerhand das Dach abschnitt. Original oder Fälschung? Zur Unterscheidung genügt oft nur ein Blick.

the original design of covering the front light unit with a band of Perspex, and then replaced it with retractable headlights after the company vacation period in 1971.

The Berlinetta was joined at the 1969 Frankfurt Show by the Daytona Spider with Borrani wire wheels—beautiful to look at and with the same virility. However, only 124 units were built, making it a rarity, so that later some people took matters into their own hands and simply sliced the roof off the hard-top version. Original or fake? Often you can tell by a single glance.

Der mächtige V12 mit
4,4 Litern Hubraum brachte
es auf 352 PS, genug für
eine Höchstgeschwindigkeit
von 275 km/h. Das formal
betörende Cabriolet
zählt heute zu den
begehrtesten Ferrari.

The powerful V12 with its 4.4-
liter capacity was capable
of 352 bhp, enough for a top
speed of 171 mph (275 kph).
The beguiling convertible
is one of today's most
coveted models.

Nur 124 Exemplare wurden
vom Spider genannten
Cabriolet gebaut.
Dementsprechend teuer sind
sie heutzutage.

Only 124 examples of the
convertible named Spider
were built. That is why they
are so expensive today.

312 P

Der 312 P, von Ferrari Mitte Dezember 1968 vorgestellt, schien auf Sieg programmiert. Seine Maschine stammte aus der Formel 1, seit ihrem ersten Einsatz in Syrakus 1966 gereift und stetig stärker geworden mit drei Ventilen je Zylinder ab Monza 1966 und 48 Ventilen insgesamt ab Monza 1967. Im 312 P leistete sie 420 PS, zehn mehr als im Grand-Prix-Wagen 312 F1 von 1968. Wo sich zwischen dessen Zylinderbänken ein verzwicktes

The 312 P, unveiled by Ferrari in mid-December 1968, seemed to be programmed to win. It had a Formula 1 engine, which had increased in reliability and power since Syracuse 1966, with three valves per cylinder after Monza 1966 and 48 valves in total after 1967. As the 312 P, it developed 420 bhp, ten more than the 312 F1 Grand Prix car of 1968. On the sports car, the tortuous exhaust system between the cylinder banks was fitted

Auspuffgewürm ringelte, war bei dem Sportwagen die Einspritzung von Lucas angesiedelt – die Abgase verließen den Motor seitlich.

Der 312 P sah aus wie ein maßstabs-gerecht verkleinerter 612 CanAm und war es auch, nur dass dessen komplexes Flügel- und Spoilerwerk verschwun-den und Scheinwerfer hinzugekommen waren. Liberalere Bestimmungen der Sportbehörde CSI hinsichtlich Höhe und

with Lucas fuel injection; the exhaust gases exited at the side.

The 312 P could easily be mistaken for a smaller version of the 612 CanAm, which in fact it was, apart from the fact that the complicated wing and spoiler sys-tem had gone, and headlights had been added. More freedom in CSI regulations with regard to height and trunk resulted in a more functional silhouette, and it was hoped that the loss of the artificial

In Le Mans startete Ferrari 1969 mit einer geschlossenen Version des 312 P. Die beiden Wagen fielen indessen in der ersten Runde und in der 13. Stunde aus.

In 1969, Ferrari started the Le Mans with a closed version of the 312 P. Both cars failed in the first round and at the 13th hour.

Kofferraum gestatteten eine Silhouette, die sich nur noch am Zweck ausrichtete, und was durch den Verlust an künstlichen Hilfen beim Abtrieb verloren ging, hoffte man durch eine radikale Keilform zurückzugewinnen.

Der Ertrag sah indessen eher mäßig aus, mit zwei zweiten Plätzen in sechs Rennen als Sahnehäubchen und frühen Ausfällen in Le Mans, wo die beiden gewöhnlich offenen 312P zu Berlinettas mutiert waren mit langen, in Kaskaden nach hinten abfallenden Dachaufbauten. Ferrari zersplitterte seine Streitkräfte an zu vielen Fronten. Und mit dem Porsche 908 war ein formidabler Gegner eingebrochen in die alte Domäne der roten Renner aus Maranello, die Dreiliterklasse.

aerodynamic aids would be compensated for by a more radical wedge shape.

The overall results were not particularly satisfying, with two second places in six races as the icing on the cake, and early failures at Le Mans, where the two usually open 312Ps were transformed into Berlinettas with very long roofs that sloped steeply at the back. Ferrari was spreading itself too wide—plus it had a formidable opponent in the Porsche 908, which broke into the three-liter class that had long been ruled by the Maranello red runners.

Das Triebwerk des 312P hatte drei Liter Hubraum wie der Zwölfzylinder des aktuellen Grand-Prix-Wagens der Scuderia, auf dem es basierte, und leistete 430 PS.

The engine of the 312P had a capacity of three liters—like the 12-cylinder engine of the current Scuderia Grand Prix car on which it was based—and achieved 430 bhp.

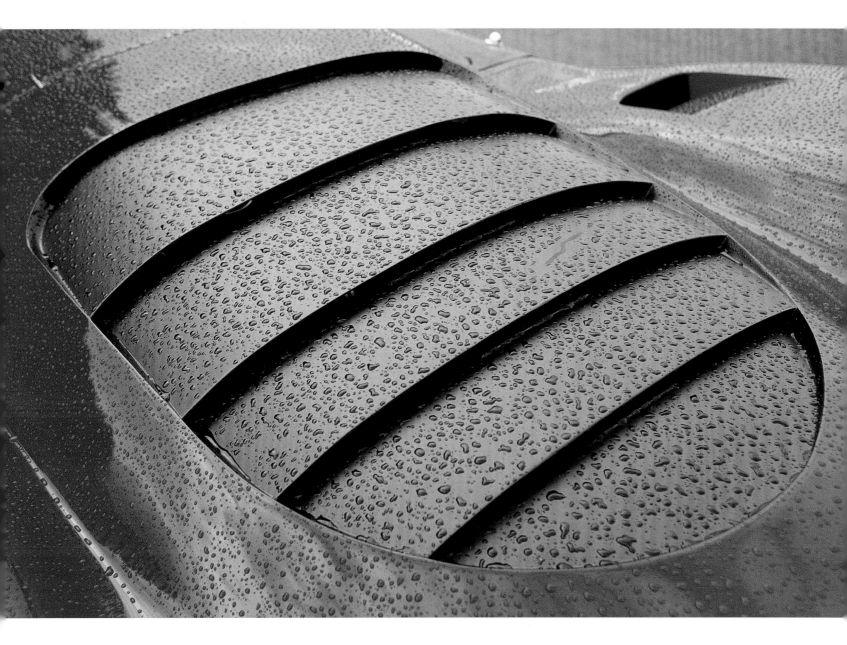

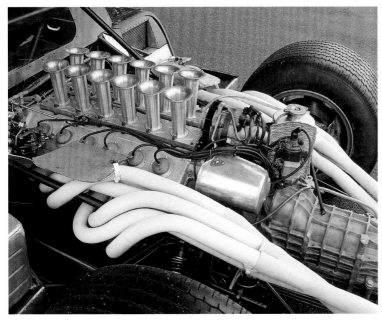

512 S
512 M

Sie waren nur Episoden zwischen den Dreilitern 312 P und 312 PB, der 512 S und später 512 M (für *modificata*). Unter ihrer Kunststoffkarosserie schaute es aus wie beim 612 CanAm und beim 312 P: ein Rohrrahmen mit genieteten und geklebten Blechteilen, angefertigt bei Cigarla & Bartinetti in Turin, das synchronisierte Fünfganggetriebe verblockt mit dem Sperrdifferential, Wasserkühler zu beiden Seiten der Maschine, Ölkühler vorn. Der Motor: mittig, 4994 cm³ und anfänglich 550 PS, Lucas-Einspritzung vor den Ventilen. Nur wenige der 25 roten Berlinettas und Spider, die zur Homologation nachgewiesen werden

The 512 S and later the 512 M (for *modificata*) were only stopgaps between the three-liter 312 P and 312 PB. Under their lightweight bodies they looked like the 612 CanAm and 312 P: a tubular chassis with riveted and glued metal components, made by Cigarla & Bartinetti in Turin, the five-speed gearbox with limited slip differential, radiators on each side of the engine, the oil cooler at the front. The engine: centrally mounted, 4994 cc, initially providing 550 bhp, with Lucas fuel injection in front of the valves. Only a few of the 25 red Berlinettas and Spiders that were built for homologation ended up in

mussten, gelangten in die Hände von Kunden, die meisten blieben in der Obhut des Werks.

Dass Mario Andretti zusammen mit Nino Vaccarella und Ignazio Giunti die 12 Stunden von Sebring am 21. März 1970 gewann, weckte nur falsche Hoffnungen. Der 512 S blieb der Underdog, vor allem gegenüber dem Porsche 917 des Gulf-Teams. Le Mans geriet gar zum Debakel. Rechtzeitig zum letzten Lauf auf dem neuen Kurs von Zeltweg am 11. Oktober stellte man den 512 M fertig, 40 kg leichter, 70 PS stärker, aerodynamischer, mit kleinen einstellbaren Spoilern und einem Ansaugkamin hinten. Jacky Ickx

customers' hands; most of them remained under guard at the factory.

When Mario Andretti, assisted by Nino Vaccarella and Ignazio Giunti, won the Sebring 12 Hours on 21 March 1970, it only served to raise false hopes. The 512 S remained the underdog, especially in comparison with the Gulf Team's Porsche 917. Le Mans was a disaster. The 512 M appeared just in time for the last round of the Championship on 11 October at the Austrian Zeltweg circuit. It was 88 pounds (40 kg) lighter, 70 bhp stronger, more aerodynamic, with small adjustable spoilers,

Die Ferrari 512 S und M waren Fahrmaschinen von brutaler Anmutung und wildem Wohlklang, mit einem Wort: schön.

The Ferraris 512 S and M were driving machines of brutal appeal and fabulous sound; in a word, beautiful.

enteilte anfänglich allen und fiel dann aus: Probleme an der Elektrik.

1971 kam es noch schlimmer: acht Porsche-Siege, drei für Alfa Romeo, keiner für den 512 M, nicht einmal für das vorzüglich präparierte Exemplar des Teams von Roger Penske mit Mark Donohue am Lenkrad.

and had a raised air intake at the rear. At the start, Jacky Ickx roared into the lead, but then had to retire with electrical problems.

Worse was to follow in 1971: eight wins for Porsche, three for Alfa Romeo, none for the 512 M, not even for the beautifully prepared version by Roger Pense with Mark Donohue at the wheel.

Wie bei den Serienwagen der Marke wurde der Schaltstock des 512 M – gekrönt durch einen hölzernen Knauf – in einer Kulisse geführt.

As with the marque's production cars, the gearstick on the 512 M – crowned by a wooden knob – moved through a shifting gear.

Der Anpressdruck auf die Hinterachse ließ sich einfach durch verstellbare Klappen variieren. Enorme Walzen vermittelten die 610 PS des 512 M an die Straße.

The tread pressure on the rear axle was varied by adjustable flaps. Vast wheels transmitted the 610 bhp of the 512 M to the road.

312 PB

Klein, leicht und handlich war der 312 PB, mit dem Ferrari die Sportwagen-WM 1972 dominierte. Von elf Läufen gewann er zehn. Die Formel-1-Riege Jacky Ickx und Clay Regazzoni war das erfolgreichste Duo.

Small, light, and a delight to handle—the 312 PB, with which Ferrari dominated the Sports Car World Championship of 1972. It won ten out of eleven races. The Formula 1 drivers Jacky Ickx and Clay Regazzoni were the most successful driver duo.

Knapp 450 PS leistete der Zwölfzylinder-Motor mit dem weiten V-Winkel von 180 Grad. Der auf 13-Zoll-Rädern stehende 312 PB brachte nur 650 Kilogramm auf die Waage.

The twelve-cylinder engine with the wide 180-degree V angle was capable of up to 450 bhp. The 312 PB, standing on 13-inch wheels, weighed in with only 1433 lbs (650 kg).

Das Formel-1-Triebwerk im 312 B von 1970 galt als Boxer-Motor, war aber eigentlich ein V12 mit Bänken im extremen Winkel von 180 Grad. Es fand sich auch im PB, um 20 auf 440 PS heruntergetunt als Waffe für die lange Strecke, dazu Übertragung und Aufhängung. Nach dem Vorbild des Porsche 908/3 war der PB klein, mit seiner knapp sitzenden Kunststoff-karosserie über 2200 mm Radstand, 585 kg leicht und rollte auf Scheiben-rädern mit bloßen Schlitzen. Lampen und zwei vertikale Finnen jenseits der Hinterachse stellten sich erst später ein. Für 1971, ein Jahr des Über-gangs, wurden zwei Spider gebaut, ohne sich sonderlich zu profilieren.

Der PB 1972 war fünf PS stärker, kompakter und 50 mm niedriger über Niederquerschnittspneus von Firestone, aber - mit einem Rahmen aus dickeren Rohren - auch schwerer, denn nach 650 kg Mindestgewicht ver-langte das Gesetz.

Acht Wagen gab es, am Ende hatte man von elf Läufen zehn gewonnen, und hätte es einen Fahrertitel gegeben, die ersten sieben Plätze wären von Ferrari-Piloten eingenommen worden. 1973 mutierte der Kampf gegen die französischen Matra zum Zwist der Nationen. Dem 312 PB jenes Jahres, mit 450 PS, 2340 mm Radstand und einer längeren Frontpartie, waren nur zwei Triumphe vergönnt, in Monza und am Nürburgring - er wurde von einem durch nichts zu kurierenden Untersteuern geplagt.

The Formula 1 engine in the 1970 312 B was considered a Boxer engine; in fact it was a V12 but with banks at an extreme angle of 180 degrees. It was also found in the PB, tuned down by 20 bhp to 440, as a weapon for the long race, together with the transmission and suspension. Following the example of the Porsche 908/3, the PB was small, with the bodywork barely stretching beyond the 7'3" (2200 mm) wheelbase; it weighed 1290 pounds (585 kg), and rode on rims with simple holes. The headlamps and two vertical fins either side of the rear axle did not appear until later. Two Spiders were built in 1971, a year of transition, without particularly distinguishing themselves. The 1972 version of the PB was five bhp stron-ger, more compact, and 2 inches (50 mm) lower, on low-profile Firestone radial tires, but because of a heavier tubular structure it was also heavier; the minimum allowed by the regulations was 650 kg (1433 pounds).

Eight cars were built; by the end of the season, Ferrari had won ten of the eleven races, and if there had been a Drivers' Sports Prototype World Championship, Ferrari drivers would have occupied the first seven places. But in 1973, the Matras appeared to spoil the party. That year, fortune only smiled twice on the 312 PB, with its 450 bhp, 7'8" (2340 mm) wheelbase, and longer front end—at Monza and on the Nürburgring; it was plagued by a tendency to understeer that simply could not be cured.

365 GTC/4

Charakteristische Merkmale des 365 GTC/4 waren sein allmählich sich hebender Bug und seine Dreiecksfenster, die über den Hinterrädern dolchspitzförmig nach hinten stachen.

Der 365 GTC/4 debütierte 1971 in Genf, ein sportlich-komfortables Coupé für zwei mit einer rudimentär ausgebildeten hinteren Sitzbank. Seine Silhouette war ein sanftes Spiel Pininfarinas mit den Motiven Welle und Keil. Im Unterschied zum Daytona wurde sein V12 von sechs seitlichen Weber-Vergasern gefüttert, was zugleich den Schwerpunkt absenkte. Die 365 GTC/4 für den Export in die USA erkannte man an vier seitlichen Positionslämpchen.

The 365 GTC/4 had its debut at the Geneva Show in 1971; it was a sporty, comfortable coupé for two with a rudimentary back seat. Designed by Pininfarina, it combined curves and angles with wedge-shaped elements. Unlike the Daytona, its V12 was powered by six double-bodied Webers on the sides, which also lowered its center of gravity. The 365GTC/4 destined for export to the USA was identified by the four small sidelights.

Dem Zug der Zeit entsprechend hatte man Chromzierrat weitgehend ausgemerzt. Aus Kunststoff bestand ein Wulst, der Kühleröffnung und Leuchten umfriedete, um milde Rempler von ihnen abzuhalten, mattschwarz wie die simple hintere Stoßstange und sogar die quadratischen Module, in welche die vier wichtigsten Rundinstrumente unmittelbar im Gesichtsfeld eingebettet waren sowie vier weitere Ührchen weiter rechts, konzentrisch zum Piloten hin geneigt.

Following the current trend, all superfluous chrome had been removed. A thin lip of synthetic material, painted matt black like the plain rear fender, was used to protect the radiator grille and headlights against light impacts, and the square modules that held the four round instrument dials in the driver's line of sight and four further gauges a little further to the right were curved round gradually so that they faced towards the driver.

Typical features of the 365 GTC/4 were its gently sloping rear section and the triangular windows, which extended, dagger-like, over the rear wheels.

Das Cockpit im Stil der
frühen Siebziger verwöhnte
mit einer Klimaanlage,
während der große V12
von sechs Doppelvergasern
gespeist wurde.

Auf einer massigen Konsole thronte ein Schalt-stock, dessen Weg durch keine Kulisse vorgeschrieben war. Darunter verbarg sich, akustisch stets präsent, das Fünfganggetriebe, anders als beim Daytona verblockt mit dem Motor. Dieser leistete 320 PS in der US-Version und 340 PS bei den GTC/4, die für den Rest der Welt bestimmt waren. Serienmäßig waren eine Klimaanlage, die aus dem 365 GT 2+2 vertraute Niveauregulierung hinten sowie Lenkhilfe und Bremskraftverstärker für die innenbelüfteten Scheibenbremsen.

A chunky console held the stick shift. This concealed, a permanent acoustic presence, the five-speed gearbox; unlike in the Daytona, it was attached to the engine. The engine developed 320 bhp for the US version, and 340 bhp on the GTC/4 for the rest of the world. It had air-condi-tioning, a system for adjusting the ride height taken from the 365 GT 2+2, as well as power steering and assisted brakes as standard.

In the typical style of the 1970s, the interior pampered the occupants with air-conditioning, while six double carburetors fed the large V12.

365 GT4 BB
BB 512
BB 512i

Den Piloten im Nacken saßen bereits die V12 der 250 LM von 1963. Die Basis erreichte die Mittelmotor-Revolution gleichwohl erst, als die Klientel gebieterisch nach konzeptioneller Identität mit den Rennsportwagen 512 S und M und 312 PB verlangte, hinter deren Sitzen sich ein V-Triebwerk im Winkel von 180 Grad breit machte, kurz und schief Boxer geheißen. Kürzel und Konstruktionsprinzip wurden für den 365 GT4 BB (für Berlinetta Boxer) übernommen, auf dem Turiner Salon 1971 als Prototyp vorgestellt und zwei Jahre später kaum verändert bei Scaglietti in Serie. Pininfarina hatte seine Hausaufgaben sorgfältig erledigt: Der BB präsentierte sich fast unzerklüftet in klaren, ruhigen Linien.

Auf dem Pariser Salon 1976 hieß er plötzlich 512, eingedenk einer wenig glorreichen Vergangenheit. Man hatte von 4390 cm³ auf deren 4942 aufgerüstet, während die Leistung um 20 auf 360 PS gesunken war, die bereits

Drivers of the 1963 250 LM had the V12 behind their heads. The mid-engined revolution finally found its way into a road car when the clientele started to demand the same configuration as found in the 512 S and M and 312 PB racing cars, which had 180-degree V engines and bore the name "Boxer." The name and construction principle were adopted for the 365 GT4 BB (Berlinetta Boxer), which made its first public appearance as a prototype at the 1971 Turin Show. Two years later, and with only slight modifications, production began at the Scaglietti plant. Pininfarina had done his homework. The BB had clear, tranquil lines.

At the 1976 Paris Salon, it was suddenly called the 512— even though the history to which it referred was less than

Wie der Daytona ab 1971 schaute auch der BB aus Klappscheinwerfern in die nächtliche Welt, seinem Aussehen nicht unbedingt zuträglich.

Like the Daytona after 1971, the BB viewed the world at night through retractable headlights, although they did not necessarily enhance its appearance.

Der 1971 präsentierte
365 GT4 BB hatte einen
Mittelmotor mit 180-Grad-V-
Winkel, der fälschlicherweise
Boxer genannt wurde.

The 365 GT4 BB presented
in 1971 possessed a mid-
engine with a 180-degree
V angle, which was falsely
termed Boxer.

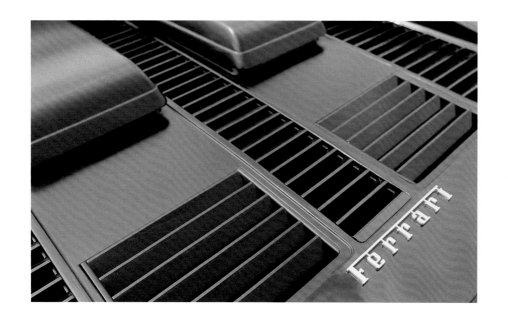

früher zur Verfügung standen. Der 512 BB hatte Trocken-sumpfschmierung. Sein Heck war länger und breiter, um die Michelin-Pneus XWX vom Kaliber 225/70 VR 15 angemessen zu beherbergen. Paarweise angeordnete Heckleuchten ersetzten die sechs Einzellampen am Vorgänger, je zwei dicke Auspuffrohre lösten sechs schlankere ab, und vorn war eine dezente Spoilerlippe gesprossen. Auf der Frankfurter IAA 1981 hatte eine K-Jetronic von Bosch die Verpflegung des 512 übernommen, für die vorher vier Weber-Dreifachvergaser zuständig gewesen waren. Das verringerte seine Potenz um weitere 20 PS, nicht aber seine liberalen Konsumgewohnheiten.

Ab Herbst 1981 übernahm die mechanische Einspritzung K-Jetronic von Bosch die Kraftstoffversorgung des BB.

glorious. The engine had been upgraded from 4390 cc to 4942, but provided just 360 bhp, 20 less than had earlier been available. The 512 BB had dry sump lubrication. Its rear end was long and wider to accommodate the imposing Michelin XWX 225/70 VR 15 tires. Two sets of two rear lights replaced the previous total of six, and two double exhaust pipes replaced the original six on the first BB; a discreet spoiler graced the front end. At the Frankfurt IAA in 1981, the four triple Webers were replaced by a Bosch K-Jetronic injection system. This caused a drop of a further 20 bhp, but had no effect on its heavy fuel consumption.

From the fall of 1981, a Bosch mechanical gasoline injection (K-Jetronic) took over the fuel provision of the BB.

365 GT4 2+2
400i
412

Pininfarina bot auf dem Pariser Salon 1972 mit dem 365 GT4 2+2 Erstaunliches: ein voluminöses Coupé mit seriös-limousinenmäßigen Zügen, Frontmotor und Heckantrieb, zunächst 340, später 310 und am Ende wieder 340 PS stark. Im Gewande altersloser Klassik verbarg sich die Mechanik des GTC/4, der Radstand war um 150 auf 2700 mm angewachsen. 1976, wieder in Paris, hatten die Puristen an einem weiteren Affront zu schlucken: Der 400 A, mit 4823 cm³ anstelle der bisherigen 4390, war serienmäßig mit einer Automatik ausgestattet. Wahlweise gab es in einer Variante GT die traditionelle Fünfgangschaltung. Ein Spoiler vorn war dazugekommen, das Leuchtenensemble hinten von sechs auf vier reduziert, der zentrale Rudge-Verschluss durch fünf Stehbolzen ersetzt.

In Paris 1979 gähnte Leere, wo einst sechs Doppelvergaser Weber 38 DCOE residiert hatten. Das i für *iniezione*

The car presented by Pininfarina at the 1972 Paris Salon was something amazing: a roomy coupé with serious lines, front-engined, rear-wheel drive, and 340 bhp (this was dropped later to 310 before finally returning to 340 bhp). The classical body housed the mechanics of the GTC/4; the wheelbase had been extended by 6 inches (150 mm) to 8'10" (2700 mm). In 1976, back in Paris, the purists were affronted—again. The 400 A, with 4923 cc instead of the previous 4390, was fitted with an automatic gearbox as standard. The traditional five-speed gearbox was offered as a GT option. A spoiler had been added at the front, the group of six rear lights reduced to four, and the Rudge wheels had been replaced by five-stud rims.

In Paris in 1979, there was a gaping hole where six twin-choke Weber 38 DCOEs had once been situated. The "i" for

Im Olympiajahr 1972 erschien der 365 GT4 2+2 – ein großes, zeitlos elegantes Coupé mit beinahe limousinenhafter Silhouette, klassischem Frontmotor und Heckantrieb.

The 365 GT4 2+2 appeared in the Olympic year of 1972—a large, timeless, and elegant coupé with an almost sedan-like silhouette and classical front engine with rear-wheel drive.

Zu Beginn seiner Karriere trug der 365 pro Seite drei Rückleuchten, die letzte Version, der 412, begnügte sich mit zwei prägnanten Lampen am klaren Heck.

zeugte von der Anwesenheit einer Bosch-Jetronic. Neu war auch die Niveauregulierung hinten. Die Baureihe kulminierte 1985 in Genf mit dem 412, dem ersten GT von Ferrari mit Antiblockiersystem. Gelinde waren mit 119 cm³ der Zuwachs an Hubraum und karg die Retuschen am äußeren Erscheinungsbild: Stoßfänger vorn und hinten in Wagenfarbe, umlaufende Abschlussbleche in Schwarz wie die Umrandung der Fenster und die Außenspiegel, ein etwas höherer Kofferraumdeckel.

iniezione indicated the presence of a Bosch-Jetronic. The suspension leveling system at the rear was another innovation. The series peaked in Geneva in 1985 with the 412, the first Ferrari GT to be fitted with anti-lock brakes. The 119 cc increase in capacity was hardly noticeable, as were the modifications to the bodywork: the front and rear fenders were color-coded with the bodywork; skirts, window frames, and wing mirrors were painted in black; the trunk was a little higher.

The 365 bore three rear lights per side at the beginning of its career. The last version, the 412, made do with two succinct lamps on its clear rear.

Der 412, die letzte Evolutionsstufe des 365, erschien im März 1985 und war der erste Ferrari mit einem Antiblockiersystem. Die Gemischaufbereitung übernahm eine mechanische Benzineinspritzung von Bosch (K-Jetronic).

The 412, the final evolutionary development of the 365, appeared in March 1985 and was the first Ferrari with an anti-lock braking system (ABS). A Bosch mechanical gasoline injection system (K-Jetronic) took over responsibility for fuel mix preparation.

Dino 308 GT4

Den Dino 308 GT4 bekleidete nicht Hausdesigner Pinin Farina, sondern dessen ebenfalls in Turin ansässiger Konkurrent Nuccio Bertone. Der Dino folgte der Formel 2+2 – mit überaus beengten Raumverhältnissen hinten.

Mit dem Dino 308 GT4 vollzog Stardesigner Nuccio Bertone auf dem Pariser Salon 1973 die Quadratur des Zirkels: einen sportiven Viersitzer einzukleiden – mit dem Triebwerk achtern. Über dessen Linie, schrieb drei Jahre später stellvertretend für viele andere das amerikanische Fachmagazin *Road & Track*, lasse sich trefflich streiten. Auf den kurzen Anstieg des Bugs folgte ein gedrungener Rumpf, aus dem sich die stark geneigte Frontscheibe erhob. Schmale Holme beiderseits des senkrecht stehenden hinteren Fensters rissen eine Schräge an, die erst an

At the Paris Salon of 1973, star designer Nuccio Bertone squared the circle with the Dino 308 GT4: a sporty four-seater—with a rear-mounted engine. Three years later, the American trade magazine *Road & Track* expressed the commonly held opinion that there was some doubt over whether the car's looks were a success. The strongly raked windshield rose up from a short trunk hood. The extensions of the rear pillars were angled so that they ended at the uppermost part of the truncated rear end. The black polyester fenders looked as though they would

der Vertikale des Stumpfhecks endete. Stoßstangen aus schwarzem Polyester harrten ängstlich der Dinge, die da hoffentlich nicht kamen, und die vier Scheinwerfer verschwanden tagsüber unter ihren Abdeckungen.

Über den 2550 mm voneinander getrennten Achsen hatte Bertone die erste Sitzreihe weit nach vorn angesiedelt, die zweite verdiente kaum ihren Namen. Der V8 im Winkel von 90 Grad, Copyright Franco Rocchi, heiserte und giftete quer zur Fahrtrichtung, ein weiteres Verpackungswunder, in klaustrophobischer Enge mit dem

have difficulty resisting the slightest knock, and the four headlights disappeared behind their covers by day.

Between the two axles, separated by 8'4" (2550 mm), Bertone had placed the front seats very far forward; the rear seats hardly deserved the name. The 90-degree V8, copyright Franco Rocchi, was transversally mounted—it was a perfect example of compactness, directly attached to the five-speed gearbox and the differential. As with the marque's boxer engine, the four overhead camshafts were driven by toothed belts.

The Dino 308 GT4 was not fitted out by company designer Pininfarina, but by his competitor Nuccio Bertone, also of Turin. The Dino followed the 2+2 formula—with very little room in the back.

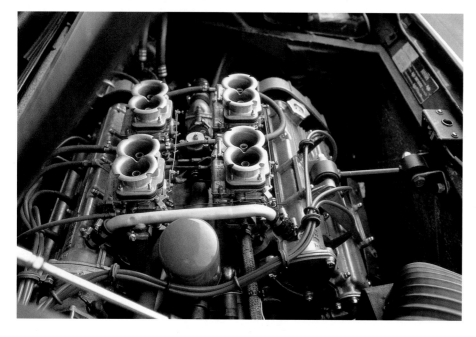

Der Dreiliter-V8, beatmet
mittels der markanten
Lufteinlässe im Anschluss an
die hinteren Fenster, agierte
quer und in qualvoller Enge.

The triangular air intake
behind the rear windows
on the 3-liter V8 operated
well hidden at the rear
and perpendicular to the
driving direction.

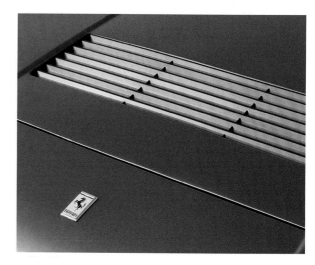

Fünfganggetriebe und dem Differential zusammengepfercht, Zahnriemen hielten wie bei den Boxer-Maschinen der Marke die vier oben liegenden Nockenwellen zur Arbeit an.

Im März 1975 rollte dem 308 der 208 GT4 zur Seite, mit seinem Zweiliter von 170 PS für den Markt in Italien bestimmt und kenntlich etwa am Fehlen der Nebelscheinwerfer und einer breiteren Kühleröffnung. Den stolzen Namen Ferrari durfte der Dino erst ab Mai 1976 tragen.

In March 1975, the 208 GT4 made its entrance alongside the 308; with a two-liter, 170 bhp engine, it was built exclusively for the Italian market, and was identifiable by the lack of fog lights and for its bigger radiator opening. The Dino was finally allowed to bear the Ferrari name in May 1976.

308 GTB
308 GTS
328 GTB
328 GTS

Auf der Pariser Show 1975 war der 308 GTB der erste von 21 678 seines Schlages bis 1989 – neuer Rekord. Pininfarina hatte über den mechanischen Komponenten des 308 GT4 Motive aus dem 246 GT und dem 365 GT4 BB miteinander verschnitten. Von Scaglietti im Anschluss an eine Kunststoff-Edition von 808 Stück nach April 1977 in Metall gewandet, war er einfach schön. Im gleichen Jahr kam der GTS, wie der Berlinetta den Dreiliter quer im Heck. Ein festes Dachteil ließ sich hinter den Sitzen verstauen.

The 308 GTB unveiled at the 1975 Paris Salon was the first of 21,678 of this automobile to be built by 1989—a new record. Pininfarina had used mechanical components from the 308 GT4, and had taken his stylistic inspiration from the 246 GT and the 365 GT4 BB. After a first run of 808 cars in fiberglass, Scaglietti switched to metal in April 1977; the result was simply beautiful. That same year, the GTS Spider appeared, like the Berlinetta with a transversely mounted 3-liter engine. The removable roof

Der 308 GTB, neuer Ferrari-Bestseller, war eine gelungene Mischung aus 246 GT und 365 BB.

The 308 GTB, the new Ferrari bestseller, was a clever combination of the 246 GT and the 365 BB.

Zwei Lamellendreiecke fanden sich statt der rückwärtigen Fensterchen.

Ab Herbst 1980 ersetzte eine K-Jetronic von Bosch die vier Doppelvergaser, Tod für 41 der ursprünglichen 255 PS. 26 davon gewann man zurück, als zwei Jahre später 32 Ventile die Arbeit aufnahmen, ausgewiesen durch die Inschrift *quattrovalvole* am Heck. Von den 12143 Einheiten des 308 bis zum Juli 1985 waren 8004 GTS. Dies galt entsprechend für den 328, der ihn auf der Frankfurter IAA 1985 ablöste. Er bot 3186 cm³ und 270 (mit Katalysator 255) PS auf und hatte auch sonst zugelegt: 25 mm

Von seinem Debüt im Herbst 1975 auf dem Pariser Salon bis zum Produktionsende 1989 verließen über 21000 Exemplare das Werk in Maranello. Die schlichte Eleganz der Pininfarina-Karosserie ist zeitlos.

was stored behind the seats. Two triangular laminated plates replaced the rear side windows.

From the fall of 1980, the four doubled-choked carburetors were replaced by a Bosch K-Jetronic, which meant a loss of 41 of the original 255 bhp. However, 26 bhp of this was saved two years later when 16 valves were added; this model was identifiable by the *quattrovalvole* on the trunk. Of the 12,143 units of the 308 produced by July 1985, 8004 were GTSs. Similar proportions applied with the 328, which replaced it at the Frankfurt IAA in 1985. The engine size had been increased to 3186 cc and 270 bhp (255 with

Over 21,000 examples left the Maranello works between its debut at the 1975 Paris Car Salon and termination of production in 1989. The simple elegance of the Pininfarina bodywork is timeless.

Länge, 8 mm Höhe, je 10 mm Breite und Radstand. Seine Front zitierte den Testa Rossa. Weg waren die Kühlrippen hinter den Scheinwerfern, größer der Grill auf der vorderen Haube, anders das Arrangement der offenen Lampen, voluminöser der schwarze Spoiler vorn, neu die Inneneinrichtung. Exklusiv für Italien gab es seit 1980 den Zweiliter 208, 2123 Stück bis zum Oktober 1989 mit 155 PS. Zu 220 verhalf ihm 1982 ein Turbolader von KKK, zu weiteren 34 ein Ladeluftkühler von 1986.

a catalytic converter), and it was bigger elsewhere, too: one inch (25 mm) in length; 5/16" (8 mm) in height; 3/4" (20 mm) in width and wheelbase. The front was inspired by the Testa Rossa. The vents behind the headlight covers had gone, while the grille on the front was bigger; the configuration of the lights had changed; a black spoiler had been added on the front; and the interior had also been changed. The two-liter 208 had been available just in Italy since 1980, 2123 of which were produced by October 1989 with 155 bhp. A KKK turbo helped it to 220 bhp, and an intercooler added in 1986 boosted it by another 34 bhp.

Der 308 GTB mutierte 1985 zum 328 GTB. Hier arbeitete der Achtzylinder mit 3,2 Litern Hubraum, und der GTS genannte Spider war der erklärte Liebling der 328-Kunden.

The 308 GTB mutated in 1985 into the 328 GTB. Here the eight-cylinder worked with a capacity of 3.2 liters, and the GTS called Spider was the declared love of 328 customers.

Mondial 8
Mondial 3.2
Mondial t
Mondial Cabriolet

Der Mondial 8 ersetzte vom Genfer Salon 1980 an den 308 GT4. Diesmal war Pininfarina der schwarze Peter zugespielt worden, auf den 2650 mm zwischen den Achsen Lebensraum für vier Personen sowie einen gut gewachsenen V8 einzurichten. Das Produkt verwöhnte indes eher durch den serienmäßigen Duft von Connolly-Tierhäuten und Segnungen der Zivilisation wie ein doppelt verstellbares Lederlenkrad, Klimaanlage, Zentralverriegelung und die elektronische Überwachung von nicht ganz geschlossenen Türen.

Ab Juli 1982 beschafften dem Dreiliter neue Köpfe mit 32 Ventilen 26 zusätzliche PS zu den ursprünglich 214, was sich ab 2000/min kraftvoll bemerkbar machte. Ein Cabriolet stellte sich ein auf dem Brüsseler Salon 1983, anfänglich

The Mondial 8 appeared at the Geneva Show of 1980, replacing the 308 GT4. This time, Pininfarina was tasked to design a car with an 8'8" (2650 mm) wheelbase with room for four people between the axles, and a well-developed V8 engine. The car pampered the occupants with the smell of the Connolly leather trim (standard), the two-way adjustable leather steering wheel, air-conditioning, central locking, and an electronic control that sounded an alarm if a door had not been properly closed.

From July 1982, new 32-valve cylinder heads gave the three-liter engine 26 additional bhp on top of the original 214, which really could be felt from 2000 rpm. The Cabriolet, shown at the Brussels Show in 1983, was initially destined exclusively for the USA. At the IAA in 1985,

Die voluminösen Lufteinlässe vor den Hinterrädern prägten die Seitenansicht des Mondial, der als Nachfolger des 308 GT4 auf den Markt kam.

The voluminous air intakes in front of the rear wheels shaped the side elevation of the Mondial, which came onto the market as the successor to the 308 GT4.

DISEGNO DI *pininfarina*

exklusiv für die USA bestimmt. Auf der IAA 1985 hatte der Mondial wie der 328 mehr Hubraum und führte fortan, von 270 PS beflügelt, den Zusatz 3.2 am Heck. Wie jener war er vorn im Umfeld der Kühleröffnung, der Lampen und des Spoilers modifiziert, war um 45 mm kürzer, fünf breiter und 25 niedriger, mit Felgen in einfacherem Design und Stoßfängern in Wagenfarbe.

Für das Mondial-Design zeichnete wieder Pininfarina verantwortlich, dennoch hielt sich die Begeisterung über die Form des 2+2-Sitzers in Grenzen.

the Mondial—like the 328—had a greater capacity, and from now on, with 270 bhp, bore the 3.2 badge on the rear. Cosmetic changes were made to the radiator grille, the headlights, and the spoiler; it was 1¾" (45 mm) shorter, ³⁄₁₆" (5 mm) wider, and one inch (25 mm) lower. The rims were plainer, and the fenders were in the same color as the car.

Pininfarina was once again responsible for the Mondial design, however, the enthusiasm for the form of the 2+2-seater was limited.

Den Mondial t gab es wieder als vollwertiges Cabriolet. Zu seinen technischen Finessen zählte das hinter dem längs montierten Motor quer eingebaute Getriebe.

In dieser waren auch die Türöffner des Mondial t (für *trasversale*) seit der Genfer Schau 1989 lackiert, geschrumpft die Hauptlampen wie die seitlichen Lufteinlässe. Die Maschine, 3405 cm³, 300 PS, war nun längs installiert, quer das Getriebe. Eine elektronische Dämpfkraftanpassung sah drei Grundeinstellungen vor.

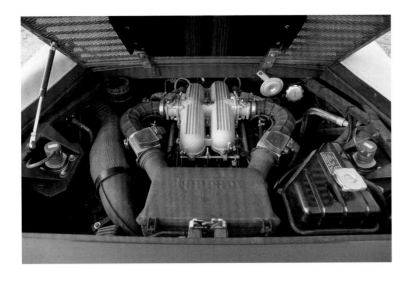

At the Geneva Show of 1989, the door handles of the Mondial t (for *trasversale*) were also red, and the main headlights and side vents were smaller. The engine of 3405 cc, providing 300 bhp, was now positioned longitudinally, while the gearbox was transversely mounted. The electronic adjustment of the damper movement offered three basic modes.

The Mondial t was also available as a full convertible. Its technical finesses included the cross-mounted transmission placed behind the lengthways-mounted engine.

288 GTO

Just schien selbst in Maranello der Trott der großen Serien einzukehren, da zeigte man auf dem Genfer Salon 1984 den 288 GTO, brutal stark, schnell und schön. Bereits vor dem Produktionsbeginn im Juli jenes Jahres war die limitierte Edition von 273 Exemplaren der jüngsten Pininfarina-Kreation gleichsam meistbietend an den Mann gebracht.

Die Ähnlichkeit zum 308 GTB, auf dem der 288 GTO fußte, ging kaum bis unter die Haut. Vorn unterschieden ihn ein größerer Spoiler und anders dimensionierte und angeordnete unbedeckte Lampen, seitlich die beiden steil aufgereckten Spiegel, athletisch geschwellte Kotflügel, horizontale Lufteinlässe unter den Türen, schräge Luftauslässe hinter den Antriebsrädern, die zugleich den historischen GTO zitierten, sowie eine kühn aufgewinkelte Heckkante und ein eigenes Auspuff-Ensemble.

Die liberale Verwendung von Fiberglas, Kevlar und Nomex verriet das Denken von Harvey Postlethwaite, der

Just as the routine of the production line seemed to have become the norm, the 288 GTO—brutally powerful, fast, and beautiful—was presented at the Geneva Show of 1984. Even before production started in July of that year, the limited edition of 273 of Pininfarina's latest creation had been sold, each one to the highest bidder.

The resemblance to the 308 GTB, on which the 288 GTO was based, was not really even skin deep. On the front were a bigger spoiler and a different layout for the (uncovered) lights; on the sides, upswept rear view mirrors and athletically muscular wings; horizontal air vents under the doors, oblique vents behind the wheels that also adorned the historic GTO; and a dynamically upswept back end that revealed an impressive set of exhaust pipes.

The liberal use of fiberglass, Kevlar and Nomex bore witness to the philosophy of Harvey Postlethwaite, who had

Er trug einen großen Namen. Der 288 GTO brillierte indessen nicht im Rennsport sondern war der schnellste Straßen-Ferrari jener Zeit mit den knapp über 300 km/h, die ihm sein Biturbo-V8 ermöglichte.

It bore a great name. However, the 288 GTO did not shine in racing sport, but was the fastest road Ferrari of its time, powered by a twin-turbo V8 that gave it a top speed of just over 185 mph (300 kph).

Der dezente Heckspoiler des 288 GTO optimierte den Anpressruck auf die Hinterräder, nur das Kult-Kürzel am Heck verriet die enorme Potenz dieses Sportwagens.

The subtle rear spoiler of the 288 GTO optimized the tread pressure on the rear wheels, only the cult abbreviation on the trunk betrayed the enormous potential of this sports car.

solch edle Kunststoffe seit 1982 auch den Grand-Prix-Wagen der Marke verordnete. Die Ausläufer des V8, dessen Volumen aus Gründen der Homologation auf 2855 cm³ abgesenkt worden war, wölbten sich bis zwischen die harten Sitze. Er war längs eingebaut, und nicht einmal der Radstand von 2450 mm, 110 mehr als im 308, hatte ihm seine Grenzen gewiesen.

Unter der reich gerippten Motorhaube aber herrschte die schlichte Symmetrie der Gewalt: Zwei Nockenwellen, 16 Ventile, ein Turbolader des japanischen Fabrikats IHI sowie ein riesiger Ladeluftkühler je Zylinderreihe ließen nicht den geringsten Zweifel an der vollzähligen Anwesenheit der 400 angegebenen PS aufkommen.

also been using these quality materials on the marque's Grand Prix cars since 1982. The exhausts of the V8, which had been reduced to 2855 cc for homologation reasons, intruded right up between the very firm GTO seats. The engine was mounted longitudinally, and not even the wheelbase of eight feet (2450 mm), 4¹/₂" (110 mm) more than the 308, managed to keep it contained.

Under the extravagantly ribbed hood, a simple symmetry of tumultuous energy reigned supreme: each bank of cylinders had two camshafts, 16 valves, a Japanese IHI turbocharger, and a huge intercooler, all of which combined to completely remove any doubts over the factory's claim to 400 bhp.

Das V8-Triebwerk verwischte akustisch jeden Unterschied zwischen einem Vier-, Sechs-, Acht- oder Zwölfzylinder und machte sich trompetend, zischend, orgelnd und pfeifend Luft.

Trumpeting, howling, and roaring, the V8 engine released its inner tension, completely denying any resemblance to a four-, six-, eight-, or twelve-cylinder.

Testarossa 512 TR F512 M

Seine Silhouette zeichnete das Segment seiner Tragfläche nach. Mit knapp zwei Metern war er fast doppelt so breit wie hoch. Seine Kühler wurden durch fünffach lamellierte Seitenschächte vom Fahrtwind angeströmt. Dies gab dem Testarossa, 1984 auf dem Pariser Salon eingeführt, sein Besonderes.

Its silhouette took its inspiration from part of an aerofoil: at just six and half feet (two meters), it was almost twice as wide as it was high. Air was channeled to its radiators through five large gills on the side. This was what made the Testarossa so special when it was first presented at the Paris Show of 1984.

Unmittelbar hinter seiner Besatzung reckte das riesige Triebwerk seine Extremitäten im Winkel von 180 Grad, im Prinzip das gleiche wie im BB 512 i, allerdings beatmet von Vierventilköpfen, die seine Leistung auf 390 PS steigerten. Wie einst am Testa Rossa waren die Zylinderkopfdeckel mit rotem Lack beschichtet. Auf

The huge 180-degree V12 engine stretched out behind the passengers, similar in principle to the one in the BB 512 i, but with four valves per cylinder that increased its power to 390 bhp. In memory of the old Testa Rossa, the cam covers were painted red. The successor to this model, the 512 TR — 38 bhp more powerful,

Das Profil des Testarossa zeichnete einen Flugzeugflügel im Querschnitt nach.

The profile of the Testarossa took its inspiration from the cross section of an aerofoil.

der Auto-Show in Los Angeles im Januar 1992 folgte der 512 TR, 38 PS stärker, 40 kg leichter, mit einer um 30 mm tiefer eingelassenen Maschine, niedrigeren Reifen sowie besseren Bremsen.

Er trug das Ferrari-Familiengesicht für die Neunziger, ein trapezförmiger vorderer Lufteinlass mit gerundeten Ecken, flankiert von größeren offenen Lampeneinheiten und unten gesäumt von einem Spoileransatz. Die Heckleuchten waren durch einen schwarzen Grill fast vertarnt,

Testa Rossa, allerdings getrennt geschrieben, hießen schon Ferrari-Rennsportwagen der Fünfziger – ebenfalls mit roten Zylinderköpfen. Für den 512 TR wählte Pininfarina-Stylist Lorenzo Ramaciotti die Horizontale als Leitmotiv.

88 pounds (40 kg) lighter, the engine 1¼ inches (30 mm) lower, and with lower profile tires and better brakes—was presented at the Los Angeles Show in January 1992.

It had the look of the Ferrari family of the nineties, with a trapezoidal grille with rounded corners, flanked by bigger open lights, and underlined by a discreet spoiler. The rear lights were almost completely hidden by the black grille, while the black air vents on the roof extensions had been removed.

Testa Rossa—spelled as two words, it was the name of Ferrari racing cars of the Fifties—also had red cylinder heads. Pininfarina stylist Lorenzo Ramaciotti chose horizontal lines as the leitmotif for the 512 TR.

Genau zehn Jahre nach
seinem Debüt vollzog man
mit dem F512 M den letzten
Schritt in der Evolution des
Testarossa, der nun aus
offenen Scheinwerfern in die
Welt blickte.

Exactly ten years after its
debut, the F512 M was the
final stage in the evolution
of the Testarossa; it now
viewed the world through
open headlights.

Das prächtige Zwölfzylinder-Aggregat begeisterte durch spontane Leistungsabgabe und perfekt abgestimmten Sound. Die mächtigen, gelochten Bremsscheiben hinter den schaufelförmigen Leichtmetallrädern sorgten für optimale Verzögerung.

während man die schwarzen Entlüftungsgitter auf den Dachausläufern völlig wegretuschiert hatte.

Die Frontpartie einer dritten Evolutionsstufe vom Herbst 1994 war angeregt von den Brüdern F355 und 456 GT. Dazu kam, wie das Kürzel M für *modificata* verhieß, ein Bündel weiterer Modifikationen, etwa 18 kg weniger, 12 PS mehr, fest stehende Scheinwerfer vorn und runde Doppellampen hinten.

The magnificent twelve-cylinder engine was an inspiration with its spontaneous performance and perfectly tuned sound. The mighty perforated brake disks behind the paddle-shaped alloy wheels ensured optimal braking.

The front section of the third stage in its evolution in the fall of 1994 was inspired by its brothers, the F355 and 456 GT. Furthermore—as indicated by the "M" for *modificata*—there were various other modifications, such as the weight reduction of 40 pounds (18 kg), an additional 12 bhp, fixed headlights at the front, and round double lights at the rear.

F40

Unter der schlichten
Bezeichnung F40 stellte
Ferrari einen absoluten High-
End-Sportwagen auf die
Räder. 320 km/h schnell und
478 PS stark.

Ferrari set a totally high-end
sports car on wheels under
the simple description F40
with its top speed of 320 kph
(199 mph) and 478 bhp.

Beim Gestalten des F40 hatte sich Pininfarina-Chefstylist Leonardo Fioravanti für einen Weg entschieden, der im Bizarr-Dramatischen und somit einer höheren Form von Schönheit mündete.

Was der greise Enzo Ferrari um die Mittagsstunde des 12. März 1987 am 40. Jahrestag seines Erstlings 125 S im Centro Civico di Maranello eigenhändig enthüllte, mochte als Sinnbild und Inbegriff der Aggression gelten, zerklüftet, durchfurcht, zersiebt und gekrönt von einem mächtigen Flügel über dem Heck.

Zwischen den Polen Ästhetik und Pragmatik war die Karosserie des F40 aus noblen Kunststoffen legiert, dreimal steifer und 20 Prozent leichter als eine vergleichbare Metallstruktur. Mit Kevlar, Kohlefaser und Fiberglas verstärkt sorgte der traditionelle Gitterrohrrahmen für das

The car that the venerable Enzo Ferrari came to unveil personally on the stroke of midday on 12 March 1987—the 40th birthday of his "firstborn," the 125 S—at the Centro Civico di Maranello was the incarnation of aggression; a menacing mixture of slopes and chasms, ridged and furrowed all over, and all topped off with an impressive wing at the rear.

Between the polar opposites of aesthetics and pragmatism, the body of the F40 was built from sophisticated plastics, three times stiffer and 20 percent lighter than any comparable metal structure. The traditional tubular

gebotene Rückgrat. Unter dem zweimal neunfach aufgebrochenen Rückfenster aber lagerte das Kraftwerk, einschüchternd allein durch seine optische Präsenz. Das Betreten gestaltete sich mühselig, da den Eindringling eine abwehrend im Wege stehende Strebe behinderte. Aber hatte er sich erst einmal in die harte Sitzschale fallen lassen, entpuppte sie sich als überraschend bequem.

Der Druck auf einen Gummiknopf entfachte umgehend ein konzertiertes Miteinander im Nacken der Passagiere, untermalt von einem Klanggemälde, dessen Bandbreite von ungewöhnlich bis infernalisch reichte und bald

structure—a veritable backbone—was reinforced with Kevlar, carbon fiber, and fiberglass. Under the rear window with its nine openings were the mechanical parts, both beautiful and intimidating to look at. Getting on board was difficult, since a structural cross-member was in the way and had to be overcome. But once installed in the hard bucket seats, it proved to be surprisingly comfortable.

The touch of a rubberized button unleashed a hurricane behind the passengers' ears, followed by a whole range of sounds from the strange to the diabolical that soon rendered conversation impossible. At maximum revs in first

For the design of the F40, Pininfarina's chief stylist Leonardo Fioravanti chose a path that ended in the bizarre and dramatic, and thus in a higher form of beauty.

jegliche Kommunikation unterband. Bei Vollgas im ersten und im zweiten Gang wölkte blauer Qualm empor, die Michelin-Walzen vom Kaliber 335/35 ZR 17 leimten fette schwarze Balken in den Asphalt, und Tempo 200 war nach baren elf Sekunden kein Thema mehr. Dabei umgab einen das unverbramte Ambiente einer Mönchszelle, und die Anschaffung des Extras Klimaanlage erwies sich als lebensnotwendig, sollte sich der knappe Fahrgastraum nicht zur Bratröhre erhitzen. 1311 betuchte Kunden nahmen diese Erfahrung gern in Kauf.

and second, clouds of blue smoke would pour out from around the large Michelin 335/35 ZR 17 tires that then expressed their displeasure at being treated this way by leaving thick black tracks on the tarmac; after a mere 11 seconds, the 124 mph (200 kph) barrier was no longer an issue. And yet the atmosphere in the cockpit was austere, a monk's cell, and the addition of the air-conditioning was essential if one wanted to avoid being roasted alive as a passenger. This was an experience that 1311 moneyed customers were only too happy to share.

Das Herz des F40 lag für jeden Passanten sichtbar unter einer großen transparenten Abdeckung. Optisch dominierten die beiden Ladeluftkühler.

The heart of the F40 lay open for all passers-by to see under the large transparent cover. Optically, the two large intercoolers dominated.

*Der V8 setzte mit 478 PS bei 7000/min
Leistung in Hülle und Fülle frei, mit drei Litern
Hubraum, 32 Ventilen, zwei Turboladern
und Ladeluftkühlern.*

*With 478 bhp, the V8 let it all hang out at
7000 rpm: three liters cubic capacity, 32 valves,
two turbochargers, and two intercoolers.*

Sonderangebot für die Piste:
der F40 GT Competizione
mit 780 PS, ursprünglich
für Le Mans vorgesehen,
in den USA bei der IMSA-
Serie eingesetzt.

Special offer for the
race track: the F40 GT
Competizione with 780 bhp,
intended originally for
Le Mans, was used in the
USA's IMSA series.

348 tb
348 ts
348 GTB
348 GTS
348 Spider

Ferrari ließ den 348 auf der Frankfurter IAA im Herbst 1989 gleich im gemischten Doppel antreten, als tb und ts, das b für Berlinetta, das s für Spider, obwohl es sich doch um einen Targa handelte. Das t (für *trasversale*) kürzelte das Quergetriebe hinter dem Längsmotor, dem aus dem Mondial bekannten V8 mit 3405 cm³, zunächst mit 300 und vom Herbst 1993 an mit 320 PS. Mit seinem kurzen Überhang

Ferrari presented the 348 at the Frankfurt IAA in the fall of 1989 as part of a mixed double, the tb and the ts, the "b" for Berlinetta, the "s" for Spider, even though it was a targa. The "t" (for *trasversale*) referred to the transversely mounted gearbox behind the longitudinally mounted engine, which was based on the 3405cc V8, initially providing 300 bhp and later, from the fall of 1993,

hinten und seinen Spoilern und Schürzen wirkte der 348 stämmig-militant. Die durch Lamellen gegliederten seitlichen Einkerbungen führten weiter vorn zu den Kühlern als beim Testa Rossa und beim Mondial. Der ts unterschied sich vom Berlinetta im Wesentlichen durch die sieben Kilo schwere Dachplanke aus Fiberglas, mit Stahl verstärkt, die flugs entfernt und hochkant hinter den Sitzen versenkt

320 bhp, that powered the Mondial. With its short overhang at the rear, its spoilers and skirts, the 348 looked stocky and aggressive. Its lateral grooves and slats were arranged further forward than on the Testarossa and Mondial. The main difference between the ts and the Berlinetta was the fiberglass steel-reinforced roof of 15 pounds (7 kg) that was easy to remove and stowed away behind

Der 348 löste den bisherigen Bestseller 328 ab und schrieb die Ferrari-Erfolgsgeschichte der Neunziger weiter.

The 348 superseded the best-selling 328, and went on to write the Ferrari story of success for the 1990s.

Zusammen mit dem Berlinetta tb kam, versehen mit dem Kürzel ts und einer Dachplanke aus Fiberglas, eine Targa-Version auf den Markt.

A targa version with the abbreviation "ts" and a removable fiberglass roof came onto the market at the same time as the closed model.

werden konnte. Fahrer und Beifahrer fehlten dann zehn Zentimeter Kniefreiheit.

Im Februar 1993 wurde im kalifornischen Beverly Hills der 348 Spider präsentiert, auch er umgehend ein Hit. Schon das straff sitzende Barett stand dem Auto gut. Hatte man es in die dafür zuständige Mulde gestopft und eine schwarze Persenning darüber geknöpft, war alles Stoffliche auf eine milde Hügellandschaft reduziert, in der sich der Grundriss des Dachs mit seinen schräg nach hinten abfallenden Holmen noch einmal abzeichnete. Dann wurde der Spider plötzlich zur offenen Kriegserklärung an den Rest der Cabrio-Welt – und der Sieger stand auch schon fest.

the seats. This cost the driver and passenger four inches (10 cm) in legroom.

The 348 Spider was presented in Beverley Hills in February 1993 to general admiration and acclaim. The tight-fitting soft-top roof suited the car well. When it was folded down, stored away in the space intended for this purpose and hidden under a stud-fastening cover, the amount of material still visible was limited to a small bump in which only the outline of the roof with its supports angled to the rear could be detected. Then the Spider suddenly became an open declaration of war on all the other convertibles in the world—and it was clear from the start who the winner would be.

Vieles aus der Formensprache
beim 348 lässt noch an
den Testarossa denken:
die Lamellen über den
Rückleuchten, die
Luftauslässe der hinteren
Haube – insgesamt die
Betonung der Horizontale.

Much of the 348's form
language is reminiscent of the
Testarossa: the slats above
the rear lights, the air outlets
of the rear hood—all in all the
emphasis on the horizontal.

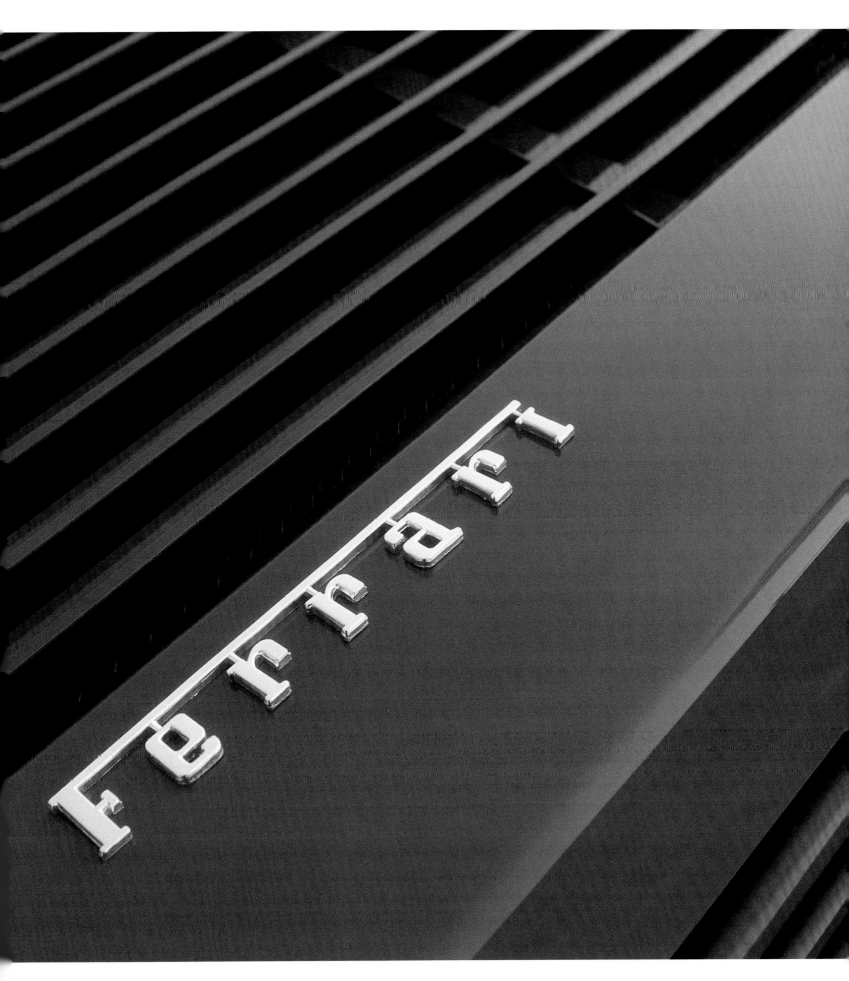

Auch im Spider sorgte
der 3,4 Liter große und
320 PS starke Achtzylinder
für vehementen Vortrieb.
Genuss in einer der
schönsten Formen.

The 3.4-liter and 320 bhp eight-cylinder provided a vehement thrust for the Spider as well. Pleasure in one of its most beautiful forms!

456 GT
456 GTA
456 M GT

Er füllte die Vakanz des Ferrari für die große Reise, die sich mit dem Heimgang des 412 anno 1989 aufgetan hatte: der 456 GT auf dem Pariser Salon im Oktober 1992. Das Pininfarina-Designstudio unter Lorenzo Ramaciotti hatte genüsslich in die Schatulle mit schönen und bewährten Details gegriffen: Das Gesicht des voluminösen Coupés verriet die Nähe zum 512 TR und zum 348, die Seitenpartie mochte Anklänge an F40 und Mythos nicht verhehlen, und das Heck erinnerte gar massiv an den Daytona. Kein Flügelwerk entstellte die klaren Linien. Allerdings war ein beweglicher Spoiler in den hinteren Stoßfänger eingearbeitet. Ein elektronisches Steuergerät veränderte seinen

When the 412 disappeared in 1989, it left a gap in the market for a Ferrari suitable for long distances, and this model filled that gap. The 456 debuted at the Paris Salon in October 1992. The Pininfarina design studio under Lorenzo Ramaciotti had dug deep into the treasure trove of beautiful, tried-and-tested solutions: the front of the spacious coupé was closely related to the 512 TR and the 348; the sides could not conceal their links to the F40 and the Mythos; and the rear bore a strong resemblance to the Daytona. There were no wings to disturb the purity of the lines, although a movable spoiler had been worked into the rear fender. An electronic device modified the

Winkel ab 110 km/h nach Tempo und Logik, bei 80 kehrte er in die Ausgangslage zurück.

Das vergleichsweise üppige Raumangebot kam vor allem den Frontpassagieren zugute. Im Umfeld der Bedienelemente herrschte ein ungewohnt metallenes Ambiente mit einer Fülle von Kipphebelchen, die sich mit knackigem Klicken vernehmen ließen. Das von einem Aluminiumbällchen gekrönte Schaltstänglein ließ sich durch sechs Fahrstufen führen, nachdem eine Drehung an dem winzigen Zündschlüsselchen endgültig die Zwienatur des 456 GT erschlossen hatte, halb potente Limousine, halb überlegener Sportwagen. Obwohl akustisch

angle at speeds above 68 mph (110 kph), returning it to its original position below 50 mph (80 kph).

The comparatively spacious interior was of particular benefit to the front passengers. An unusual metallic ambience prevailed around the control elements with an abundance of rocker switches that when activated gave a satisfying "click." The gear lever crowned by a small aluminum ball led you through the six forward gears, after a quarter-turn of the tiny ignition key had revealed the split personality of the 456 GT: it was part high-performance sedan, part superior sports car. While the soundproofing was effective, the powerful V12 covered the entire range

Im Segment des 456 GT herrschten eigene Regeln. Bevorzugt wurden Blautöne, auch gelb. Nur eine Minderheit votierte für klassisches Ferrarirot.

The 456 GT club had its own rules. Most preferred one of the blue finishes, and some the yellow. Only a few voted for classic Ferrari red.

Das Gesicht des 456 GT zeugte von der genetischen Nähe zu 512 TR und 348. Noch schien die Schaltkulisse ein schier unverzichtbares Requisit.

The appearance of the 456 GT showed that it was a close relative of the 512 TR and the 348. Even the gear lever surround seemed an essential piece of equipment.

klug gezähmt, bespielte der mächtige V12 das ganze Spektrum vom baritonalen Grummeln zum schmetternden Trompeten. Die opulente Serienausstattung umspannte nicht zuletzt eine Servotronic, die das Lenken bis hin zu 70 km/h erleichterte, ohne den Kontakt zur Fahrbahn zu verfremden.

from a baritone grumble to a blaring trumpet. The opulent standard features included progressive power steering that made turning the wheel easier up to 44 mph (70 kph) without affecting road holding.

Customer requests for an automatic version of the 456 GT were met in 1996 with the GTA (the "A" stood for

Kundenwünsche nach einer Automatik für den 456 GT wurden 1996 mit dem GTA (das A stand für Automatik) erfüllt. Modifikationen an Radaufhängungen, Karosserie und im Interieur ab 1998 schlugen sich im Modellnamen durch ein zusätzliches M nieder – für *modificata*. Selbst das hatte Tradition.

automatic). Changes to the wheel suspension, bodywork, and to the interior from 1998 were indicated by another addition to the 456 GT—"M" for *modificata*. Even this was a kind of tradition.

442 PS, geboren von fünfeinhalb Litern Hubraum, trieben den Viersitzer auf knapp über 300 km/h. Er war eine gelungene Collage aus bewährten Stilelementen.

The 442 bhp achieved by the 4.5-liter engine brought the four-seater to 185 mph (300 kph). It was a clever mix of tried-and-tested style elements.

F333 SP

Der F333 SP, im Januar 1994 enthüllt, war gedacht für die WSC (für World Sports Car)-Rennen der International Motor Sport Association (IMSA) in den USA.

Als treibende Kräfte hinter dem Projekt wirkten Ferrari North America unter dem Präsidenten Gian Luigi Buitoni und Giampiero Moretti, der sich die Sporen im Zeichen des schwarzen Hengstes bereits im 512S verdient hatte und seit dem Debüt des F333 SP in Road Atlanta im April 1994 zum lebenden Inventar der WSC-Tournee zählte. Die Karosserie aus Kohlefaser und Nomex konnte selbst in der Hitze des Gefechts partiell zügig entfernt werden. Kohlefaser, mit Aluminium zu einem Monocoque verquickt, trug überdies zum rigiden Rückgrat des Zweisitzers bei. Auf der knappen Parzelle zwischen den Achsen fand

The F333, unveiled in January 1994, was intended for the WSC (World Sports Car Championship) races run under the auspices of the International Motor Sport Association (IMSA) in the USA.

The driving force behind the project was Ferrari North America, under the presidency of Gian Luigi Buitoni and Giampiero Moretti. Moretti had already won his spurs for the little black horse at the wheel of a 512S, and since the debut of the F333 SP at Road Atlanta in April 1994 had been considered essential to the endeavor. The bodywork of carbon fiber and Nomex could quickly be partly removed if necessary in the heat of battle. The carbon fiber, combined here with aluminum to form the monocoque,

Mit dem F333 SP kehrte Ferrari 1994 nach Jahrzehnten der Abstinenz wieder zurück in die Szene der Sportwagenrennen. Den Renneinsatz überließ man engagierten Privatteams.

With the F333 SP, Ferrari returned in 1994 to the sports car racing scene once more, after decades of abstinence. The racing operation was left to dedicated private teams.

sich auch das Getriebe eingezwängt. Die fünf Fahrstufen wurden sequentiell eingelegt. Das Triebwerk: ein V12 mit 3997 cm³ und fünf aus Titan gefertigten Ventilen je Zylinder, Gabelwinkel 65 Grad, über 650 PS stark.

Ganz ähnlich, plauderte Gian Luigi Buitoni aus, werde die Maschine des F130 beschaffen sein – das war der Werkscode für den F50 …

contributed to the rigidity of this two-seater. The gearbox was mounted on the narrow area between the two axles. The five gears were changed by means of a sequential box. The engine was a 3997 cc, 65-degree V12 with five titanium valves per cylinder, providing more than 650 bhp.

Gian Luigi Buitoni "let slip" that the engine for the F130 —the factory name for the F50—would be quite similar …

Das Lista-Team des Schweizer Industriellen Fredy Lienhard startete mit dem F333SP erfolgreich bei den Rennen der World Sports Car Series. Der Motor mit vier Litern Hubraum und einer Leistung von mehr als 650 PS war natürlich ein Zwölfzylinder. 40 Exemplare wurden gebaut, das letzte 2002.

Swiss industrialist Fredy Lienhard's Lista team started successfully with the F333SP at the World Sports Car Series races. The four-liter engine with a performance of more than 650 bhp was, of course, a twelve-cylinder. 40 units were constructed, the last one in 2002.

F355 Berlinetta
F355 GTS
F355 Spider
F355 Challenge

Der F355 wurde von Ferrari-Präsident Luca di Monte-zemolo am 24. Mai 1994 in Maranello 50 Journalisten vorgestellt, als Berlinetta und GTS. Das Exterieur des 348 war sorgsam entrümpelt und dabei gewissermaßen die Urform des Ferrari-Dreiers freigelegt worden. Die Ziffer am Ende des Sigels 355 stand nicht länger für die Summe der Zylinder, sondern für die Zahl der Ventile pro Brennraum des V8, eines Federgewichts von drei Zentnern.

Der F355 versöhnte Extreme miteinander, die ehemals unvereinbar schienen. Bei niedrigem Tempo ging etwa dem Piloten eine Servolenkung zur Hand – einst ein Tabu ebenso wie die Vorstellung, dass ein Ferrari dieses Genres einmal die Dämpfereinstellungen sportlich und komfortabel anbieten könnte. Und dem Urschrei früherer Generationen hatte er eher klassische Musik entgegenzusetzen,

The Berlinetta and GTS versions of the F355 were unveiled by Ferrari President Luca di Montezemolo on 24 May 1994 at Maranello to a group of fifty handpicked journalists. The exterior of the 348 had been carefully stripped down, in a way revealing the original shape of the Ferrari 3-liter. The last figure of the code number 355 no longer indicated the number of cylinders, but represented the number of valves per cylinder of the V8, a featherweight of a mere three hundredweight.

The F355 brought together seemingly irreconcilable extremes. At low speeds the driver could count on the help of power steering—once as much of a taboo as the idea that this type of Ferrari could ever have suspension designed for comfort as well as speed. The primal screams of past generations had clearly been replaced by classical

Am F355 war die Urform des Ferrari-Dreiers freigelegt wie eine
platonische Idee. Schöpfer Sergio Pininfarina mochte seine
»muskulöse Solidität«.

The original shape of the Ferrari 3-liter was exposed in the
F355 like a platonic idea. Its creator Sergio Pininfarina liked its
"muscular solidity."

Betrachter betörte der Spider
mit grenzenloser Offenheit,
Fahrer mit einer Synthese aus
erotischen Klangsequenzen
und überschäumendem
Temperament des
potenten Achtzylinders.

The Spider beguiled the
viewer with its unlimited
openness, and the driver
with a hardly beatable
synthesis of its exuberant
temperament and the erotic
sound sequences of its potent
eight cylinders.

sorgfältig ins neue Ferrari-Image hineinkomponiert. Es
gab ihn auch mit einer rein mechanischen Lenkung und
- gegen Aufpreis - knüppelharten Rennsitzen aus Ver-
bundwerkstoff statt der kommoden Serien-Fauteuils.

Die Käufer des Spiders aber, der sich noch ein Jahr von
seinem Vorgänger vertreten ließ, lösten nur noch den Zen-
tralverschluss am Rahmen der Windschutzscheibe, führten das Verdeck per Hand zurück, bis ein Signal ertönte,
und auf Knopfdruck versank das Stoffdach in einer Höhle
vor dem Motorraum. Wer sportliche Ambitionen hegte,
war im Wettstreit um einen Markenpokal auf den Renn-
pisten bestens bedient mit dem F355 Challenge von 1995.
1997 rüstete man den F355 unter der Bezeichnung 355 F1
mit einem hydraulischen Kupplungs- und Schaltsystem
aus. Damit hielt die Wippenschaltung hinter dem Lenkrad, Premiere 1989 in Nigel Mansells F1-Ferrari, Einzug in
ein Straßenauto.

music, carefully composed to go with the new Ferrari
image. It was possible to have it with purely mechanical
steering and, for an extra price, to have rock-hard racing
seats made from composite material instead of the comfortable standard ones.

Owners of the Spider, though—who had to make do
with the previous model for another year—simply undid
a central catch above the windshield, pulled the roof back
by hand until an alarm sounded, and pressed a switch
for the soft top to disappear inside a recess in front of the
engine compartment. And those with sporting ambitions
could acquire the 1995 F355 Challenge competition version to tussle on the racetrack for a trophy. In 1997 Ferrari
fitted out the F355 under the name of 355 F1 with a hydraulic clutch and transmission. Thus it was that the paddles
behind the steering wheel, first tested in Nigel Mansell's
F1 Ferrari in 1989, found their way into a road car.

3,5 Liter Hubraum, 380 PS,
40 Ventile – nüchterne Daten
eines der drehfreudigsten
Motoren der neunziger
Jahre. Das Interieur war von
unaufgeregter Sachlichkeit.

A capacity of 3.5 liters,
380 bhp, five valves per
cylinder—that's the bare
data of one of the most
rpm-friendly engines of the
1990s. The interior was of
sober functionality.

F50

Seine Premiere auf dem Genfer Salon 1995 ließ das gewohnt perfekte Timing vermissen: Er kam zu früh, weil sein Name bereits das fünfzigste Jubiläum der Firma vorwegnahm, er war zu spät dran, da ihn jedermann schon 1993 erwartet hatte, Spider und Berlinetta zugleich in einer Auflage von 349 Exemplaren. Das Hardtop saß mit ein wenig Routine nach einer halben Stunde.

Der F50 bot Logis für zwei in gepflegter Unwirtlichkeit, nachdem man extrem breite Schwellen überwunden hatte, Schalensitze aus Komposit-Material in zwei Größen, ein karges Equipment, in dessen Mitte die Klimaanlage fremdartig anmutete, Analog-Display für Drehzahl und Tempo, Digitalanzeige für Tankinhalt, Öldruck, Öl- und Wassertemperatur sowie den gerade eingelegten Gang, ein Hauch von Connolly-Leder.

All dies verbarg schütter den Rennwagen, 520 PS stark, 325 km/h schnell. Er war ein kunstvoll gegliederter Keil

The appearance of the F50 at the Geneva Show of 1995 seemed to have come at the wrong time. It was too early, because its name anticipated the company's 50th birthday; it was too late because it had been expected in 1993: Spider and Berlinetta together in a production run of just 349. With a little bit of practice, the roof could be fitted in just half an hour.

The F50 would accommodate two in the somewhat inhospitable cockpit, once the two very wide sills had been negotiated. The interior was austere apart from the incongruity of the air-conditioning: it had composite construction bucket seats that were available in two sizes; rev and speed displays were analog, while the fuel gauge, oil pressure and temperature, water temperature, and the gear indicator were all digital; and there was the pervasive smell of Connolly leather.

Under this thin veneer of civilization was a pure racing car, powered by a 520 bhp engine giving a top speed

Der F50, von Ferrari-Präsident di Montezemolo charakterisiert als Formel-1-Wagen, mit dem man auch Brötchen holen konnte, war der ultimative Sportwagen für die Straße.

Ferrari President Luca di Montezemolo summed up the F50 as a Formula 1 vehicle that could also be used to fetch the bagels; it was the ultimate sports car for the road.

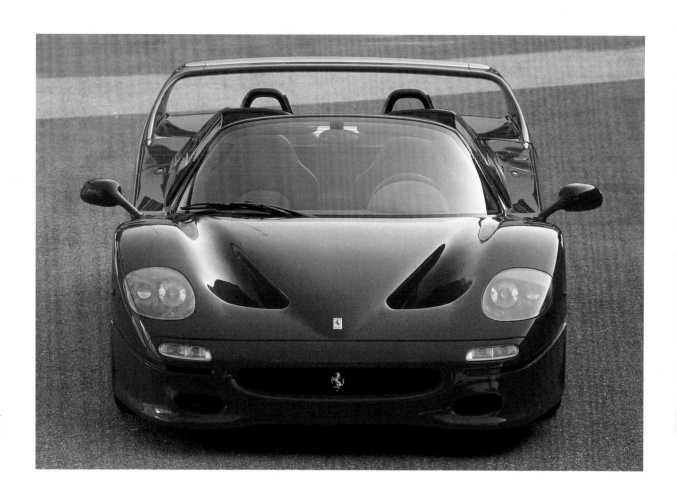

Der F50 schien die Straße förmlich aufzusaugen. Seine im Windkanal optimierte Aerodynamik erzeugte Unter- und Anpressdruck und sorgte auch jenseits von 300 km/h für stabile Fahrzustände.

The F50 seemed to literally suck up the road. Its aerodynamics, optimized in the wind tunnel, produced a vacuum and down force, and ensured that driving was stable even at speeds beyond 200 mph (300 kph).

mit elliptischen Lufteinlässen in den Flanken, einer stark gewinkelten und gerundeten Windschutzscheibe, breiten Anpressflächen hinter dem Cockpit und einem hoch in den Fahrtwind gereckten Flügel. Der glatte Boden war als Diffusor ausgebildet, High-Tech-Werkstoffe verringerten das Gewicht und erhöhten die Stabilität: Aus Titan waren Radnaben und Pleuel, aus Magnesium die Räder, aus Kohlefaser-Legierungen die Karosserie und das ultrarigide Chassis, zwei Zentner leicht und aufwändig im Ofen gebacken. So konnten V12 und Kraftübertragung als tragende Elemente verwendet werden. Der Motorblock bestand aus Stahlguss, für geringe Wandstärken und kompakte Ausmaße. Die Aufhängungen arbeiteten nach dem Pushrod-System: mit Federn und Stoßdämpfern quer zu den tragenden Teilen – auch da glich der F50 dem wilden Vetter 412 T2.

Offene Kulissenschaltung mit Karbonknauf, ein Zwölfzylinder mit 520 PS und betörendem Sound sowie großzügig dimensionierte Bremsscheiben waren einige der Zutaten, die den F50 als automobiles Kunstwerk adelten.

An open shifting gate with a carbon gear knob, a 12-cylinder engine with 520 bhp and a bewitching sound, and generously dimensioned brake disks were just some of the components that entitled the F50 to be regarded as a motorized work of art.

of 200 mph (325 kph). It was an artistically shaped wedge with elliptical air intakes in the sides and a strong curve to the windshield; the shape increased the down force behind the cockpit area, and a raised wing dominated the rear. The smooth base was designed as a diffuser. High-tech materials reduced the weight and increased stability: wheel hubs and con rods were made of titanium, the wheels of magnesium, the chassis and body were made of carbon fiber; it weighed just 220 pounds (100 kg), and was baked in an oven at incredibly high temperatures. The V12 engine and the transmission were thus strong enough to be used as load-bearing structures. The engine block was cast iron for thinner walls and compact dimensions. The suspension followed the pushrod system with horizontally mounted springs and dampers; here too, the F50 resembled its wilder cousin, the 412 T2.

550 Maranello
550 Barchetta
575 M Maranello
575 GTC
575 M Superamerica

Präsentiert wurde der 550 Maranello von seinen geistigen Vätern Luca di Montezemolo und Sergio Pininfarina persönlich am 20. Juli 1996 vor 229 handverlesenen Journalisten, Schauplatz: der Mediensaal des Nürburgrings. Seine Silhouette folgte dem Prinzip lange Motorhaube, weit hinten platzierte Fahrgastzelle, massiver Überhang vorn – einst mit dem Daytona auf die Spitze getrieben. Pate standen auch der 250 GTO mit seinen seitlichen Belüftungsschlitzen und der sanft aufgewellten hinteren Abreißkante und der 275 GTB/4. Die Typenbezeichnung verwies, leicht aufgerundet, auf den aus dem 456 GT bekannten V12 mit 5475 cm³ mit einem Bankwinkel von 65 Grad, 485 PS stark. Der Radstand des großen Bruders war für den kommoden GT für zwei um 130 auf

The 550 Maranello was personally presented by its spiritual fathers, Luca di Montezemolo and Sergio Pininfarina, to 229 handpicked journalists in the Media Hall of the Nürburgring on 20 July 1996. Its silhouette followed the pattern of a long hood, passenger cell set well back, and solid overhang at the front that had once reached the heights with the Daytona. It also borrowed from the 250 GTO, with its side air vents and the gently rounded spoiler lip on the rear, and the 275 GTB/4. The model number, slightly rounded up, was a reference to the 465 GT's 5475 cc, 65-degree V12 with 485 bhp. Its big brother's wheelbase had been shortened for the comfortable two-

Im 550 fanden sich die Gene des 456 GT, dessen sportive Alternative für zwei er darstellte.

The 550 had the 456 GT's genes, and was its sporty alternative for two.

2470 mm verkürzt worden. Wie jener hatte
der 550 einen mit der Alu-Karosserie ver-
schweißten Gitterrahmen aus Stahlrohr,
wie bei jenem war das Sechsganggetriebe
nach dem Transaxle-Prinzip mit dem
Differential an der Hinterachse verblockt.

2002 mutierte der Maranello zum
575 M mit mehr Leistung und dezenten
optischen Retuschen.

seater GT by five inches (130 mm) to 8'1¼" (2470 mm). The 550 also had a steel tube frame that was welded to the aluminum body, and its six-gear transmission was mated to the rear axle differential following the transaxle principle.

In 2002 the Maranello was transformed into the 575 M, with more performance and discreet visual modifications.

550 Maranello. 550 Barchetta. 575 M Maranello. 575 GTC. 575 M Superamerica

Im Herbst 2002 folgte, gleichsam als Treueprämie für 448 handverlesene Kunden, ein Barchetta mit fetten Überrollbügeln, einer flachen Frontscheibe und anmutig sich verjüngenden Kopfstützen. Im Februar 2002 rüstete man nach mit dem 575 M, auf Wunsch mit dem System Selespeed, das den Gangwechsel nach dem Antippen zweier Paddel hinter dem Lenkkranz vornahm. Wieder standen das 575 für den Hubraum und das M für *modificata*. 515 PS waren dabei herausgesprungen.

Der Barchetta war als reine Fahrmaschine für eine überschaubare Klientel konzipiert und umgehend vergriffen – eine sichere Kapitalanlage.

In the fall of 2002, a Barchetta with thick rollover bars, flat windshield, and attractively tapered headrests was launched as a thank-you for 448 handpicked customers. In February 2002, the 575 M was modified so that the Selespeed system could be used to change the gears after touching two paddles behind the steering column. Once again, the 575 indicated the engine capacity, and the "M" was for *modificata*. The output was 515 bhp.

The Barchetta was designed as a pure driving machine for a specific clientele—and sold instantly; a surefire capital investment.

Der 550 Barchetta zählte gewiss zu den schönsten Medien für die Begegnung mit Sonne und Wind. Für die Wechselfälle nordischer Witterung hingegen war er nicht unbedingt gerüstet.

The 550 Barchetta was undoubtedly one of the loveliest ways to experience sun and wind. However, it was not quite so well suited to changeable weather.

2003 wurde die Wettbewerbsversion GTC geschaffen, auf die vorge-
schriebenen 1100 kg verschlankt, mit 605 PS bei 6300/min. Militant war
ihr Auftritt, weniger imposant ihre Bilanz vor allem in der FIA GT Championship bis 2005. Gekrönt und abgerundet wurde die Baureihe im Herbst
2004 durch den Superamerica in einer Mini-Auflage von 559, mit dem V12
von 540 PS aus dem 612 Scaglietti, vor allem jedoch einem nach hinten
wegschwenkbaren elektrochromatischen Glasdach.

2003 saw the advent of the GTC competition version, pared down to
the requisite 2200 pounds (1100 kg), with 605 bhp at 6300 rpm. It looked
ready for battle but its results were disappointing, especially in the FIA
GT Championships up to 2005. The series peaked and came to an end in
the fall of 2004 with the Superamerica, in a mini edition of 559 automobiles. It had the 540 bhp V12 of the 612 Scaglietti, and was remarkable for
its retractable electrochromatic glass roof.

*2004 krönte der Superamerica die Baureihe – mit einem nach hinten
wegschwenkbaren elektrochromatischen Glasdach.*

*The series peaked in 2004 with the Superamerica—remarkable especially for its
retractable electrochromatic glass roof.*

360 Modena Berlinetta
360 Spider
360 Challenge Stradale

Im 360 Modena artikulierte sich die Formensprache von Pininfarina im Zusammenwirken mit dem Windkanal.

Mit seinem Namen verneigte man sich vor der quirligen norditalienischen Metropole, wo die V8-Triebwerke der Firma im einstigen Karosseriewerk Scaglietti hergestellt wurden. Die Zahl 360 bildete, wie im 550 Maranello, das leicht nach oben abgerundete Motorvolumen ab. Vor seiner Präsentation 1999 beim Genfer Salon führte man diverse Prototypen einem wahren Hundeleben zu, marterte Motoren auf dem Prüfstand, setzte mögliche

Its name was a homage to the lively north Italian metropolis, where the company's V8 engines were made at the former Scaglietti bodywork factory. As with the 550 Maranello, the 360 represented the engine capacity, rounded upwards. Before its presentation at the 1999 Geneva Show, a number of prototypes were run through the mill; engines were sacrificed on the test stand; shapes were experimented with, and finally the ideal silhouette

Formen und schließlich die ideale Silhouette zwecks Feinschliffs Tausende von Stunden dem Kunst-Orkan des Windkanals aus.

Dies bezeugten, zugleich Querverweis auf die zeitgenössischen Formel-1-Wagen der Scuderia, die zweigeteilt gähnenden Nüstern unterhalb der Scheinwerfer, durch die der große Wasserkühler und der Wärmetauscher der Klimaanlage angeströmt wurden. Dass man dafür die

was exposed to a man-made hurricane in the wind tunnel to ensure refined lines.

This was confirmed, in cross reference to the Scuderia Formula 1 cars of the time, by the split yawning nostrils below the headlights, the large radiator, and the heat exchanger in the air-conditioning. The nose of the 360 Modena was drawn upwards as an aid to the downforce. Air was channeled almost without obstruction,

Pininfarina's design language is articulated in collaboration with the wind tunnel in the 360 Modena.

Schnauze des 360 Modena hochgezogen hatte, diente dem Abtrieb. Fast unbehindert zischte nun der Fahrtwind den glatten Wagenboden entlang und, beschleunigt durch zwei Diffusoren, aus trichterförmigen Schächten zwischen den zweimal zwei Auspuffrohren wieder heraus. Keinerlei hässliche aerodynamische Hilfen entstellten die schöne Linie des 295 km/h schnellen Coupés.

Als überaus rigides Skelett diente eine Spaceframe-Struktur, nur 270 kg schwer und aus Aluminium wie Kraftwerk und Karosserie. Die Räder wurden an doppelten Querlenkern geführt, elektronisch geregelte Stoßdämpfer unterstützten Stabilisatoren vorn und hinten, und Sensoren bewirkten, dass der Aufbau unter allen Umständen in der Horizontale blieb. Der Lenker des Modena hatte die Wahl zwischen drei Stufen der Antriebsschlupfregelung je nach Laune, Umfeld und Fahrkunst. Großzügig dimensionierte innenbelüftete Scheibenbremsen wirkten dem ungestümen Treiben von 400 PS schier unerschütterlich entgegen. Diese wurden bei 8500/min freigesetzt durch einen Kurzhuber mit fünf Ventilen pro Zylinder, als Teil des Ästhetik unter einem Acrylfenster in der hinteren Haube zur Schau gestellt. Auch dem Ohr gereichten sie zur Freude durch sorgsam komponierten Designersound mit einer enormen Bandbreite zwischen beflissenem Hecheln und grellem Fanfarenschmettern. Dem Auge

along the smooth underside of the car, and, accelerated by two diffusers, it exited through funnel-shaped shafts between the two pairs of exhaust pipes. There were no ugly aerodynamic aids to spoil the perfect lines of this 185 mph (295 kph) coupé.

A spaceframe structure formed the ultra strong skeleton of just 594 pounds (270 kg); it was made of aluminum like the engine and body. The wheels were carried on double aluminum transverse links; electronically controlled shock absorbers supported the stabilizers front and rear; and sensors made sure that the car always remained in the horizontal. Drivers of the Modena had the choice of three levels of traction control according to their mood, environment, and level of skill. Generously proportioned disk brakes, cooled from the inside, were totally oblivious to the 400 bhp. They were given their head at 8500 rpm by the short stroke with five valves per cylinder, which was presented as if in a glass showcase at the rear. It was no less pleasing to the ear thanks to the carefully composed "designer" sound with a tremendous range from an initial dull roar to a high-pitched scream. The complex yet beautiful technology pleased the eye: two red air vents with flap-controlled transverse bulkhead; airflow sensor with electric throttle flaps; two air filters; and oil fillers for the dry sump lubrication at the head of the

Moderne Zeiten auch im Interieur des neuen Bestsellers, hochwertige Materialien allenthalben. Geschaltet wurde gegen einen saftigen Aufpreis über Wippen am Lenkrad – analog zur Formel 1.

Modern times and top-quality materials reign inside the new bestseller. In return for a juicy surcharge, the gears could be shifted via a rocker switch on the steering wheel—just as in Formula 1.

bot sich komplexe und dennoch schöne Technologie: die beiden roten Luftsammler mit klappengesteuertem Querschott, die Luftmassenmesser mit den elektrischen Drosselklappen, die beiden Luftfilter und den zu Häupten des Getriebes angesiedelten Einfüllstutzen fürs Ölreservoir der Trockensumpfschmierung im Differentialgehäuse. Man ahnte tosendes Innenleben darunter: vier Nockenwellen mit Phasenschieber auf der Auslassseite, die flache, im Winkel von 180 Grad gekröpfte Kurbelwelle, die acht Steuerklappen in den Hochleistungs-Ansaugtrichtern.

Diese blieben bis zu 5500/min in den kurzen Trichtern geschlossen, wodurch der Motor seine Atemluft über die fast doppelte Saugrohrlänge einsog. Darüber gaben sie den Hochleistungs-Ansaugtrakt frei.

Zum Schalten der sechs Fahrstufen konnte der Pilot des 360 Modena entweder das gewohnte massive Knüppelchen mit krispem Klack durch die Schlitze der gleichfalls klassischen Aluminiumkulisse führen oder - gegen

transmission in the differential housing. All this hinted at just what was going on out of sight: four camshafts with phase shifter on the exit side; the flat 180-degree crankshaft; the eight control flaps in the high-performance intake funnels.

Up to 5500 rpm, these remained closed in the short funnels, which meant that the engine sucked in air along almost twice the length of the inlet manifold. Over that, the high-performance air intake was released.

To shift between the six gears, the driver of the 360 Modena could either use the solid little stick that clicked smartly through the slots in the aluminum frame, or—for a surcharge that roughly equaled the price of a high-specification small car—leave the gear-shifting to an electro-hydraulic system operated by two paddles behind the steering wheel. Half the customers opted for the second choice, not least because it brought a Grand Prix ambience into the cockpit.

Der 360 Spider, eines der schönsten Autos seiner Ära, bot die Möglichkeit, den Belcanto des Achtzylinders ungefiltert zu genießen.

The 360 Spider, one of the most beautiful cars of its era, was an opportunity to enjoy the bel canto of the eight-cylinder unfiltered.

Per Knopfdruck stülpte sich der Spider
eine kleine Kappe über, was seine Jünger
möglichst vermieden.

*The Spider donned a cap at the touch of a button,
but its disciples did their best to avoid this.*

einen Aufpreis im Gegenwert eines gut ausgestatteten Kleinwagens – dieses Hand-Werk mittels zweier Paddel hinter dem Lenkkranz einem elektrohydraulischen System überlassen. Die Hälfte der Klientel entschied sich für die zweite Lösung, zumal sie Grand-Prix-Anmutung ins Cockpit fächelte.

Zu den schönsten Autos der Welt zählte zweifellos der 360 Spider, anno 2000 in Monaco inmitten adäquat fürstlichen Ambientes vorgestellt. Das Rückgrat des 360 war von vornherein auch dafür ausgelegt worden, einen offenen Aufbau zu tragen. Das knappe Verdeck öffnete sich auf Knopfdruck in 20 Sekunden und verschwand dann rückstandslos. Weit weniger sanft ging ab Frühjahr 2003 der 360 Challenge Stradale mit Insassen und Umwelt um, 110 kg leichter und 25 PS stärker als der Berlinetta, allzeit bereit zu vielerlei Schandtaten auf Straße und Piste.

The 360 Spider, presented in Monaco in 2000 in an appropriately royal setting, is without doubt one of the most beautiful cars in the world. The frame of the 360 was designed from the outset to carry an open construction. The roof opened in 20 seconds at the touch of a button, and disappeared from sight completely. The 360 Challenge Stradale, 242 pounds (110 kg) lighter and 25 bhp faster and launched in the spring of 2003, treated its passengers—and the environment—less gently than the Berlinetta, and was always ready to show off on road and race track.

Nur die größeren Räder und die Karbon-Blende am Heck waren die optischen Erkennungsmerkmale des Challenge Stradale.

The distinctive optical features of the Challenge Stradale were only the rear carbon shade and the larger wheels.

In der Silhouette identifiziert der Kenner die seitlichen Lufteinlässe für Motorkühlung und Ansaugluft als elegante Hilfsmittel einer effizienten Aerodynamik. Große, gelochte und innenbelüftete Bremsscheiben garantierten optimale Verzögerung. Der V8 mit seinen 425 PS begeisterte im Challenge Stradale mit extrem alertem Reagieren aufs Gaspedal und phänomenalem Drehvermögen - nichts für zarte Gemüter.

In the silhouette, the expert can identify the side air intakes for engine cooling and induction air as elegant aids for an efficient aerodynamic. Large, perforated ventilated brake disks guaranteed optimal braking. The 425 bhp V8 in the Challenge Stradale appeals with its extreme responsiveness to the accelerator and a phenomenal torque—definitely not for those of a nervous disposition.

Enzo Ferrari
FXX

Im Hausgebrauch hieß das Projekt FX, dann erwog man die Bezeichnung F60, am Ende entschied man sich für das sperrige Ferrari Enzo Ferrari, von jedermann kurz und frech Enzo genannt. Seine Mission bestand darin, die kesse Konkurrenz von Bugatti, Lamborghini und McLaren zurechtzuweisen. Folglich besann man sich auf Kernwerte des Hauses, versah praktisch einen Formel-1-Rennwagen mit einem zweiten Sitz und bekleidete das Ganze mit einem knappen Trikot von wüster Schönheit.

Darin und darunter verbarg sich zum Stückpreis von über 1000 Euro pro PS Technologie vom Feinsten, noble Kunststoffe wie zum Beispiel Kohlefaser für das Chassis und die riesengroßen Bremsscheiben für buchstäblich atemberaubende Verzögerungen.

First of all, within the company, the project was called "FX," and then "F60" was contemplated, but in the end they opted for the somewhat cumbersome Ferrari Enzo Ferrari, which everyone simply shortened to Enzo. Its mission was simple: to take down a peg the cheeky competition from Bugatti, Lamborghini, and McLaren. The company's core values were all represented, and as a practical touch a Formula 1 racing car was given a second seat; the whole thing was then dressed in a tight-fitting body of wild beauty.

Within and underneath lay—at a price of over 1000 euros per bhp—the very latest and very best technology, elegant materials such as carbon fiber for the chassis, and vast brake disks for literally breathtaking slowing down.

Die Nase wie die gesamte Frontpartie des Enzo war eine gezielte Anspielung auf die Formel-1-Monoposti der Marke. Es gab nur 399 Exemplare. Soviel Exklusivität hatte ihren Preis: 645 000 Euro im Sommer 2004.

The nose, like the entire front section of the Enzo, was a deliberate reference to the marque's Formula 1 single-seaters. Only 399 were ever made. All this exclusivity came at a price: 645,000 euros in the summer of 2004.

Drei schwarze Tunneleinfahrten, die links und rechts zum Öl- und Wasserkühler und unter der Nase zu den beiden Venturi-Kanälen am flachen Unterboden führten, schluckten den Fahrtwind. Dieser leimte den Enzo bei hohem Tempo an die Fahrbahn, unterstützt von einem visuell unauffälligen variablen Aerodynamiksystem, und zischte aus bedrohlich anmutenden Heckdiffusoren wieder heraus. Nachdem der Pilot den Enzo durch weit vorn angeschlagene Flügeltüren betreten und ihn zum Leben erweckt hatte, ging ihm, unterlegt mit einem Concerto Grosso von höllischer Sinfonik, ein Sechsliter-V12 mächtig zur Hand. Dessen 660 PS schossen das bizarre Coupé nebst Insassen in baren 9,5 Sekunden auf Tempo 200, irgendwann ins Nirwana jenseits von 350 km/h und insgesamt wieder an die Spitze des Feldes.

Nur 399 stolze Eigner durften ab 2002 an solchen Erlebnissen teilhaben, lediglich 29 Erwählte plus Ferrari-Ikone Michael Schumacher gelangten in den Besitz der ultimativen Lesart FXX von 2006, mit 6262 cm³ und 800 (in

Three black tunnel entrances that ran along to the left and right of the oil and water coolers and under the nose of the two Venturi channels on the flat bottom swallowed the head wind. Thus the Enzo was glued fast to the road surface at high speeds, assisted by a practically invisible variable aerodynamics system. The air was released again through the somewhat threatening rear diffusers. Once the driver had climbed into the Enzo through the doors, which were positioned far forward and lifted upwards, and brought it to life, he found himself with a six-liter V8 in his hands, accompanied by a concerto grosso with a devilish sound. Its 660 bhp catapulted the strange coupé and its passengers to 124 mph (200 kph) in just 9.5 seconds, then on to the Nirvana beyond 215 mph (350 kph), and thus back to the top of its field.

Only 399 proud owners would ever be able to experience these incredible delights after its premiere in 2002, and a mere 29 chosen ones—plus Ferrari icon Michael Schumacher—would count themselves among the owners

Er trug den großen Namen des legendären Firmengründers und bot folglich das Feinste vom Feinen: Karbon überall, Aufhängungen wie in der Formel 1, ultimativen aerodynamischen Feinschliff, einen Premium-V12.

It bore the name of the company's legendary founder, and consequently consisted exclusively of the very best of everything: carbon everywhere, Formula 1 suspension, the ultimate aerodynamic finishing touches, and a premium V12.

einer Evolutionsstufe vom Oktober 2007 sogar 860) PS, Kostenpunkt anderthalb Millionen Euro. Zusätzliche Heckflügelchen, eine im Windkanal optimierte Form des Unterbodens sowie leichtgewichtige Bridgestone-Pneus sorgten für Benimm im Extrembereich. Da von hinten ohnehin keine Gefahr drohte, hatte man auf Rückspiegel gänzlich verzichtet.

of the ultimate version FXX, which appeared in 2006, with 6262cc and 800bhp (a next level in its evolution in October increased it to 860), at a price tag of some one and a half million euros. Additional winglets on the rear, the shape of the underside optimized in the wind tunnel, and lightweight Bridgestone tires ensured that it behaved itself when it reached the extremes. And, as there was never any risk of anything coming up behind, it had no rear view mirror.

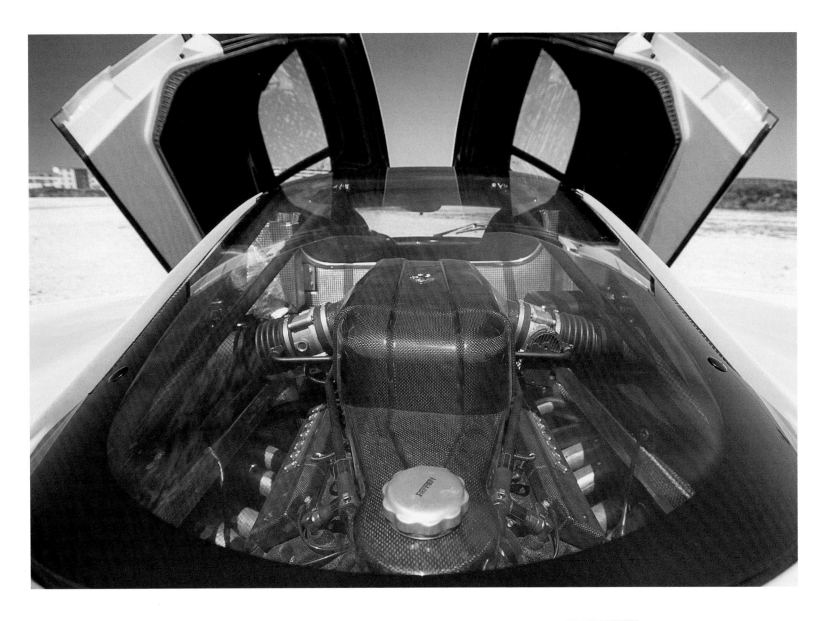

Die leichten Türen öffneten nach oben und entfernten dabei Teile des Dachs, und in gläserner Transparenz ging ein V12 seiner Arbeit nach, der in der Tat nichts zu verbergen hatte.

The light doors opened upwards, removing a part of the roof, and a V12 that had nothing to hide performed its role under transparent glass.

*Der ausfahrbare Heckspoiler
und der Diffusor machten
Aerodynamik sichtbar.*

*The extendable rear spoiler
and the diffuser made
aerodynamics visible.*

Im oben abgeflachten Lenkrad waren die Leucht-dioden eines zusätz-lichen Drehzahlmessers, Blinkerknöpfe und weitere Bedienelemente versammelt.

The steering wheel was flat at the top, and contained the LEDs for an additional rev counter, indicator buttons, and other control elements.

Am Samstag vor dem Grand Prix de France 2007 schickt sich
Siebenfach-Champion Michael Schumacher an, mit dem
französischen Fußballstar Zinedine Zidane in einem Ferrari FXX
ein paar Runden über den Kurs von Magny-Cours zu drehen.

On the Saturday before the Grand Prix de France 2007,
seven-times world champion Michael Schumacher took
French football star Zinedine Zidane for several spins
around the Magny-Cours track in a Ferrari FXX.

612 Scaglietti

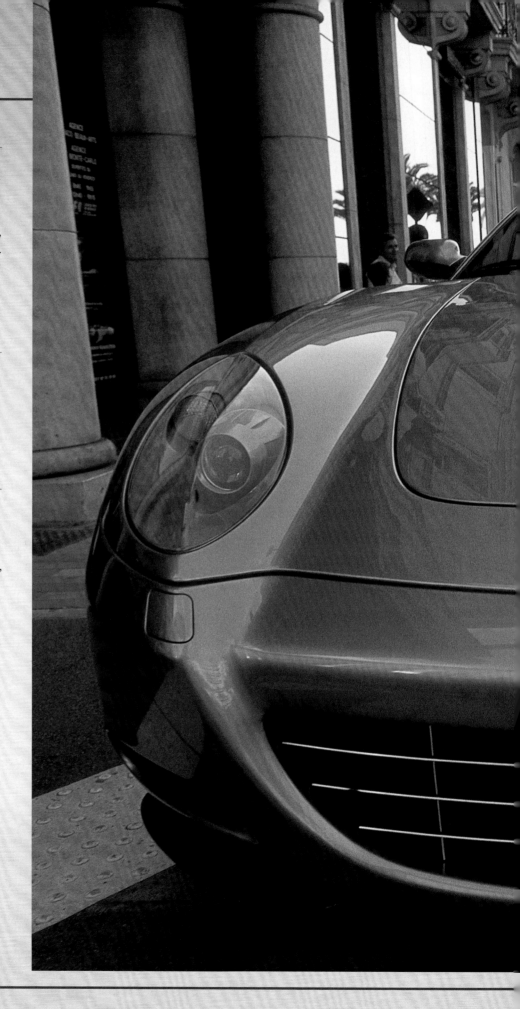

Der 612 Scaglietti, Debüt Anfang 2004 auf der Detroit Auto Show, war der Nachfolger des 456M GT. Die Typenbezeichnung für das jüngste Familien-Angebot der Marke stand für sechs Liter und zwölf Zylinder, Hommage zugleich an die altehrwürdige Carrozzeria Scaglietti, bis 1970 Hoflieferant, dann geschluckt vom Ferrari-Kosmos, heute mit der Produktion der Achtzylindermodelle befasst. Das Kürzel GT fehlte aus gutem Grund, denn der Neue war ein Sportwagen für vier fern jeglicher Askese. Man hatte den Radstand des 456 GT um 350 auf 2950 mm erweitert und seine Länge um 237 auf 4902 mm.

Für die schmissige Linie des großen Coupés zeichnete einmal mehr Star-Couturier Pininfarina verantwortlich, der wie üblich Kreationen aus der gemeinsamen

The 612 Scaglietti, which was first presented at the Detroit Auto Show early in 2004, was the successor to the 456M GT. The model number for the latest addition to the marque's family stood for six liters and twelve cylinders. The name was a homage to the venerable Carrozzeria Scaglietti, which had held the "royal warrant" until 1970 before being taken over by Ferrari, and was now occupied with the production of the eight-cylinder versions. The "GT" was missing for good reason, because the "newbie" was a sports car for four, and beyond any asceticism. The wheelbase of the 456 GT had been increased by 14 inches (350 mm) to 9 feet 8 inches (2950 mm), and its length by 9⅓ inches (237 mm) to 16 inches (4902 mm).

Star designer Pininfarina was once again responsible for the racy lines of this large sedan, and as usual he included

Mit unvergleichlicher Grandezza setzte der 612 Scaglietti die Tradition potenter und luxuriöser 2+2-Sitzer der Nobel-Firma fort. Hinter windschlüpfigen Einschalungen leuchteten Bi-Xenon-Lampen.

The 612 Scaglietti continued the marque's tradition of powerful and luxurious 2+2 automobiles with incomparable grandezza. Bi-xenon lamps shone through the covered headlights.

Geschichte zitierte und zu einer höchst eigenständigen Symbiose verquickte. Die Insassen umgab ein Ambiente von luxuriöser Sachlichkeit mit einer Mixtur von Rindsleder, Metall und Kunststoff im Heavy-Metal-Look. Drei Viertel der Klientel votierte bereits für die halbautomatische F1-Schaltung.

Das Sechsgang-Getriebe war in Transaxle-Bauweise mit der Hinterachse verblockt. Der lange Radstand gestattete es, den sorgfältig überarbeiteten Abkömmling des V12 aus dem 575M Maranello hinter der Vorderachse in das Doppelquerlenker-Fahrwerk zu versenken. So entstand die zeitgemäße Architektur, die sich hinter dem paradoxen Wortmonster Front-Mittelmotor verbirgt.

Überall war der Einfluss der Gestione Sportiva zu spüren, deren Anliegen darin bestanden hatte, die Renngene der Marke in diesem exemplarischen Reiseauto nicht verkümmern zu lassen. Zu den Zeugnissen ihres Wirkens zählte der unter der Heckschürze des imposanten Hinterviertels gähnende Diffusor, mit dem sich Ästhetik und Dynamik des 612 Scaglietti auf einer höheren Ebene wieder begegneten.

features from their shared history, combining them in a completely separate symbiosis. Passengers were wrapped in an ambience of luxurious simplicity, with a mix of leather, metal and plastic in a heavy metal look. Three-quarters of the clientele opted for the semi-automatic F1 transmission.

The six-gear drive was transaxle-linked to the rear axle. The long wheelbase meant that the carefully revamped offspring of the V12 could be lowered onto the 575M Maranello in the double wishbone chassis behind the front axle. This resulted in the contemporary architecture, hidden behind the apparent contradiction of a front mid-engine.

The influence of Gestione Sportiva was evident everywhere; its aim had been to make sure the marque's racing genes were present in this exemplary touring car. Evidence of their achievements included the imposing rear quarter's yawning diffuser under the apron, in which the aesthetics and dynamics of the 612 Scaglietti again came together on a higher level.

Eingezogene Flanken bringen
Spannung in die fließende
Silhouette des 612, der wie
alle seine Vorgänger von
Haus-Designer Pininfarina
gezeichnet wurde. Mit
sicherer Hand kreierte er
einen eleganten Gran Turismo
in der großen Tradition
der Marke.

Inset flanks add excitement
to the flowing silhouette
of the 612 which, like all
its predecessors, bears the
signature of the company
designer Pininfarina. His sure
hand created an elegant Gran
Turismo in the old tradition of
the marque.

Die eingezogenen Flanken des Scaglietti spielten auf ein Frühwerk Pininfarinas an – den Berlinetta 375 MM, den Regisseur Roberto Rossellini 1954 der schönen Schwedin Ingrid Bergman geschenkt hatte.

The indented flanks of the Scaglietti were a reference to an earlier work by Pininfarina—the Berlinetta 375 MM, which film director Roberto Rossellini gave to the beautiful Swedish actress Ingrid Bergman in 1954.

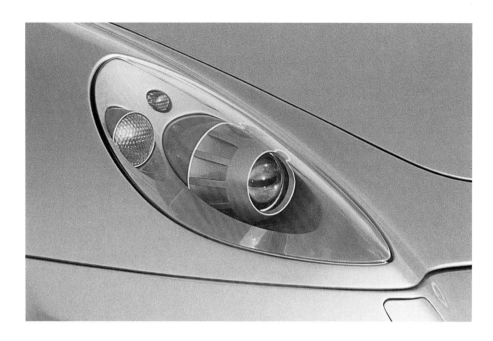

Im Blickfeld des Piloten lag
der große Tourenzähler, ab
7200/min rot unterlegt,
flankiert vom bis 340 km/h
reichenden Tacho sowie
einem Bildschirm mit
diversen Informationen.

The large rev counter,
highlighted in red from
7200 rpm, flanked by the
speedometer that went up
to 220 mph (340 kph) and
a screen with all kinds of
information, were all in the
driver's line of sight.

F430 Berlinetta
F430 Spider
F430 Challenge
430 Scuderia
430 Scuderia Spider 16M

Schönheit paarte sich im F430 Spider mit Sicherheit: In den Rahmen der Windschutzscheibe zum Beispiel hatten seine Väter eine robuste Stahlstruktur eingebaut, die ihn überdies noch einmal versteifte.

The F430 Spider combined beauty with safety: in the windscreen frame, for instance, its fathers included a strong steel structure to further reinforce it.

Wie sein Vorgänger war der F430, präsentiert bei den Ferrari Days auf dem Nürburgring Anfang September 2005, um eine Spaceframe-Struktur herum gebaut und in Leichtmetall gehüllt, mit größeren Lufteinlässen, anderen Frontleuchten, einer Heckpartie, die an den Enzo gemahnte, und einem riesigen, von vier senkrechten Finnen strukturierten Diffusor. Unter einem transparenten Fenster indes fand sich ein völlig neuer Kurzhuber, nahe verwandt dem aktuellen Maserati-V8, mit 4,3 Litern und 490 PS bei 8500/min.

Like its predecessor the F430, first presented at the Ferrari Days on the Nürburgring early in September 2005, was built around a spaceframe structure and clothed in aluminum, although with bigger air intakes, different headlights, and a vast diffuser with four vertical fins. Under a transparent panel in the middle was a brand new engine, closely related to the current Maserati V8, of 4300 cc and 490 bhp at 8500 rpm.

As an option, the familiar Formula 1 gearshift exercised its unbridled potency via the six-gear drive to the rear axle.

Stofflliches war auf ein Minimum reduziert und zog sich, von sieben elektrohydraulischen Motörchen aktiviert, binnen 20 Sekunden vollautomatisch unter einen Deckel zurück.

The fabric was pared down to the minimum and, activated by seven electrohydraulic motors, withdrew automatically under a cover within 20 seconds.

Wahlweise vermittelte die bekannte Formel-1-Schaltung seine ungestüme Potenz über ein Sechsganggetriebe an die Hinterachse. Alle Systeme zur Regelung der Fahrdynamik wurden über ein Drehschalterchen am griffigen Volant aktiviert, dem *manettino* (Hebelchen). Optional lieferbar: eine Bremsanlage mit Scheiben aus Karbon und Keramik.

Im März 2005 stellte sich Zuwachs ein in Gestalt des F 430 Spider, ein weiteres Pininfarina-Opus und in der gewohnten Schönheit, im selben Jahr die Variante Challenge als Waffe für den Markenpokal, mit identischer Leistung, aber Keramikbremsen und trotz eines rigiden Überrollkäfigs von 1450 auf 1225 kg Leergewicht abgemagert. Auf der Frankfurter IAA 2007 weckte der 430 Scuderia weitere Begehrlichkeiten, ein Leichtgewicht für die Straße mit 1350 kg. 20 Mehr-PS hoben die Literleistung von 114 auf 118 PS, die Spitze von 315 auf 320 km/h und das maximale Drehmoment auf 470 Nm an und drückten den Sprint bis Tempo 100 von vier auf unter 3,7 Sekunden.

Im Rahmen des Saison-Finales in Mugello 2008 rollte man ihm die Spider-Version 16 M zur Seite, auf 499 Exemplare limitiert. Mit dem Zusatz 16 M zelebrierte Ferrari sich selbst - man verzeichnete in diesem Jahr den 16. Konstrukteurstitel in der Formel 1.

All the systems used to control the driving dynamic were activated using a rocker switch on the steering wheel, the *manettino* (little lever). One option was a braking system with disks made of carbon and ceramic.

A new addition followed in March 2005 in the form of the F430 Spider, another Pininfarina opus of the usual beauty. Later that year, the Challenge version appeared as a weapon in the now established tussle between the brands; its performance was the same, it had ceramic brakes and, despite having a rigid roll cage, had slimmed down from 3200 pounds (1450 kg) to 2700 pounds (1225 kg) unladen. The 430 Scuderia kindled further passions at the Frankfurt IAA 2007; a lightweight for the road at 2975 pounds (1350 kg). An additional 20 bhp increased the performance per liter from 114 to 118 bhp, the top speed from 195 to 198 mph (315 to 320 kph) and the maximum torque to 347 lb-ft (470 Nm), and the sprint to 60 mph (100 kph) was reduced from four to less than 3.7 seconds.

The Spider version 16 M, produced in a limited edition of 499 units, was provided for the end-of-season event in Mugello in 2008. The addition of the 16 M was a Ferrari celebration of itself—it was the year of Ferrari's 16th constructors' title in Formula 1.

Dank pingeliger Feinarbeit an der Abgasentsorgung schmeichelte sich der 430 Scuderia mit sogar noch aufreizenderer Melodik ein als die Standard-Version. In seine Entwicklung eingebunden: Haus-Ikone Michael Schumacher.

Thanks to painstaking finishing touches to the exhaust system, the 430 Scuderia delighted with an even more enchanting melodiousness than the standard version. Included in the development: Ferrari icon Michael Schumacher.

599 GTB Fiorano

Dank Front-Mittelmotor-Bauweise lagen 85 Prozent des Leergewichts zwischen den Achsen des Fiorano.

Er wurde seinem Namen gerecht wie kaum ein Zwei-ter vor ihm, der 599 GTB Fiorano, der auf dem Gen-fer Salon 2006 in der Nachfolge des 575 M einen wahren Heißhunger auf Ferrari entfachte. In der Triade hatte man das Volumen des V12 von 5999 cm³ griffig eingedampft,

The 599 GTB Fiorano lived up to its name like no other car had ever done before, creating a passion for Ferrari when it was first shown at the Geneva Show of 2006 as the successor to the 575 M. The three-figure model num-ber stood for the V12's cubic capacity of 5999; Fiorano

das Fiorano stand für die einschlägigen Zutaten, welche die dort ansässige Gestione Sportiva beigesteuert hatte.

Das Triebwerk mit 620 knorrigen PS bei 7600/min, dem stämmigen maximalen Drehmoment von 608 Nm bei 5600/min und einem angemessen-dramatischen

stood for the pertinent ingredients that the local Gestione Sportiva contributed.

The engine provided a rugged 620 bhp at 7600 rpm; the equally sturdy maximum torque of 448 lb-ft (608 Nm) at 5600 rpm, and the appropriately dramatic soundtrack,

The front-mid engine construction of the Fiorano meant that 85 percent of its unladen weight was positioned between the axles.

Soundtrack blickte auf ein bewegtes Vorleben im Enzo zurück, nur dass es nun in Front-Mittelmotor-Architektur auf einer Parzelle des Alu-Spaceframes hinter der Vorderachse angesiedelt worden war. Vor allem im Bunde mit dem sequentiellen F1-Superfast-Getriebe, das die sechs Fahrstufen in je 100 Millisekunden einlegte, machte es sich zum willigen Handlanger des Piloten und vermochte den agilen 1,9-Tonner nebst Insassen auf Wunsch und bei sich bietender Gelegenheit in 3,7 Sekunden auf 100 und anschließend in die einsamen Höhen von 330 km/h zu wuchten. Speziell auf den Charakter des 599 GTB abgestellt worden war der *manettino* rechts am Lenkrad, der Einstellungen für Low-Grip-Situationen, Sport und Rennen vorsah. Dass der Fiorano nie die gebotene Bodenhaftung verlor, dafür war vor allem die raffinierte Ausformung des Wagenbodens zuständig.

Allein schon das Interieur verlieh der Zwienatur dieses Ferrari Ausdruck: viel feines Leder auf der Beifahrerseite, eher sachorientiert im Umfeld des Piloten, voller Hightech-Elemente mit der Anmutung von Aluminium und Kohlefaser, ein Werkstoff, der auch in die optional erhältlichen diabolisch geformten, aber sanft zupackenden Rennschalensitze eingearbeitet worden war.

looked back on an eventful earlier life in the Enzo, except that it was now positioned in front mid-engine architecture on a section of the aluminum spaceframe behind the front axle instead of the rear. With the help of the sequential F1 Superfast transmission that shifted into each of the six gears in 100 milliseconds, it was the driver's willing accomplice, shifting the agile two-ton vehicle and passengers to 60 mph (100 kph) in 3.7 seconds (whenever the opportunity presented itself, of course), and to the dizzying heights of 205 mph (330 kph).

The *manettino* on the right of the steering wheel was for choosing the settings for low-grip conditions, sports and racing, and was designed specifically for the nature of the 599 GTB. That the Fiorano held the road so well was due mainly to the clever styling of the underside.

The interior by itself expressed the dual personality of this Ferrari: lots of fine leather on the passenger side, quite pared-down and practical on the driver's; full of high-tech elements with the appeal of aluminum and carbon fiber, a material that was also worked into the optional, diabolically shaped, firm but gentle bucket seats.

Aus jedem Blickwinkel gerät
das 4665 Millimeter lange
und fast zwei Meter breite
Coupé zur Augenweide, eine
mobile Skulptur des Haus-
Michelangelo Pininfarina,
wie üblich nicht ohne Déjà-
vu-Anmutung.

From every angle, the 15'4"
(4665 mm) long, almost
6½-foot (two-meter) wide
coupé is a treat for the
eyes; a mobile sculpture by
Pininfarina, as always not
without a touch of déja vu.

Dass man selbst von Tempo 330 sicher wieder zum Stillstand gelangte, besorgten effiziente Bremsen, auf Wunsch mit Keramik-Karbon-Scheiben zum Gegenwert eines Kleinwagens in Vollausstattung.

Breathtakingly efficient brakes brought the car back safely to a standstill from 205 mph (330 kph); for roughly the same price as a small car with all the bells and knobs, they could be fitted with ceramic carbon disks.

California

Er reanimierte einen besonderen Ferrari-Mythos. Deshalb ließ man sich für seine Enthüllung etwas ganz Besonderes einfallen: Sie fand bereits 14 Tage vor der eigentlichen Präsentation beim Pariser Salon im Oktober 2008 vor einem buntscheckigen Dreifach-Forum statt – 2000 geladenen Gästen in Maranello und Los Angeles, ab 22 Uhr überdies vor virtuellen Zaungästen im Internet mittels einer eigens eingerichteten Website. Mit der historischen Ikone California teilte er den Namen und visuelle Anspielungen wie einen Lufteinlass auf der Fronthaube sowie seitliche Schlitze. Der Zustand luftiger Offenheit ließ sich als Tribut an den Geist der neuen Zeit binnen 14 Sekunden herstellen, indem sich via Knopfdruck ein knappes Metalldach faltete und hinter den beiden Notsitzen in der zweiten Reihe im oberen Teil des Kofferraums verschwand.

This car revived an exceptional Ferrari myth. Which is why the team thought up something very special for its launch. It was held two weeks before the actual presentation at the Paris Salon in October 2008 in front of a motley collection of people in three locations: 2000 invited guests in Maranello and in Los Angeles—and after 10 pm, an unknown number of virtual onlookers on the Internet, courtesy of its own website.

It not only shared its name with the historic and iconic California, but it also shared visual delights, such as an air intake on the front hood and gills on the sides. The characteristic state of airy openness was created in 14 seconds by pressing a button on a floating console to open the small folding metal roof, and stowing it away behind the two dickey seats in the upper part of the trunk.

It was the company's first product to carry the V8 at the front, in the front mid-engine construction, with 4297 cc, a boisterous 460 bhp at 7750 rpm, and an appropriately

Wieder arbeitete Haus-Designer Pininfarina mit Tradition: Der Lufteinlass auf der Fronthaube sowie seitliche Schlitze hinter den Vorderrädern erinnern an den illustren Vorgänger gleichen Namens.

Once again the experts at Pininfarina used tradition: the air inlets on the hood and side slits behind the front wheels are reminiscent of the illustrious predecessor of the same name.

Als erstes Produkt des Hohen Hauses trug er seinen V8 vorn in Front-Mittelmotor-Bauweise, mit 4297 cm³, 460 rüstigen PS bei 7750/min und einem angemessen aggressiv gestylten Sound, der nur noch von ferne an das krispe Wüten seines Kollegen im F430 erinnerte. Neu auch die Durchreiche für sperrige Habseligkeiten zwischen Fond und Gepäckabteil, Mehrlenkerachse hinten, Direkteinspritzung, vor allem jedoch die Doppelkupplung: Ohne

aggressive, stylish sound that was only dimly reminiscent of its colleague's confident roar in the F430.

Actually new were the between-seats opening for bulky items from the passenger cell through to the luggage compartment, the multi-link axle in the rear, fuel injection, and above all the double clutch anticipating the future standard: now, powered by the two little paddles behind the steering wheel and with no discernible judder,

*Manche unterstellten dem California einen zu
dicken Hintern. Aber der machte schon Sinn
als Abschluss einer stetig steigenden Silhouette
und als Behältnis für das gefaltete Metalldach,
nachdem sich die Insassen zu offenem Reisen
entschlossen hatten.*

*Some claim that the California had a big rear.
But it did make sense, as the stylistic conclusion
to a constantly ascending silhouette and housing
for the folded metal roof—once the passengers
had decided to travel "open".*

merklichen Ruck flossen jetzt die Fahrstufen des Sieben-
ganggetriebes ineinander.

Luxus, Komfort und Bequemlichkeit, welche den Ferrari
California auszeichneten, standen indes in keinem Augen-
blick dem Fahrspaß im Wege, den er vermittelte, nicht
einmal sein stattliches Gewicht - leer schon 1625 kg. Unter
vier Sekunden auf Tempo 100 und 310 km/h Spitze, das
sprach für sich.

the various stages of the seven-gear transmission flowed
smoothly into each other.

Luxury and comfort were key features of the Ferrari
California and in no way impaired the driving fun that it
provided, not even its impressive weight—3580 pounds
(1625 kg) when empty. It reached 60 mph (100 kph) in less
than four seconds, and 194 mph (310 kph), wherever it was
possible—well, that spoke for itself.

Bei einer Besichtigung des Interieurs fallen das unten abgeflachte Volant, die schwebende Konsole etwa mit dem Knopf für den Rückwärtsgang und das große Display des Info-Centers ins Auge.

Looking at the interior, the steering wheel (which is flattened at the bottom), the floating console with the button for reverse, and the large display on the info center catch the eye.

458 Italia
458 Spider

Traditionell verbergen sich hinter der nüchternen Ferrari-Zahlenkombination des 458 die Motordaten – nämlich 4,5 Liter Hubraum und acht Zylinder. Freilich schwingt bei der Namensgebung dieses rassigen Mittelmotor-Coupés auch nationaler Stolz mit: Italia! Das betörend schöne Pininfarina-Design setzt dem 2012 verstorbenen Sergio Pininfarina nachträglich ein weiteres Denkmal. Die Frontpartie hebt sich deutlich von den Nüstern des 360 Modena und des F430 ab: durch ein breites Maul mit seinen seitlich integrierten Winglets. Über diesem zentralen Lufteinlass schiebt sich eine LED-Lichtleiste zwischen zwei vergitterte Luftschlitze. In die stark konturierte Taille, deren Bogen bis in den vorderen Kotflügel geschlagen ist, mündet eine nicht minder betonte hintere Flanke. Die seitlichen Schweller – kleine Anleihe beim Enzo – sowie das Auspuff-Trio – Reminiszenz an den F40 – erinnern an Pininfarinas großes Design-Repertoire.

In keeping with tradition, the model number of the Ferrari 458 refers to the engine specifications—4.5 liter displacement and eight cylinders. Of course, the name of this thoroughbred mid-engine coupé also conveys a swelling of national pride: Italia! The hauntingly beautiful Pininfarina design is a posthumous homage to Sergio Pininfarina, who passed away in 2012. The radiator grille is markedly different to the apertures of the 360 Modena and the F430, with its broad muzzle and side winglets. Slotted in above this central air intake is an LED light strip between two ventilation grilles. The exaggerated rear flank flows into the heavily contoured waist, the curve of which follows through up to the front fender. The side panels—borrowed from the Enzo—and the triple exhaust—reminiscent of the F40—serve as reminders of Pininfarina's extensive design repertoire.

Die breite Panorama-Schnauze mit integrierten Winglets steht dem 458 ebenso gut zu Gesicht wie die gewaltige Windschutzscheibe oder die von Luftschlitzen flankierte Frontlichtbatterie.

The broad panorama muzzle with integrated winglets suits the character of the 458 just as well as the powerful windshield and the front lighting battery, which is flanked by two ventilation grilles.

Der 458 brilliert nicht nur mit seinen Fahrleistungen, sondern besticht auch durch seine wohlproportionierten Rundungen. In nur 14 Sekunden verschwindet das Alu-Dach des Spiders über dem Mittelmotor.

Der 458 rauscht in knapp 3,4 Sekunden durch die 100-km/h-Barriere und hat nach 20,3 Sekunden bereits einen Kilometer zurückgelegt. Mit seinen 570 PS im Rücken erreicht er mühelos 326 Stundenkilometer, denn schließlich muss er pro PS nur 2,42 Kilo seines Leergewichts bewegen und verfügt über eine ausgefeilte Aerodynamik. Sein durchschnittlicher Spritverbrauch liegt deutlich unter der Schmerzgrenze von 20 Litern. Die Schallgrenze – also voller Ferrari-Sound – wird bei gleichzeitiger Entfaltung eines maximalen Drehmoments von 540 Newtonmetern bei 6000 Touren erreicht. Ein Bypass sorgt dafür, dass der Italia bei niedrigen Drehzahlen die Klappe hält. Der tief liegende Schwerpunkt des Sportwagens trägt zu der hervorragenden Straßenlage ebenso bei wie das adaptive Fahrwerk. Die Spider-Version hat das Stoffverdeck abgelegt und verfügt über ein Alu-Dach, das sich in nur 14 Sekunden versenkt.

The 458 speeds through the 60-mph barrier in just under 3.4 seconds, and takes just about twenty seconds to cover the first 1000 yards. It reaches 202 miles per hour effortlessly with the 570 bhp in the back, thanks to the sophisticated aerodynamics and the fact that it only needs to shift 5$\frac{1}{3}$ pounds of its empty weight per bhp. Its average mileage is well beyond the acceptance limit of 11 mpg. Its noise threshold—the full Ferrari sound—is reached when the engine hits the maximum torque of 398 lb-ft at 6000 revs. A bypass ensures that the Italia keeps schtum at low speeds. The sports car's low center of gravity contributes just as much to its outstanding road holding as the adaptive chassis. The Spider version does away with the soft top in favor of an aluminum roof that can be retracted in just 14 seconds.

The 458 boasts both a dazzling driving performance and enchantingly well-proportioned curves. The Spider's aluminum roof can be concealed above the mid-engine in just 14 seconds.

Der 458, dessen V8-Triebwerk 570 PS freisetzt, besitzt - gemessen an seiner Länge - einen langen Radstand von 2650 Millimetern, der bei hohem Tempo für einen Geradeauslauf ohne unerwünschte Adrenalin-Ausschüttung sorgt.

The 458, whose V8 engine unleashes 570 bhp, has a comparatively long wheelbase of 8 ft 8 in, which keeps the car running straight—and the adrenalin under control at high speeds.

Links: Das unten abgeflachte Lenkrad mit manettino, Starterknopf und mehreren Bedienelementen vermittelt Formel-1-Feeling. Kraftvoll: die Bremsen (oben). Infernalischer Tonableiter: das Auspufftrio (unten).

Left: The steering wheel with flattened bottom section, manettino, starter button and many other controls gives the car a Formula 1 feel. Powerful: the brakes (top). Infernal roar: the triple exhaust (bottom).

Der 90-Grad-V8-Motor mit zwei oben liegenden, variabel gesteuerten
Nockenwellen und gewaltigem Ansaugtrakt wurde 2011 zur
»Engine of the Year« gekürt.

The 90° V8 engine with two variable overhead
camshafts and massive air intake was crowned
"Engine of the Year" in 2011.

FF

Ein Ferrari, der sich freudig durch den Schnee wühlt und in diesem winterlichen Element den bewährten Allradradlern von nördlich der Alpen Paroli bietet, ist ein Novum, mit dem Ferrari der große Wurf in der Allrad-Gilde gelungen ist. Der 2+2-Sitzer bietet eine große Heckklappe und umlegbare Rücksitze: Mit dem FF erschließt Ferrari eine vierte Dimension, die viel Platz für Gepäck bietet, zumal das hintere Abteil

A Ferrari happily carving its way through the snow, taking on the tried and tested all-wheel-drive vehicles from north of the Alps, is something of a novelty—one with which Ferrari has successfully made the leap into the all-wheel-drive club. The 2+2-seater FF offers a large tailgate and repositionable rear seats, giving Ferrari an extra dimension that offers plenty of space for luggage, not least with the 16 cu ft of

Sportliche Kombination: der allradgetriebene FF mit zwei plus zwei Sitzen, viel Stauraum und großer Heckklappe.

Sporty combination: the all-wheel-drive FF with two plus two seats, ample storage space and a large tailgate.

Augenweide: Der Zwölfzylinder, der aus seinen 6,2 Litern 660 PS und 683 Nm holt. Er ermöglicht den 100-km/h-Sprint unter vier Sekunden und eine Spitze von 335 km/h. Auch das Interieur, mit einzeln umklappbaren Rücksitzen, lässt keine Wünsche offen.

ohnehin mit 450 Litern Stauraum aufwartet. Die Zuladung wird freilich auf 390 Kilo beschränkt.

Als Frontmittelmotor-Sportwagen ausgelegt, ist das Gewicht des Ferrari Four – kurz FF – ausgewogen tariert: 47 Prozent liegen auf den Vorderachsen, 53 Prozent belasten die Hinterräder. Ein technischer Leckerbissen: der Allradantrieb mit Siebengang-Doppelkupplungsgetriebe, angeordnet nach dem Transaxle-Prinzip, und das integrierte Torque-Vectoring-Differenzial, das die Hinterachse direkt bedient. Vorn an der Kurbelwelle ist ein zusätzliches Zweiganggetriebe angeflanscht. Dieses sorgt für die Kraftumverteilung, wenn die Hinterräder die 660 PS des 6,2-Liter-V12 einmal nicht bewältigen sollten und durchdrehen. Das kann gelegentlich passieren, doch die an den Bordcomputer gekoppelten Sensoren registrieren es sofort. Dieser Computer, in dem viel Know-how aus der Formel 1 steckt, dirigiert die Kraftverteilung dann blitzschnell auch auf die vorderen Walzen. Natürlich unterstützt eine *launch control* das Anfahren, und mit dem *manettino* lässt es sich aus fünf Fahrdynamik-Programmen wählen. Deren erstes wird durch eine Schneeflocke symbolisiert, die beim FF eine besondere Bedeutung hat. Mit einer Beschleunigung auf Tempo 100 in 3,7 Sekunden und einer Spitzengeschwindigkeit von 335 km/h ist der FF kein Rentier, sondern ein Rennpferd.

storage space in the rear section. The additional load, however, is limited to 860 lbs.

Designed as a front-mid-engine sports car, the weight of the Ferrari Four—"FF" for short—is distributed evenly, with 47% on the front axle and 53% on the rear wheels. The all-wheel drive with 7-speed, dual-clutch transmission configured to the transaxle principle, and the integrated torque vectoring differential that directly serves the rear axle, make this vehicle a real technological treat. In the front, flanged onto the crankshaft, there is an additional two-speed transmission which redistributes the power if the rear wheels are struggling to cope with the 660 bhp from the 6.2-liter V12 engine, and start to spin. This may happen occasionally, but the sensors connected to the onboard computer will detect it immediately. This computer—the product of extensive Formula 1 expertise—then redistributes the power to the front wheels in the blink of an eye. Naturally, this process is supported by a launch control system, and can be chosen from five different driving dynamics programs using the *manettino*. The first of these is marked with a snowflake symbol, which is very important to the FF. With an acceleration of 0–62 mph in 3.7 seconds and a top speed of 208 mph, the FF is a racehorse, not a reindeer.

A feast for the eyes: the V12 engine, which gets 660 bhp and 504 lb-ft off its 6.2 liters, rushes the car to 60 mph within less than four seconds, and lets it hit a top speed of 208 mph. With its fold-back rear seats, the interior, too, leaves nothing to be desired.

Lediglich von fünf vertikalen und zwei horizontalen Gittern unterbrochen, wirkt das Ferrari-Maul ziemlich gierig.

Interrupted by only five vertical and two horizontal bars, the Ferrari's muzzle hints at the car's insatiable character.

F12berlinetta

*Rasse und Klasse:
Formvollendet gestaltet von
Pininfarina und dem Ferrari-
Styling-Center, wartet der
F12 Berlinetta mit enormem
Potenzial auf.*

Ausgerechnet im Todesjahr des berühmten Auto-mobil-Couturiers Sergio Pininfarina präsentiert Ferrari mit dem F12 die wohl formvollendetste Symbiose des hauseigenen Styling Centers und der Turiner Edelschmiede. Der bildhübsche F12, unter dessen Outfit aus zwölf verschiedenen Aluminium-Legierungen ein Kraftpaket mit 740 PS pulsiert, ist der bislang stärkste Ferrari

Just as the industry is still mourning the famous auto-mobile couturier, Sergio Pininfarina, Ferrari's F12 marks the year of his passing in style with what is probably the most complete symbiosis yet of its in-house Style Centre and Turin class and glamor. The picture-perfect F12, whose 12-alloy aluminum exterior conceals a pulsating power package of 740 bhp, is the most powerful

für den Straßengebrauch. Neben seiner Potenz kann das 6,2-Liter-Triebwerk mit mehr Effizienz bei Spritverbrauch und Emissionen aufwarten. Ohne zusätzliches Geflügel – Ferrari-Präsident Luca di Montezemolo verabscheut solcherlei Spoilerwerk – erzielt der F12 enormen Anpressdruck. Gegenüber dem 599 GTB Fiorano fällt der F12 kompakter und 70 Kilo leichter aus; sein Schwerpunkt

road-use Ferrari yet. In addition to its potency, the 6.2-liter engine also offers greater efficiency in terms of fuel consumption and emissions. Without any additional wings—Ferrari President Luca di Montezemolo abhors such spoilers—the F12 achieves an enormous amount of downforce. Compared to the 599 GTB Fiorano, the F12 is more compact and 155 lbs lighter; it has a lower center of

Breeding and class: with its perfect design by Pininfarina and the Ferrari Style Centre, the F12 Berlinetta oozes enormous potential.

*Seitliche Endrohrpaare
begrenzen die Diffusoranlage.*

*Side-mounted tailpipe pairs
flank the diffusor system.*

liegt tiefer, und auf den Antriebsachsen im Heck lasten
54 Prozent des Fahrzeuggewichts.

Das völlig überarbeitete Fahrwerk mit adaptiven Stoßdämpfern, äußerst wirksame Karbon-Keramik-Bremsen,
die präzise Lenkung und das perfekte Handling des F12
animieren zum Ertasten des Grenzbereichs. Sehen lassen
können sich die Beschleunigungswerte: 3,1 Sekunden
bis 100 km/h und deren 8,5 bis Tempo 200. Die Spitzengeschwindigkeit – jenseits der Autobahn-Realität – wird
vom Werk mit 340 km/h angegeben. Form und Funktion
strahlt auch das geschmackvolle Leder-Interieur aus. Tief
in die Sitzschale eingebettet, blickt der F12-Fahrer auf
ein Display im oberen Segment des Karbon-Volants mit
Ledergriffzonen, und wartet auf die optische Bestätigung
der Schaltvorgänge. Zu diesem Mini-Blitzgewitter gesellt
sich der Donner des V12, dessen voller Sound durch zwei
Schallröhren vom Motorraum direkt ins Cockpit geleitet
werden kann. Von den Lesern einer großen Fachpublika-
tion zum besten Sportwagen Europas gekürt und mit dem
Goldenen Lenkrad geehrt, sammelt dieser Beau schon bei
Markteinführung Meriten.

gravity, and the drive axles in the rear bear 54% of the
vehicle's weight.

The completely reworked chassis with adaptive
dampers, extremely effective carbon-ceramic brakes,
the precise steering and the perfect handling of the F12
encourage you to push it to the limit. The acceleration
specifications are clear for all to see: 0 to 62 mph in 3.1 seconds, and 0 to 124 in 8.5. The top speed—ignoring the reality of the motorway—is stated by the factory as 211 mph.
The tasteful leather interior absolutely radiates form and
functionality. Settled low in the bucket seat, the F12 driver
looks at a display in the top segment of the carbon steering
wheel with leather grip zones, and waits for visual con-
firmation of the speed shifts. This mini lightning storm is
complimented by the thunder of the V12, the full sound
of which can be channeled directly from the engine compartment to the cockpit through two sound tubes. Voted
Europe's best sportscar by the readers of a large specialist publication and awarded the Golden Steering Wheel,
this beauty has won plaudits right from the moment of its
market launch.

*Die F12-Front integriert
ein ausgeklügeltes
Luftführungssystem in
das aerodynamische
Gesamtkonzept.*

*The front of the F12 includes a
sophisticated air channeling
system in its aerodynamic
overall concept.*

Unter der langgestreckten Motorhaube entwickelt der weit hinter der Vorderachse platzierte V12 740 PS, die ihn in 3,1 Sekunden auf Tempo 100 beschleunigen und eine Spitzengeschwindigkeit von 340 km/h ermöglichen.

Under the long hood and far behind the front axle, the V12 engine churns out 740 bhp, which accelerates it from 0 to 62 mph in 3.1 seconds and allows a top speed of 211 mph.

LaFerrari

Er ist der Ferrari schlechthin, präsentiert auf dem Genfer Salon 2013: der auf 499 Einheiten limitierte LaFerrari. »Es verkörpert genau das, was unser Unternehmen ausmacht«, so Ferrari-Präsident Luca di Montezemolo, »nämlich Exzellenz in jeder Hinsicht, ganz gleich, ob in Bezug auf technische Innovation, Leistung, visionäres Design oder pures Fahrvergnügen.« In der Rennabteilung von Ferrari entstand das handlaminierte und speziell gehärtete Kohlefaser-Chassis mit einem fix positionierten, auf den jeweiligen Besitzer zugeschnittenen Fahrersitz. Pedalerie und Lenkrad werden entsprechend angepasst. Die Erfahrungen der Formel-1-Piloten Fernando Alonso und Felipe Massa mit dem KERS-System flossen in den Entwicklungsprozess dieses Hybrid-Supersportwagens ein.

It is the epitome of the Ferrari, presented at the Geneva International Motor Show 2013: the 499-unit limited edition LaFerrari. "It is the perfect embodiment of what makes our company special," says Ferrari President Luca di Montezemolo. "Excellence in all areas; be it technical innovation, performance, visionary design or pure driving pleasure." The hand-laminated, specially hardened, carbon-fiber chassis was born in Ferrari's racing department, and the fixed-position driver's seat is customized to suit the needs of each individual owner. The pedals and steering wheel are then adapted accordingly. The experience of Formula 1 drivers Fernando Alonso and Felipe Massa with the KERS system were factored into the development process for this hybrid super sports car.

Türen und Motorhaube hoch zur Präsentation des Supersportwagens LaFerrari mit dem Hy-KERS-System auf dem Genfer Salon 2013. Gut sichtbar ist das Chassis aus vier verschiedenen Kohlefaserarten.

Doors and hood raised for the presentation of the LaFerrari super sports car with the Hy-KERS system at the Geneva International Motor Show 2013, revealing a great view of the chassis, which is made of four different types of carbon fiber.

Zwei Elektromotoren versorgen Antriebsräder und Fahrzeugsysteme mit einer Gesamtleistung von 163 PS. Dazu addieren sich die 800 PS des 6,2-Liter-Zwölfzylinders, der bis auf 9250 Touren hochgedreht werden kann. Aerodynamische Effizienz, vornehmlich durch Leitbleche und Diffusoren im unteren Bereich erzielt, erübrigt den Anpressdruck eines Heckflügels – selbst jenseits von 350 km/h. Es darf innerlich abgehoben werden!

Two electric motors supply the drive wheels and vehicle systems with a total of 163 bhp. This is added to the 800 bhp from the 6.2-liter, twelve-cylinder engine, which can be revved up to 9250 rpm. The aerodynamic efficiency, achieved mainly through use of deflectors and diffusors in the bottom section, means there is no need for the downforce supplied by a rear wing – even at speeds way beyond 210 mph. Prepare to be amazed!

Auf 499 Exemplare limitiert ist dieses Hybrid-Modell, das alle bisherigen Straßen-Ferrari in jeder Hinsicht übertrifft. Zu den 800 PS des V12 mit Direkteinspritzung gesellen sich noch 163 PS der Elektromotoren.

This hybrid model—limited to 499 units—outperforms all previous Ferrari road models in every respect. The 800 bhp from the V12 with direct injection is boosted by another 163 bhp from the electric motors.

Technische Daten

Spider (Barchetta) Touring (1948–1953): 212 Export 1951 | Coupé Ghia (1950–1952): 195 Inter 1950 | Spider Vignale (1951–1953): 166 MM 1953

	Spider (Barchetta) Touring (1948–1953): 212 Export 1951	Coupé Ghia (1950–1952): 195 Inter 1950	Spider Vignale (1951–1953): 166 MM 1953
Motor	V12 60°, vorn längs	V12 60°, vorn längs	V12 60°, vorn längs
Hubraum	2562 cm³	2341 cm³	1995 cm³
Bohrung × Hub	68 × 58,8 mm	65 × 58,8 mm	60 × 58,8 mm
Kraftstoffversorgung	3 Weber 36 DCF	1 Weber 36 DCF	3 Weber 32 IF4/C
Leistung	170 PS bei 6500/min	135 PS bei 6000/min	160 PS bei 7200/min
Getriebe	5-Gang, unsynchronisiert	5-Gang, 3+4 synchronisiert	5-Gang, unsynchronisiert
Chassis	verschweißter Rohrrahmen	verschweißter Rohrrahmen	verschweißter Rohrrahmen
Aufhängung vorn	Trapez-Dreieckslenker, Querblattfedern	Trapez-Dreieckslenker, Blattfedern	Trapez-Dreieckslenker, Querblattfedern
Aufhängung hinten	Starrachse, Halbelliptikfedern	Starrachse, Halbelliptikfedern	Starrachse, Halbelliptikfedern
Bremsen	hydraulische Trommelbremse	hydraulische Trommelbremse	hydraulische Trommelbremsen
Radstand	2200 mm	2500 mm	2250 mm
Länge × Breite × Höhe	4000 × 1600 × 1200 mm	4100 × 1450 × 1350 mm	4100 × 1650 × 1130 mm
Gewicht	900 kg (leer)	960 kg (leer)	800 kg (trocken)
Fahrleistungen			
Höchstgeschwindigkeit	ca. 200 km/h – approx. 125 mph	192 km/h – 119 mph	ca. 200 km/h – approx. 125 mph
0–100 km/h		9,9 s	

	250 MM Coupé Pinin Farina (1953–1954): 250 MM Coupé PF 1953	250 GT Europa Pinin Farina (1953–1956): 250 GT 1955	375 MM Spider, 375 Plus (1953–1954): 375 Plus 1954
Motor	V12 60°, vorn längs	V12 60°, vorn längs	V12 60°, vorn längs
Hubraum	2953 cm³	2953 cm³	4954 cm³
Bohrung × Hub	73 × 58,8 mm	73 × 58,8 mm	84 × 74,5 mm
Kraftstoffversorgung	3 Weber 36 DCF	3 Weber 36 DC13	3 Weber 46 DCF/3
Leistung	240 PS bei 7200/min	220 PS bei 7000/min	345 PS bei 6000/min
Getriebe	4-Gang	4-Gang	4-Gang
Chassis	verschweißter Rohrrahmen	verschweißter Rohrrahmen	verschweißter Rohrrahmen
Aufhängung vorn	Trapez-Dreieckslenker, Querblattfedern	Trapez-Dreieckslenker, Schraubenfedern	Trapez-Dreieckslenker, Querblattfedern
Aufhängung hinten	Starrachse, Halbelliptikfedern	Starrachse, Halbelliptikfedern	de-Dion-Achse, Querblattfedern
Bremsen	hydraulische Trommelbremsen	hydraulische Trommelbremsen	hydraulische Trommelbremsen
Radstand	2400 mm	2600 mm	2600 mm
Länge × Breite × Höhe	3988 × 1600 × 1257 mm	4458 × 1676 × 1371 mm	4190 × 1638 × 1092 mm
Gewicht	945 kg (leer)	1307 kg (mit vollem Tank)	900 kg (trocken)
Fahrleistungen			
Höchstgeschwindigkeit	200 km/h – 129 mph	205 km/h – 127 mph	270 km/h – 168 mph
0–100 km/h		6 s	

	750 Monza (1954–1955): 750 Monza 1954	410 S Spider & Coupé (1955): 410 S 1955	410 Superamerica (1956–1959): 410 SA Series I 1955
Motor	4 Zylinder in Reihe, vorn längs	V12 60°, vorn längs	V12 60°, vorn längs
Hubraum	2999 cm³	4961 cm³	4522 cm³
Bohrung × Hub	103 × 90 mm	88 × 68 mm	84 × 68 mm
Kraftstoffversorgung	2 Weber 58 DCO A/3	3 Weber 46 DCF/3	3 Weber 42 DCZ
Leistung	250 PS bei 6000/min	380 PS bei 7000/min	340 PS bei 7000/min
Getriebe	5-Gang, unsynchronisiert	4-Gang	4-Gang
Chassis	verschweißter Rohrrahmen	verschweißter Rohrrahmen	verschweißter Rohrrahmen
Aufhängung vorn	Trapez-Dreieckslenker, Querblattfedern	Trapez-Dreieckslenker, Schraubenfedern	Trapez-Dreieckslenker, Schraubenfedern
Aufhängung hinten	de-Dion-Achse, Querblattfedern	de-Dion-Achse, Querblattfedern	Starrachse, Halbelliptikfedern
Bremsen	hydraulische Trommelbremsen	hydraulische Trommelbremsen	hydraulische Trommelbremsen
Radstand	2250 mm	2350 mm	2800 mm
Länge × Breite × Höhe	4166 × 1651 × 1054 mm		
Gewicht	760 kg (trocken)	1200 kg (trocken)	1200 kg (trocken)
Fahrleistungen			
Höchstgeschwindigkeit	265 km/h – 165 mph	303,5 km/h – 188.5 mph (1000 km Buenos Aires 1956)	265 km/h – 165 mph
0–100 km/h			5,8 s

	250 GT Boano/Ellena (1956–1958): 250 GT Boano 1957	250 GT Tour de France (1956–1959): 250 GT TdF 1958	500 Testa Rossa – TRI 62 (1956–1962): 500 TRC 1957
Motor	V12 60°, vorn längs	V12 60°, vorn längs	4 Zylinder in Reihe, vorn längs
Hubraum	2953 cm³	2953 cm³	1984 cm³
Bohrung × Hub	73 × 58,8 mm	73 × 58,8 mm	90 × 78,8 mm
Kraftstoffversorgung	3 Weber 36 DCZ	3 Weber 36 DCZ3	2 Weber 40 DCO/A3
Leistung	240 PS bei 7000/min	260 PS bei 7000/min	180 PS bei 7000/min
Getriebe	4-Gang	4-Gang	4-Gang
Chassis	verschweißter Rohrrahmen	verschweißter Rohrrahmen	verschweißter Rohrrahmen
Aufhängung vorn	Trapez-Dreieckslenker, Schraubenfedern	Trapez-Dreieckslenker, Schraubenfedern	Trapez-Dreieckslenker, Schraubenfedern
Aufhängung hinten	Starrachse, Halbelliptikfedern	Starrachse, Halbelliptikfedern	Starrachse, Schraubenfedern
Bremsen	hydraulische Trommelbremsen	hydraulische Trommelbremsen	hydraulische Trommelbremsen
Radstand	2600 mm	2600 mm	2250 mm
Länge × Breite × Höhe	4458 × 1676 × 1372 mm	4350 × 1600 × 1350 mm	3937 × 1638 × 965 mm
Gewicht	1307 kg (mit vollem Tank)	1160 kg (mit vollem Tank)	680 kg (trocken)
Fahrleistungen			
Höchstgeschwindigkeit	203,5 km/h – 126.5 mph	245 km/h – 152 mph	ca. 245 km/h – approx. 152 mph
0–100 km/h	6 s	7,6 s	

Specifications

	290S, 315S, 335S (1957): 335S 1957	250GT Cabriolet (1957–1962): 250GT Cabriolet Series II 1961	250GT California Spyder (1957–1962): 250GT California Spyder SWB 1961
Engine	V12 60°, 4 OHC, vorn längs	V12 60°, vorn längs	V12 60°, vorn längs
Displacement	4023 cm³	2953 cm³	2953 cm³
Bore × stroke	77 × 72 mm	78 × 58,8 mm	73 × 58,8 mm
Fuel supply	6 Solex 40 PII	3 Weber 36 DCL	3 Weber 40 DCL/6
Output	390 PS bei 7800/min	240 PS bei 7000/min	280 PS bei 7000/min
Transmission	4-Gang	4-Gang + Overdrive	4-Gang
Chassis	verschweißter Rohrrahmen	verschweißter Rohrrahmen	verschweißter Rohrrahmen
Suspension front	Trapez-Dreieckslenker, Schraubenfedern	Trapez-Dreieckslenker, Schraubenfedern	Trapez-Dreieckslenker, Schraubenfedern
Suspension rear	de-Dion-Achse, Querblattfedern	Starrachse, Halbelliptikfedern	Starrachse, Halbelliptikfedern
Brakes	hydraulische Trommelbremsen	Scheibenbremsen	Scheibenbremsen
Dimensions Wheelbase	2350 mm	2600 mm	2400 mm
Length × width × height	4204 × 1651 × 1041 mm	4700 × 1690 × 1330 mm	4200 × 1720 × 1370 mm
Weight	880 kg (trocken)	1200 kg (trocken)	1050 kg (trocken)
Performance Maximum speed	ca. 300 km/h – approx. 185 mph	225 km/h – 140 mph	248 km/h – 154 mph
0–62 mph			

	250GT Coupé Pinin Farina (1958–1960): 250GT Coupé PF 1958	250GT Berlinetta SWB (1959–1962): 250GT Berlinetta SWB 1961	400 Superamerica (1959–1963): 400SA Coupé Aerodinamico 1962
Engine	V12 60°, vorn längs	V12 60°, vorn längs	V12 60°, vorn längs
Displacement	2953 cm³	2953 cm³	3967 cm³
Bore × stroke	73 × 58,8 mm	73 × 58,8 mm	77 × 71 mm
Fuel supply	3 Weber 36 DCL	3 Weber 36 DCL	3 Weber 40 DCL/6
Output	240 PS bei 7000/min	280 PS bei 7000/min	340 PS bei 7000/min
Transmission	4-Gang	4-Gang	4-Gang + Overdrive (5.)
Chassis	verschweißter Rohrrahmen	verschweißter Rohrrahmen	verschweißter Rohrrahmen
Suspension front	Trapez-Dreieckslenker, Schraubenfedern	Trapez-Dreieckslenker, Schraubenfedern	Trapez-Dreieckslenker, Schraubenfedern
Suspension rear	Starrachse, Halbelliptikfedern	Starrachse, Halbelliptikfedern	Starrachse, Halbelliptikfedern
Brakes	hydraulische Trommelbremsen	Scheibenbremsen	Scheibenbremsen
Dimensions Wheelbase	2600 mm	2400 mm	2600 mm
Length × width × height	4700 × 1725 × 1340 mm	4150 × 1690 × 1260 mm	4670 × 1770 × 1300 mm
Weight	1150 kg (trocken)	1120 kg (mit vollem Tank)	1362 kg (mit vollem Tank)
Performance Maximum speed	201,6 km/h – 125.3 mph	233 km/h – 145 mph	272 km/h – 169 mph
0–62 mph	6 s	8,2 s	9,4 s

	250GTE Coupé 2+2 (1960–1963): 250GTE Coupé 2+2 1962	Dino 246SP, 196SP, 286SP, 248SP, 268SP (1961–1962): Dino 268SP 1962	250GTO (1962–1964): 250GTO Series I 1963
Engine	V12 60°, vorn längs	V8 90°, hinten längs	V12 60°, vorn längs
Displacement	2953 cm³	2645 cm³	2953 cm³
Bore × stroke	73 × 58,8 mm	77 × 71 mm	73 × 58,8 mm
Fuel supply	3 Weber 36 DCS	4 Weber 40 IF2/C	6 Weber 38 DCN
Output	240 PS bei 7000/min	260 PS bei 7500/min	297 PS bei 7400/min
Transmission	4-Gang + Overdrive	5-Gang, unsynchronisiert	5-Gang, 2–5 synchronisiert
Chassis	verschweißter Rohrrahmen	verschweißter Rohrrahmen	verschweißter Rohrrahmen
Suspension front	Trapez-Dreieckslenker, Schraubenfedern	Trapez-Dreieckslenker, Schraubenfedern	Trapez-Dreieckslenker, Schraubenfedern
Suspension rear	Starrachse, Halbelliptikfedern	Trapez-Dreieckslenker, Schraubenfedern	Starrachse, Halbelliptikfedern
Brakes	Scheibenbremsen	Scheibenbremsen	Scheibenbremsen
Dimensions Wheelbase	2600 mm	2320 mm	2400 mm
Length × width × height	4700 × 1700 × 1350 mm	3828 × 1582 × 1022 mm	4325 × 1600 × 1210 mm
Weight	1488 kg (mit vollem Tank)	870 kg (trocken)	900 kg (trocken)
Performance Maximum speed	219,5 km/h – 136.4 mph	290 km/h – 180 mph	250 km/h – 155 mph
0–62 mph	8,5 s		5,6 s

	250GT Lusso (1962–1964): 250GT Lusso 1963	250LM (1963–1965): 250LM 1964	330GT 2+2 (1964–1967): 330GT 2+2 1964
Engine	V12 60°, vorn längs	V12 60°, hinten längs	V12 60°, vorn längs
Displacement	2953 cm³	3286 cm³	3967 cm³
Bore × stroke	73 × 58,8 mm	77 × 58,8 mm	77 × 71 mm
Fuel supply	3 Weber 36 DCS	6 Weber 38 DCN	3 Weber 40 DFI
Output	250 PS bei 7000/min	320 PS bei 7700/min	300 PS bei 6600/min
Transmission	4-Gang	5-Gang, unsynchronisiert	4-Gang + Overdrive
Chassis	verschweißter Rohrrahmen	verschweißter Rohrrahmen	verschweißter Rohrrahmen
Suspension front	Trapez-Dreieckslenker, Schraubenfedern	Trapez-Dreieckslenker, Schraubenfedern	Trapez-Dreieckslenker, Schraubenfedern
Suspension rear	Starrachse, Halbelliptikfedern	Trapez-Dreieckslenker, Schraubenfedern	Starrachse, Schraubenfedern, Halbelliptikfedern
Brakes	Scheibenbremsen	Scheibenbremsen	Scheibenbremsen
Dimensions Wheelbase	2400 mm	2400 mm	2650 mm
Length × width × height	4410 × 1750 × 1290 mm	4270 × 1700 × 1115 mm	4840 × 1715 × 1365 mm
Weight	1363 kg (mit vollem Tank)	820 kg (trocken)	1380 kg (leer)
Performance Maximum speed	240 km/h – 149 mph	287 km/h – 178 mph (Achsübersetzung: 3,548 : 1)	234 km/h – 145 mph
0–62 mph	8,2 s		6,9 s

500 Superfast (1964–1966): 500 Superfast 1964

Motor	V12 60°, vorn längs
Hubraum	4962 cm³
Bohrung × Hub	88 × 68 mm
Kraftstoffversorgung	3 Weber 40 DCZ/6
Leistung	400 PS bei 6500/min
Getriebe	5-Gang
Chassis	verschweißter Rohrrahmen
Aufhängung vorn	Trapez-Dreieckslenker, Schraubenfedern
Aufhängung hinten	Starrachse, Schraubenfedern, Halbelliptikfedern
Bremsen	Scheibenbremsen
Radstand — Maße	2650 mm
Länge × Breite × Höhe	4820 × 1780 × 1280 mm
Gewicht	1400 kg (leer)
Fahrleistungen	
Höchstgeschwindigkeit	280 km/h – 174 mph
0–100 km/h	8 s

275 GTB. GTS. GTB/4. Spider NART (1964–1968): 275 GTB/4 1967

Motor	V12 60°, 4 OHC, vorn längs
Hubraum	3286 cm³
Bohrung × Hub	77 × 58,8 mm
Kraftstoffversorgung	6 Weber 40 DCN
Leistung	300 PS bei 8000/min
Getriebe	5-Gang
Chassis	verschweißter Rohrrahmen
Aufhängung vorn	Trapez-Dreieckslenker, Schraubenfedern
Aufhängung hinten	Trapez-Dreieckslenker, Schraubenfedern
Bremsen	Scheibenbremsen
Radstand — Maße	2400 mm
Länge × Breite × Höhe	4410 × 1725 × 1200 mm
Gewicht	1050 kg (leer)
Fahrleistungen	
Höchstgeschwindigkeit	260 km/h – 162 mph
0–100 km/h	5,6 s

275/330 P/P2. 330 P3/P4 (1965–1967): 330 P4 1967

Motor	V12 60°, 4 OHC, 36 Ventile, hinten längs
Hubraum	3967 cm³
Bohrung × Hub	77 × 71 mm
Kraftstoffversorgung	Einspritzung
Leistung	450 PS bei 8200/min
Getriebe	5-Gang
Chassis	verschweißter Rohrrahmen, mit Blechen verstärkt
Aufhängung vorn	Trapez-Dreieckslenker, Schraubenfedern
Aufhängung hinten	Trapez-Dreieckslenker, Schraubenfedern
Bremsen	belüftete Scheibenbremsen
Radstand — Maße	2400 mm
Länge × Breite × Höhe	4185 × 1810 × 1000 mm
Gewicht	800 kg (trocken)
Fahrleistungen	
Höchstgeschwindigkeit	320 km/h – 199 mph

330 GTC/GTS. 365 GTC/GTS (1966–1970): 365 GTC 1969

Motor	V12 60°, vorn längs
Hubraum	4390 cm³
Bohrung × Hub	81 × 71 mm
Kraftstoffversorgung	3 Weber 40 DFI
Leistung	320 PS bei 6600/min
Getriebe	5-Gang
Chassis	verschweißter Rohrrahmen
Aufhängung vorn	Trapez-Dreieckslenker, Schraubenfedern
Aufhängung hinten	Trapez-Dreieckslenker, Schraubenfedern
Bremsen	Scheibenbremsen
Radstand — Maße	2400 mm
Länge × Breite × Höhe	4470 × 1670 × 1300 mm
Gewicht	1300 kg (leer)
Fahrleistungen	
Höchstgeschwindigkeit	243 km/h – 151 mph
0–100 km/h	6,4 s

365 California (1966–1967): 365 California 1966

Motor	V12 60°, vorn längs
Hubraum	4390 cm³
Bohrung × Hub	81 × 71 mm
Kraftstoffversorgung	3 Weber 40 DFI
Leistung	320 PS bei 6600/min
Getriebe	5-Gang
Chassis	verschweißter Rohrrahmen
Aufhängung vorn	Trapez-Dreieckslenker, Schraubenfedern
Aufhängung hinten	Starrachse, Schraubenfedern, Halbelliptikfedern
Bremsen	Scheibenbremsen
Radstand — Maße	2650 mm
Länge × Breite × Höhe	4900 × 1780 × 1330 mm
Gewicht	1320 kg (leer)
Fahrleistungen	
Höchstgeschwindigkeit	245 km/h – 152 mph

Dino 206 S (1966): Dino 206 S 1966

Motor	V6 65°, 4 OHC, hinten längs
Hubraum	1987 cm³
Bohrung × Hub	86 × 57 mm
Kraftstoffversorgung	Einspritzung
Leistung	220 PS bei 9000/min
Getriebe	5-Gang, unsynchronisiert
Chassis	verschweißter Rohrrahmen mit Verstärkungen
Aufhängung vorn	Trapez-Dreieckslenker, Schraubenfedern
Aufhängung hinten	Trapez-Dreieckslenker, Schraubenfedern
Bremsen	Scheibenbremsen
Radstand — Maße	2280 mm
Länge × Breite × Höhe	3875 × 1680 × 985 mm
Gewicht	580 kg (trocken)
Fahrleistungen	
Höchstgeschwindigkeit	260 km/h – 162 mph

350/612/712 CanAm (1967–1971): 712 CanAm 1971

Motor	V12 60°, 4 OHC, 48 Ventile, hinten längs
Hubraum	6900 cm³
Bohrung × Hub	
Kraftstoffversorgung	Einspritzung
Leistung	720 PS bei 8000/min
Getriebe	5-Gang
Chassis	Semi-Monocoque mit Verstärkungen
Aufhängung vorn	Trapez-Dreieckslenker, Querlenker unten, Führungs- und Schubstreben, Schraubenfedern
Aufhängung hinten	Querlenker oben und unten, Schubstreben, Schraubenfedern
Bremsen	belüftete Scheibenbremsen
Radstand — Maße	2400 mm
Länge × Breite × Höhe	4360 × 2190 × 970 mm
Gewicht	680 kg (trocken)
Fahrleistungen	
Höchstgeschwindigkeit	340 km/h – 211 mph

365 GT 2+2 (1967–1971): 365 GT 2+2 1968

Motor	V12 60°, vorn längs
Hubraum	4390 cm³
Bohrung × Hub	81 × 71 mm
Kraftstoffversorgung	3 Weber 40 DFI
Leistung	320 PS bei 6600/min
Getriebe	5-Gang
Chassis	verschweißter Rohrrahmen mit Metallverstärkungen
Aufhängung vorn	Trapez-Dreieckslenker, Schraubenfedern
Aufhängung hinten	Trapez-Dreieckslenker, Schraubenfedern, hydropneumatische Höhenverstellung
Bremsen	Scheibenbremsen
Radstand — Maße	2650 mm
Länge × Breite × Höhe	4980 × 1790 × 1345 mm
Gewicht	1825 kg (mit vollem Tank)
Fahrleistungen	
Höchstgeschwindigkeit	244 km/h – 152 mph
0–100 km/h	7,3 s

Dino 206 GT. 246 GT/GTS (1967–1974): Dino 246 GT 1972

Motor	V6 65°, 4 OHC, hinten quer
Hubraum	2418 cm³
Bohrung × Hub	92,5 × 60 mm
Kraftstoffversorgung	3 Weber 40 DCF 14
Leistung	195 PS bei 7500/min
Getriebe	5-Gang
Chassis	verschweißter Rohrrahmen
Aufhängung vorn	Trapez-Dreieckslenker, Schraubenfedern
Aufhängung hinten	Trapez-Dreieckslenker, Schraubenfedern
Bremsen	belüftete Scheibenbremsen
Radstand — Maße	2340 mm
Länge × Breite × Höhe	4230 × 1700 × 1115 mm
Gewicht	1230 kg (mit vollem Tank)
Fahrleistungen	
Höchstgeschwindigkeit	238,4 km/h – 148.1 mph
0–100 km/h	7,4 s

365 GTB/4 Daytona. GTS/4 Daytona (1968–1973): 365 GTS/4 Daytona 1971

Motor	V12 60°, 4 OHC, vorn längs
Hubraum	4390 cm³
Bohrung × Hub	81 × 71 mm
Kraftstoffversorgung	6 Weber 40 DCN 20
Leistung	352 PS bei 7500/min
Getriebe	5-Gang
Chassis	verschweißter Rohrrahmen
Aufhängung vorn	Trapez-Dreieckslenker, Schraubenfedern
Aufhängung hinten	Trapez-Dreieckslenker, Schraubenfedern
Bremsen	Scheibenbremsen
Radstand — Maße	2400 mm
Länge × Breite × Höhe	4425 × 1760 × 1245 mm
Gewicht	1625 kg (mit vollem Tank)
Fahrleistungen	
Höchstgeschwindigkeit	274,8 km/h – 170.8 mph
0–100 km/h	6,1 s

312 P (1968–1969): 312 P 1969

Motor	V12 60°, 4 OHC, 48 Ventile, hinten längs
Hubraum	2989 cm³
Bohrung × Hub	77 × 53,5 mm
Kraftstoffversorgung	Einspritzung
Leistung	430 PS bei 9800/min
Getriebe	5-Gang
Chassis	Semi-Monocoque
Aufhängung vorn	Trapez-Dreieckslenker, Schraubenfedern
Aufhängung hinten	Trapez-Dreieckslenker, Schraubenfedern
Bremsen	belüftete Scheibenbremsen
Radstand — Maße	2370 mm
Länge × Breite × Höhe	4230 × 1980 × 950 mm
Gewicht	680 kg (trocken)
Fahrleistungen	
Höchstgeschwindigkeit	320 km/h – 199 mph

512 S/M (1969–1970): 512 M 1970

Motor	V12 60°, 4 OHC, 48 Ventile, hinten längs
Hubraum	4994 cm³
Bohrung × Hub	87 × 70 mm
Kraftstoffversorgung	Einspritzung
Leistung	610 PS bei 9000/min
Getriebe	5-Gang
Chassis	Semi-Monocoque
Aufhängung vorn	Trapez-Dreieckslenker, Schraubenfedern
Aufhängung hinten	Trapez-Dreieckslenker, Schraubenfedern
Bremsen	belüftete Scheibenbremsen
Radstand — Maße	2400 mm
Länge × Breite × Höhe	4360 × 2000 × 970 mm
Gewicht	930 kg (leer)
Fahrleistungen	
Höchstgeschwindigkeit	340 km/h – 211 mph

312 PB (1970–1973): 312 PB 1972 · 305 GTC/4 (1071–1972): 365 GTC/4 1971 · 365 GT4 BB, BB 512/512i (1971–1984): BB 512i 1984

312 PB 1972	365 GTC/4 1971	BB 512i 1984	
V12 180°, 4 OHC, 48 Ventile, hinten längs	V12 60°, 4 OHC, vorn längs	V12 180°, 4 OHC, hinten längs	Engine
2991 cm³	4390 cm³	4943 cm³	Displacement
80×49,6 mm	81×71 mm	82×78 mm	Bore×stroke
Einspritzung	6 Weber 38 DCOE	Einspritzung	Fuel supply
440 PS bei 11000/min	320 PS bei 6200/min	340 PS bei 6000/min	Output
5-Gang	5-Gang	5-Gang	Transmission
Semi-Monocoque	verschweißter Rohrrahmen	verschweißter Rohrrahmen	Chassis
obere und untere Trapez-Dreieckslenker, Schraubenfedern	Trapez-Dreieckslenker, Schraubenfedern	Trapez-Dreieckslenker, Schraubenfedern	Suspension front
einfache Querlenker oben und Trapez-Dreieckslenker unten, Schraubenfedern	Trapez-Dreieckslenker, Schraubenfedern	Trapez-Dreieckslenker, Schraubenfedern	Suspension rear
belüftete Scheibenbremsen	Scheibenbremsen	belüftete Scheibenbremsen	Brakes
2220 mm	2550 mm	2500 mm	Dimensions Wheelbase
3770×1960×954 mm	4570×1780×1270 mm	4400×1830×1120 mm	Length×width×height
655 kg (trocken)	1877 kg (mit vollem Tank)	1600 kg (mit vollem Tank)	Weight
			Performance
320 km/h – 199 mph	244 km/h – 152 mph	288 km/h – 179 mph	Maximum speed
	7,5 s	5,9 s	0–62 mph

365 GT4 2+2, 400i, 412 (1972–1989): 412 1986 · Dino 308 GT4 (1973–1980): Dino 308 GT4 1976 · 308 GTB/GTS, 328 GTB/GTS (1975–1989): 308 GTB 1979

412 1986	Dino 308 GT4 1976	308 GTB 1979	
V12 60°, 4 OHC, vorn längs	V8 90°, 4 OHC, hinten quer	V8 90°, 4 OHC, hinten quer	Engine
4943 cm³	2927 cm³	2927 cm³	Displacement
82×78 mm	81×71 mm	81×71 mm	Bore×stroke
Einspritzung	4 Weber 40 DCNF	4 Weber 40 DCNF	Fuel supply
340 PS bei 6000/min	236 PS bei 7700/min	255 PS bei 7700/min	Output
5-Gang	5-Gang	5-Gang	Transmission
verschweißter Rohrrahmen	verschweißter Rohrrahmen	verschweißter Rohrrahmen	Chassis
Trapez-Dreieckslenker, Schraubenfedern	Trapez-Dreieckslenker, Schraubenfedern	Trapez-Dreieckslenker, Schraubenfedern	Suspension front
Trapez-Dreieckslenker, Schraubenfedern	Trapez-Dreieckslenker, Schraubenfedern	Trapez-Dreieckslenker, Schraubenfedern	Suspension rear
belüftete Scheibenbremsen	belüftete Scheibenbremsen	belüftete Scheibenbremsen	Brakes
2700 mm	2550 mm	2340 mm	Dimensions Wheelbase
4810×1800×1315 mm	4320×1800×1180 mm	4230×1720×1120 mm	Length×width×height
1805 kg (leer)	1320 kg (mit vollem Tank)	1320 kg (mit vollem Tank)	Weight
			Performance
250 km/h – 155 mph	248,3 km/h – 154.3 mph	255,3 km/h – 158.6 mph	Maximum speed
6,7 s	6,8 s	6,5 s	0–62 mph

Mondial 8/3.2/t/Cabriolet (1980–1993): Mondial 3.2 1989 · 288 GTO (1984–1986): 288 GTO 1985 · Testarossa, 512 TR, F512 M (1984–1996): F512 M 1995

Mondial 3.2 1989	288 GTO 1985	F512 M 1995	
V8 90°, 4 OHC, 32 Ventile, hinten quer	V8 90°, 4 OHC, 32 Ventile, 2 Turbolader, 2 Ladeluftkühler, hinten längs	V12 180°, 4 OHC, 48 Ventile, hinten längs	Engine
3185 cm³	2855 cm³	4942 cm³	Displacement
83×73,6 mm	80×71 mm	82×78 mm	Bore×stroke
Einspritzung	Einspritzung	Einspritzung	Fuel supply
270 PS bei 7000/min	400 PS bei 7000/min	440 PS bei 6750/min	Output
5-Gang	5-Gang	5-Gang	Transmission
verschweißter Rohrrahmen	verschweißter Rohrrahmen	verschweißter Rohrrahmen	Chassis
Trapez-Dreieckslenker, Schraubenfedern	Trapez-Dreieckslenker, Schraubenfedern	Trapez-Dreieckslenker, Schraubenfedern	Suspension front
Trapez-Dreieckslenker, Schraubenfedern	Trapez-Dreieckslenker, Schraubenfedern	Trapez-Dreieckslenker, Schraubenfedern	Suspension rear
belüftete Scheibenbremsen	belüftete Scheibenbremsen	belüftete Scheibenbremsen	Brakes
2650 mm	2450 mm	2550 mm	Dimensions Wheelbase
4535×1795×1235 mm	4290×1910×1120 mm	4480×1975×1135 mm	Length×width×height
1410 kg (leer)	1317 kg (leer)	1631 kg (leer)	Weight
			Performance
254 km/h – 158 mph	303 km/h – 188 mph	305 km/h – 190 mph	Maximum speed
6,7 s	4,8 s	5,1 s	0–62 mph

F40 (1987–1992): F40 1990 · 348 GTB/GTS/Speciale/Spider (1989–1994): 348 ts 1992 · 456 GT, 456 M GT/GTA (1992–2002): 456 GT 1994

F40 1990	348 ts 1992	456 GT 1994	
V8 90°, 4 OHC, 32 Ventile, 2 Turbolader, 2 Ladeluftkühler, hinten längs	V8 90°, 4 OHC, 32 Ventile, hinten längs	V12 65°, 4 OHC, 48 Ventile, vorn längs	Engine
2936 cm³	3405 cm³	5474 cm³	Displacement
82×69,5 mm	85×75 mm	88×75 mm	Bore×stroke
Einspritzung	Einspritzung	Einspritzung	Fuel supply
478 PS bei 7000/min	300 PS bei 7000/min	442 PS bei 6250/min	Output
5-Gang	5-Gang	6-Gang	Transmission
Stahlrohrrahmen, Kunststoffkarosserie	Monocoque, Stahl-Spaceframe, hinten Rohr-Hilfsrahmen	verschweißter Rohrrahmen mit Aluminium-Karosserie	Chassis
Trapez-Dreieckslenker, Schraubenfedern	Trapez-Dreieckslenker, Stabilisator, Schraubenfedern	Trapez-Dreieckslenker, Schraubenfedern	Suspension front
Trapez-Dreieckslenker, Schraubenfedern	Trapez-Dreieckslenker, Stabilisator, Schraubenfedern	Trapez-Dreieckslenker, Doppel-Schraubenfeder-Dämpfer-Einheiten	Suspension rear
belüftete Scheibenbremsen	belüftete Scheibenbremsen	belüftete Scheibenbremsen	Brakes
2450 mm	2450 mm	2600 mm	Dimensions Wheelbase
4430×1980×1130 mm	4230×1895×1170 mm	4730×1920×1300 mm	Length×width×height
1254 kg (leer)	1420 kg (leer)	1790 kg (leer)	Weight
			Performance
321 km/h – 199 mph	277 km/h – 172 mph	302 km/h – 188 mph	Maximum speed
4,6 s	5,6 s	5,2 s	0–62 mph

Glossary see page 423

F 333 SP (1994–2002):
F 333 SP 1995

Motor	V12 65°, 4 OHC, 60 Ventile, hinten längs
Hubraum	3997 cm³
Bohrung × Hub	85 × 58,7 mm
Kraftstoffversorgung	Einspritzung
Leistung	über 650 PS bei 11000/min
Getriebe	5-Gang, sequenziell
Chassis	Monocoque aus Kohlefaser-Verbundstoff und Aluminium-Honigwaben-Struktur, Motor als mittragendes Element
Aufhängung vorn	Feder-Dämpfer-Einheiten
Aufhängung hinten	Feder-Dämpfer-Einheiten
Bremsen	belüftete Scheibenbremsen
Radstand	2740 mm
Länge × Breite × Höhe Maße	4775 × 1994 × 1016 mm
Gewicht	860 kg (leer)
Fahrleistungen	
Höchstgeschwindigkeit	298 km/h – 185 mph
0–100 km/h	3,7 s

F 355 Berlinetta, GTS, Spider, Challenge (1994–1998)
F 355 Spider 1995

Motor	V8 90°, 4 OHC, 40 Ventile, hinten längs
Hubraum	3496 cm³
Bohrung × Hub	85 × 77 mm
Kraftstoffversorgung	Einspritzung
Leistung	380 PS bei 8200/min
Getriebe	6-Gang
Chassis	Monocoque, hinterer Rohr-Hilfsrahmen
Aufhängung vorn	Trapez-Dreieckslenker, Schraubenfedern
Aufhängung hinten	Trapez-Dreieckslenker, Schraubenfedern
Bremsen	belüftete Scheibenbremsen
Radstand	2450 mm
Länge × Breite × Höhe	4250 × 1900 × 1170 mm
Gewicht	1512 kg (leer)
Fahrleistungen	
Höchstgeschwindigkeit	295 km/h – 183 mph
0–100 km/h	5,3 s

F 50 (1995–1997):
F 50 1995

Motor	V12 65°, 4 OHC, 60 Ventile, hinten längs
Hubraum	4698 cm³
Bohrung × Hub	85 × 69 mm
Kraftstoffversorgung	Einspritzung
Leistung	520 PS bei 8500/min
Getriebe	6-Gang
Chassis	Verbundstoff aus Kohlefaser, Kevlar- und Nomex-Honigwaben-Struktur, hinterer Rohr-Hilfsrahmen
Aufhängung vorn	Trapez-Dreieckslenker, Feder-Dämpfer-Einheiten
Aufhängung hinten	Trapez-Dreieckslenker, Feder-Dämpfer-Einheiten
Bremsen	belüftete Scheibenbremsen
Radstand	2580 mm
Länge × Breite × Höhe	4480 × 1986 × 1120 mm
Gewicht	1230 kg (leer)
Fahrleistungen	
Höchstgeschwindigkeit	325 km/h – 202 mph
0–100 km/h	3,87 s

550, 575 M (1996–2006):
575 M Maranello 2002

Motor	V12 65°, 4 OHC, 48 Ventile, vorn längs
Hubraum	5748 cm³
Bohrung × Hub	89 × 77 mm
Kraftstoffversorgung	Elektronische Einspritzung
Leistung	515 PS bei 7215/min
Getriebe	6-Gang
Chassis	Stahlrohrrahmen mit Aluminium-Karosserie
Aufhängung v/h	doppelte Dreieckslenker, elektronisch gesteuerte Feder-Dämpfer-Einheiten
Bremsen	belüftete Scheibenbremsen
Radstand Maße	2500 mm
Länge × Breite × Höhe	4550 × 1935 × 1277 mm
Gewicht	1730 kg (leer)
Fahrleistungen	
Höchstgeschwindigkeit	325 km/h – 202 mph
0–100 km/h	4,25 s

360 (1999–2005):
360 Spider 2003

Motor	V8 90°, 4 OHC, 40 Ventile, hinten längs
Hubraum	3586 cm³
Bohrung × Hub	85 × 79 mm
Kraftstoffversorgung	Elektronische Einspritzung
Leistung	400 PS bei 8500/min
Getriebe	6-Gang
Chassis	Aluminium-Monocoque mit Hilfsrahmen
Aufhängung v/h	doppelte Querlenker, elektronisch gesteuerte Feder-Dämpfer-Einheiten
Bremsen	belüftete Scheibenbremsen
Radstand	2600 mm
Länge × Breite × Höhe	4477 × 1992 × 1235 mm
Gewicht	1450 kg
Fahrleistungen	
Höchstgeschwindigkeit	295 km/h – 183 mph
0–100 km/h	4,6 s

Enzo Ferrari, FXX (2002–2006):
Enzo Ferrari 2002

Motor	V12 65°, 4 OHC, 48 Ventile, hinten längs
Hubraum	5998 cm³
Bohrung × Hub	92 × 75,2 mm
Kraftstoffversorgung	Elektronische Einspritzung
Leistung	660 PS bei 7800/min
Getriebe	6-Gang
Chassis	Kohlefaser-Monocoque, hinterer Rohr-Hilfsrahmen
Aufhängung v/h	doppelte Dreieckslenker, Schubstreben, quer liegende Feder-Dämpfer-Einheiten
Bremsen	belüftete Scheibenbremsen
Radstand	2650 mm
Länge × Breite × Höhe	4702 × 2035 × 1147 mm
Gewicht	1365 kg (leer)
Fahrleistungen	
Höchstgeschwindigkeit	350 km/h – 217 mph
0–100 km/h	3,65 s

612 Scaglietti (2004–2010)
612 Scaglietti 2004

Motor	V12 65°, 4 OHC, 48 Ventile, vorne längs
Hubraum	5748 cm³
Bohrung × Hub	89 × 77 mm
Kraftstoffversorgung	Elektronische Einspritzung
Leistung	540 PS bei 7250/min
Getriebe	6-Gang
Chassis	Spaceframe
Aufhängung v/h	doppelte Dreieckslenker, Dämpfer mit Koaxial-Schraubenfedern
Bremsen	belüftete Scheibenbremsen
Radstand Maße	2950 mm
Länge × Breite × Höhe	4902 × 1957 × 1344 mm
Gewicht	1840 kg
Fahrleistungen	
Höchstgeschwindigkeit	320 km/h – 199 mph
0–100 km/h	4,2 s

F 430 (2004–2009):
F 430 Spider 2006

Motor	V8 90°, 4 OHC, 32 Ventile, Mittelmotor längs
Hubraum	4308 cm³
Bohrung × Hub	92 × 81 mm
Kraftstoffversorgung	Saugrohreinspritzung
Leistung	490 PS bei 8500/min
Getriebe	6-Gang
Chassis	Spaceframe
Aufhängung v/h	Federbeine, doppelte Dreieckslenker
Bremsen	belüftete Scheibenbremsen
Radstand	2600 mm
Länge × Breite × Höhe	4510 × 1925 × 1235 mm
Gewicht	1520 kg (leer)
Fahrleistungen	
Höchstgeschwindigkeit	315 km/h – 196 mph
0–100 km/h	4,1 s

599 GTB Fiorano (2006–2012):
599 GTB Fiorano 2008

Motor	V12 65°, 4 OHC, 48 Ventile, vorne längs
Hubraum	5999 cm³
Bohrung × Hub	92 × 75,2 mm
Kraftstoffversorgung	Saugrohreinspritzung
Leistung	620 PS bei 7600/min
Getriebe	6-Gang, Transaxle
Chassis	Spaceframe
Aufhängung v/h	Federbeine, doppelte Dreieckslenker
Bremsen	belüftete Scheibenbremsen
Radstand	2750 mm
Länge × Breite × Höhe	4665 × 1960 × 1335 mm
Gewicht	1690 kg (leer)
Fahrleistungen	
Höchstgeschwindigkeit	330 km/h – 205 mph
0–100 km/h	3,7 s

California (2008–…)
California 2008

Motor	V8 90°, 4 OHC, 32 Ventile, vorne längs
Hubraum	4297 cm³
Bohrung × Hub	94 × 77,5 mm
Kraftstoffversorgung	Saugrohreinspritzung
Leistung	460 PS bei 7750/min
Getriebe	7-Gang, Doppelkupplung
Chassis	Spaceframe
Aufhängung vorn	Federbeine, doppelte Dreieckslenker
Aufhängung hinten	Federbeine, Längslenker, Querlenker
Bremsen	belüftete Scheibenbremsen
Radstand Maße	2670 mm
Länge × Breite × Höhe	4563 × 1902 × 1308 mm
Gewicht	1650 kg (leer)
Fahrleistungen	
Höchstgeschwindigkeit	310 km/h – 193 mph
0–100 km/h	3,9 s

458 (2009–…):
458 Italia 2012

Motor	V8 90°, 4 OHC, 32 Ventile, Mittelmotor längs
Hubraum	4499 cm³
Bohrung × Hub	94 × 81 mm
Kraftstoffversorgung	Direkteinspritzung
Leistung	570 PS bei 9000/min
Getriebe	7-Gang, Doppelkupplung
Chassis	Spaceframe
Aufhängung vorn	Federbeine, adaptive Dämpfer, doppelte Querlenker, Stabilisator
Aufhängung hinten	Mehrlenkerachse
Bremsen	belüftete Scheibenbremsen
Radstand	2650 mm
Länge × Breite × Höhe	4527 × 1937 × 1211 mm
Gewicht	1380 kg (leer)
Fahrleistungen	
Höchstgeschwindigkeit	320 km/h – 199 mph
0–100 km/h	3,4 s

FF (2011–…)
FF 2012

Motor	V12 65°, 4 OHC, 48 Ventile, vorn längs
Hubraum	6262 cm³
Bohrung × Hub	94 × 75,2 mm
Kraftstoffversorgung	Direkteinspritzung
Leistung	660 PS bei 8000/min
Getriebe	7-Gang, Doppelkupplung, Allradantrieb
Chassis	Spaceframe
Aufhängung vorn	Federbeine, adaptive Dämpfer, doppelte Querlenker, Stabilisator
Aufhängung hinten	Mehrlenkerachse
Bremsen	belüftete Scheibenbremsen
Radstand	2990 mm
Länge × Breite × Höhe	4907 × 1953 × 1379 mm
Gewicht	1790 kg (leer)
Fahrleistungen	
Höchstgeschwindigkeit	335 km/h – 208 mph
0–100 km/h	3,7 s

F13 (2012 ...) — F12berlinetta 2012 / LaFerrari (2013-...) — LaFerrari 2013

F12berlinetta 2012	LaFerrari 2013	
V12 65°, 4 OHC, 48 Ventile, vorn längs	V12 65°, 4 OHC, 48 Ventile, Mittelmotor längs; 2 Elektromotoren	**Engine**
6262 cm³	6262 cm³	Displacement
94×75,2 mm	94×75,2 mm	Bore×stroke
Direkteinspritzung	Direkteinspritzung	Fuel supply
740 PS bei 8250/min	800 PS bei 9000/min (V12) + 163 PS (Elektromotoren)	Output
7-Gang, Doppelkupplung	7-Gang, Doppelkupplung	**Transmission**
Spaceframe	Monocoque aus Kohlefaser-Verbundstoff	**Chassis**
		Suspension front
Federbeine, adaptive Dämpfer, doppelte Querlenker, Stabilisator	Federbeine, adaptive Dämpfer, doppelte Querlenker, Stabilisator	
Mehrlenkerachse	Mehrlenkerachse	Suspension rear
belüftete Scheibenbremsen	belüftete Scheibenbremsen	Brakes
2720 mm	2650 mm	**Dimensions** Wheelbase
4618×1942×1273 mm	4702×1992×1116 mm	Length×width×height
1525 kg (leer)	ca. 1365 kg (leer)	Weight
		Performance
340 km/h – 211 mph	> 350 km/h – 217 mph	Maximum speed
3,1 s	< 3 s	0–62 mph

Glossary

Engine
Displacement
Bore×stroke
Fuel supply
Output
Transmission
Chassis
Suspension front/rear
Brakes
Dimensions Wheelbase
Length×width×height
Weight
Performance
Maximum speed
0–62 mph

Engine
Displacement
Bore×stroke
Fuel supply
Output
Transmission
Chassis
Suspension front/rear
Brakes
Dimensions Wheelbase
Length×width×height
Weight
Performance
Maximum speed
0–62 mph

Engine
Displacement
Bore×stroke
Fuel supply
Output
Transmission
Chassis
Suspension front
Suspension rear
Brakes
Dimensions Wheelbase
Length×width×height
Weight
Performance
Maximum speed
0–62 mph

Allgemein	General
Aluminium	aluminum
aus	made of
doppelte	double
einfache	single
hinten	rear
längs	longitudinal
mit	with
oben	on top
oder	or
quer	transverse
über	over
unten	below
vorn	front

Motor	Engine
Direkteinspritzung	direct injection
Einspritzung	injection
Elektromotoren	electric motors
Elektronische Einspritzung	electronic injection
Ladeluftkühler	intercooler
Mittelmotor	mid-engine
OHC (oben liegende Nockenwelle)	OHC (overhead camshaft)
... PS bei .../min	...bhp at ...rpm
Saugrohreinspritzung	manifold injection
synchronisiert	synchromesh
Turbolader	turbocharger
Ventile	valves
4 Zylinder in Reihe	straight 4

Getriebe	Transmission
Doppelkupplung	dual clutch
...-Gang	...-speed
manuell	manual
sequenziell	sequential
unsynchronisiert	non-synchromesh

Chassis	Chassis
belüftete Scheibenbremsen	ventilated disks
Blattfedern	leaf springs
Dämpfer	dampers
de-Dion-Achse	de Dion tube
Doppel-Schraubenfeder-Dämpfer-Einheiten	dual coil spring damper units
Dreieckslenker	wishbones
elektronisch gesteuerte	electronically controlled
elektronische Stabilitäts- und Traktionskontrolle	electronic stability and traction control
Feder-Dämpfer-Einheiten	spring damper units
Federbeine	spring struts
Führungs- und Schubstreben	tie rods and push rods
Halbelliptikfedern	semi-elliptical springs
Hilfsrahmen	subframe
hinterer Rohr-Hilfsrahmen	rear tubular subframe
Honigwaben-Struktur	honeycomb structure
hydraulische Trommelbremse	hydraulic drums
hydropneumatische Höhenverstellung	hydropneumatic level control
Karbon-Keramik-Verbundstoff	carbon-ceramic composite
Karosserie	body
Koaxial-Schraubenfedern	coaxial coil spring
Kohlefaser	carbon fiber
Kunststoffkarosserie	plastic body
Längslenker	longitudinal control arm
Mehrlenkerachse	multilink suspension
mit Blechen verstärkt	sheet-metal reinforced
mit Metallverstärkungen	metal reinforced
mit Verstärkungen	reinforced
Motor als mittragendes Element	reinforcement-contributing engine
obere und untere	upper and lower
quer liegende	transversely set
Querblattfedern	transverse leaf springs
Querlenker	transverse arms
Rohr-Hilfsrahmen	tubular subframe
Scheibenbremsen	disk brakes
Schraubenfedern	coil springs
Schubstreben	push rods
Stabilisator	anti-roll bar
Stahl	steel
Stahlrohrrahmen	tubular steel frame
Starrachse	beam axle
Trapez-Dreieckslenker	trapezoidal wishbones
über Schubstreben betätigte	push-rod activated
Verbundstoff	composite
Verbundstoff aus Kohlefaser, Kevlar- und Nomex-Honigwaben-Struktur	carbon- and aramid-fiber honeycomb-structure composite
verschweißter Rohrrahmen	welded tubular frame

Maße	Dimensions
leer	empty
mit vollem Tank	curb weight
trocken	dry weight
100 mm	3.94 in
100 kg	220.5 lbs

Fahrleistungen	Performance
Achsübersetzung	axle ratio

Dank für Enthusiasmus und unermüdliche Unterstützung an: For their unflagging support and enthusiasm we would like to thank:

Dr. Darius Ahrabian · Jean-Jacques Bailly · Pierre Bardinon · Mario Bernardi · Andreas Birner · Henri Chambon · Adriano Cimarosti · David Cottingham · Diethelm Doll
Jürgen Dorschner · Helmut Eberlein · Herbert Engel · Jochen Frick · Michael Gabel · Ennio Gianaroli · Peter Gläsel · Hubert Hahne · Maria Homann · Lukas Hüni
Hartmut Ibing · Manfred Jung · Peter Kaus · Reinhard Kehm · Thomas Kellermann · Roland Kessler · Thomas Kiesele · Stephan Köhler · Uwe Meissner · Gerd Meranius
Hans Mischler · Karl Müller · Martha Naudascher · Albert Obrist · Holger Richter · Jean Sage · Walter Schäfer · Klaus Scholtyssek · Ulf Schossow · Jürgen Schultzke
Christoph, Engelbert & Heinz Stieger · Klaus Ulrich · Hans-Jürgen Zapf

Original title: *Ferrari*
ISBN 978-3-8331-1231-7

Photography: Rainer W. Schlegelmilch
Text: Hartmut Lehbrink, Jochen von Osterroth (Updates)
Historical photographs p. 4 (top row 2nd left), p. 9: Archiv Diethelm Doll
Layout: Oliver Hessmann
Project Management: Joachim Schwochert

Special edition

Project management for h.f.ullmann: Lars Pietzschmann

Translations into English: Mo Croasdale in association with First Edition Translations Ltd, Cambridge, UK;
Edited by David Price in association with First Edition Translations Ltd, Cambridge, UK
Translations into English for the new updates (pp. 19, 392-417): Ian Farrell in association with Delivering iBooks & Design, Barcelona

Cover design: Oliver Hessmann

Overall responsibility for production: h.f.ullmann publishing GmbH, Potsdam, Germany

Printed in China, 2013

ISBN 978-3-8480-0437-9

10 9 8 7 6 5 4 3 2 1
X IX VIII VII VI V IV III II

www.ullmann-publishing.com
newsletter@ullmann-publishing.com